ABOUT ISLAND PRESS

Island Press is the only nonprofit organization in the United States whose principal purpose is the publication of books on environmental issues and natural resource management. We provide solutions-oriented information to professionals, public officials, business and community leaders, and concerned citizens who are shaping responses to environmental problems.

In 1994, Island Press celebrates its tenth anniversary as the leading provider of timely and practical books that take a multidisciplinary approach to critical environmental concerns. Our growing list of titles reflects our commitment to bringing the best of an expanding body of literature to the environmental community throughout North America and the world.

Support for Island Press is provided by The Geraldine R. Dodge Foundation, The Energy Foundation, The Ford Foundation, The George Gund Foundation, William and Flora Hewlett Foundation, The James Irvine Foundation, The John D. and Catherine T. MacArthur Foundation, The Andrew W. Mellon Foundation, The Joyce Mertz-Gilmore Foundation, The New-Land Foundation, The Pew Charitable Trusts, The Rockefeller Brothers Fund, The Tides Foundation, Turner Foundation, Inc., The Rockefeller Philanthropic Collaborative, Inc., and individual donors.

Lifelines

ALSO BY TIM PALMER

The Wild and Scenic Rivers of America
Yosemite: The Promise of Wildness
The Snake River: Window to the West
The Sierra Nevada: A Mountain Journey
Endangered Rivers and the Conservation Movement
Youghiogheny: Appalachian River
Stanislaus: The Struggle for a River
Rivers of Pennsylvania
California's Threatened Environment: Restoring the Dream (editor)

Lifelines
The Case for River Conservation

Tim Palmer

ISLAND PRESS
Washington, D.C.
Covelo, California

Photographs copyright © 1994 by Tim Palmer
Front cover photograph: Animas River downstream from
Durango, Colorado

Library of Congress Cataloging-in-Publication Data
Palmer, Tim.
    Lifelines : the case for river conservation / Tim
Palmer.
        p.   cm.
    Includes bibliographical references and index.
    ISBN 1-55963-219-4 (cloth : alk. paper). —
ISBN 1-55963-220-8 (pbk. : alk. paper)
        1. Stream conservation—United States.
    2. Ecosystem management—United States.   I. Title.
QH76.P355   1994
333.91'6216—dc20   94-8951
                                                    CIP

Printed on recycled, acid-free paper

Manufactured in the United States of America
10 9 8 7 6 5 4 3 2 1

*To Hugh Harper for his lifelong work with
land and water, for his friendship,
and for his inspiration to "keep moving"*

Contents

A selection of photographs follows page 116.

Preface

During the past two decades, profound changes have taken place in the way we treat our rivers in the United States, giving cause for both hope and distress. Proposals for large, destructive dams seldom surface anymore, and some of the foulest pollution has been stopped, but this progress has opened the way to myriad other concerns.

The newly recognized problems are at once more subtle, complicated, and common than the old problems. While massive dams built by the federal government no longer threaten many rivers in the United States, smaller dams for hydropower do. Concerns for water quality have graduated from issues of municipal sewage and conventional industrial discharges to an epidemic of toxic wastes and the blight of polluted runoff that comes not only from single point sources, but from whole landscapes in both urban and rural America. The new view and the new conservation of rivers embrace an awareness of instream flows, riparian habitat, and ecosystem management. The biological importance of rivers is now regarded by concerned people as paramount, its ramifications vital not only to conservation but to the future of our culture, country, and hemisphere.

Properly caring for waterways as centerpieces of local ecosystems marks a starting point toward properly caring for our planet. In this way, rivers create pathways to an ecologically oriented society. Protecting our streams where we live answers the question: What can one person do amid an array of global problems and seemingly hopeless forces beyond our control or influence?

With *Endangered Rivers and the Conservation Movement*, published in 1986, I related the history of river conservation. In 1993, *The Wild and Scenic Rivers of America* explored the National Wild and Scenic Rivers

System in depth. The gap between those two volumes is the largest piece—the fundamental case for the preservation and intelligent management of our rivers in today's perplexing world. *Lifelines: The Case for River Conservation* documents the need for a new level of awareness and maps out a path for action to avert the plunder of our remaining river legacy, which is shrinking by the day.

Chapter 1 offers an overview of the values of natural rivers, of the threats to them, and of the possibilities for reform. This introductory discussion may be regarded as a primer on river conservation. Chapter 2 focuses on the salmon, species that are deeply in trouble and that symbolize the health of our waterways. Chapter 3 covers the waning era of big-dam construction, and Chapter 4 addresses the continuing challenge of hydropower development. Chapters 5, 6, 7, and 8 consecutively probe the issues of water quality, instream flows, riparian or waterfront habitat, and the greater ecosystems of rivers and their watersheds. Chapter 9 reflects on the need for vision, hope, and action.

Lifelines probes the gulf between rhetoric and reality in the way we treat our rivers. It examines what's happening to our waterways—stories of alarming reality as well as bright success in stemming the tide of loss. The following pages investigate the real needs and real possibilities in conservation, for which the only alternative is the grim reality of a world without the wonder of natural rivers.

Chapter One

Sustaining the Lifelines
of a Continent

❧ A Fading Brilliance

From willow-crowded shores, sweet with the scent of summer growth, I walked along the headwaters of the Salmon River in Idaho. At a clearing where bunchgrass and the deeper green of sedges blanketed the shore, I sat to hear the liquid song of the river and to be mesmerized by the flashing quickness of the flow. The glistening, riffling continuity marked one of the basic aspects of nature: water flowing toward the sea. Then I saw the fish.

Silver, brilliant in evening light, the river master surfaced, rolled forward like a diminutive dolphin, and disappeared forever from my sight. A brief acquaintance, the fish was there and gone in one plunging instant. But another fish surfaced. Then another, and then more. Not just creatures of the currents, those salmon were part of the *mass* of the river, and my evening became filled with one of the most wondrous migrations on earth, a journey as inspiring as that of Arctic terns flying 18,000 miles from north to south, as dramatic as caribou by the thousands fording braided channels in Alaska. After living several years in the ocean, the salmon were returning to the rivers. Some fish barely parted the water with their dorsal fins; others surged with impatient force above the wet edge, muscling their way upward, very close, now, to the spawning grounds for which they had swum thousands of miles at sea and 930 miles up the Columbia, Snake, and Salmon rivers.

Twenty-five years have passed since I sat on that shore in the wilds of the northern Rockies. Today I would have to sit a long time in order to see a fish. Today, the salmon are in very serious trouble.

On many streams where salmon once spawned, dams block their

upriver paths. At one of those sites lacking fish ladders, salmon swim against the current, leap as instinct demands, and smash into the face of the dam. The fish had evaded all the previous hazards, but battled and beaten, they collapse into the current. Lacking any alternative, uncompromisingly driven by the urge to ascend the river, to reproduce, to *survive* as a unique creature, they repeat the futile leap against the dam until, bruised and exhausted, they confront the concrete impasse to their species one final time. Then, with their lives unfulfilled, they die.

Not one species but many, salmon of various types ascend the rivers at various times. Some of the major "runs" and many of the minor ones are already extinct, having come and gone without so much as an adequate biological record, without mourning, without dynamite to correct the problems of dams. Now, the remaining runs in the Salmon River appear to be facing the same deadly fate owing to the eight downstream dams that block their path—lethal barriers despite fish ladders. The federal government built the dams so that barges could ship grain to foreign markets, and now the dams provide northwesterners with some of the cheapest electricity in the nation. The cost of extirpation of these species is omitted from the utility bills that arrive each month in the mail.

✍ An Urgency Across the Land

Family records indicate that my ancestors touched shore in America in 1637, no doubt finding a wealth of wild rivers in New England. The settlers depended on the streams for sustenance. They surely would have feasted on the swarming rafts of Atlantic salmon, free for the picking, a pitchfork being adequate for fishing. All rivers then surged from countless headwaters at springs and snowbanks and flowed down to our three oceans—the Atlantic, Pacific, and Arctic. Abundant runoff raged wild and high in springtime, clear and cool in summer. Rivers nourished the greatest abundance of life this continent has ever known. One might think of it as "North America National Park." Imagine an untouched Mississippi! The Great Lakes as a drinkable wilderness! The wildlife glories of Yellowstone—everywhere! Yet it was even better than that, because much of the continent, especially the East and South, was richer than Yellowstone, being humid, temperate, and at a low elevation, far more conducive to the propagation of life.

While my ancestors from the Pilgrim days on down possessed so much, they never lived in harmony with the land, but subdued it to the limits of their technology, as we are still doing today. Now we see the results: a lot of people possessing only a fraction of the original, natural, free wealth of the continent. Those who say we cannot afford to protect rivers are referring to only the final remnant that has somehow escaped wholesale development and rearrangement. It is about this final trace that we now argue so much. It is about this token of our ancestors' heritage that we are still pressed at every turn to compromise.

From the coasts of Maine and Florida to the shores of California and Alaska, our rivers are beleaguered by dams, pollution, diversions, and streamside development. The qualities that once seemed limitless are today utterly forgotten at waterways as massive as the Missouri, Tennessee, and Sacramento. Many people living along the Ohio River don't even *know* that it is dammed; in fact, it is not free-flowing at all. Sluggish, currentless, rainbow-oiled waters are all that many residents have ever known, all they ever *imagined*.

The abundance of water and of the life it holds were once real, but only aspects of that abundance remain. With the pressures of an American population that grows even in eras of economic recession, rivers continue to be regarded as a resource for expedient consumption.

Progress in conservation has been made, but too often we define environmental progress as a slower rate of loss. It is considered an accomplishment when a stream is reclaimed, not to healthful conditions but to anything outdistancing the toxic dumps we have come to expect of rivers ranging from West Virginia's Kanawha to California's Alamo. At a time when environmental awareness has perhaps reached a modern zenith, policies and practices continue to degrade the very basis of ecosystems and communities—the arteries that provide water, a parade of life, and a proud identity to otherwise increasingly faceless cities, towns, and countrysides.

Yet who does not desire a river of life? Who would reject a river where children can swim on summer afternoons, where anglers can cast a fly or a worm for food or sport, where homeowners can live in admiration of the fruitful shores and stroll with joy in their hearts on a summer evening? Rivers, quite simply, are part of the American ideal, as expressed in the pioneering Anglo settlement at the mouth of the James River, the tales of Mark Twain, and the paradisiac scenes on calendars, postcards, and advertisements for products as far removed from rivers as chewing tobacco.

Our rivers are fundamental to the quality of our lives, but by some perverse ingratitude they go largely unrecognized in the process of building America. In spite of important gains in pollution control, economic analysis that halts new dam proposals, and a handful of wild and scenic river designations, rivers remain a poor orphan to the nation that we continue to develop. Rivers remain victims of a wringing of wealth that ignores the source of that wealth, calling to mind an old story: the goose that laid the golden egg was killed because of the greedy belief that many eggs could be gleaned at once.

‫ The Nation's Heritage

Rivers are central to America's existence—to *people's* existence. Coursing in our veins as rivers do on earth, water constitutes 75 percent of our own body weight. With uneasy concern, the president of the organization called American Rivers remarked, "My twelve-year-old daughter is three-quarters Potomac River." A light-hearted interpretation of the Creation says people were invented so that water could *walk* from place to place. Central to our regard for rivers is the fact that we drink from them. More than half the water used in this country comes from streams, and the rest comes from groundwater, inextricably tied to the surface flow because rivers recharge the aquifers, and the aquifers in turn seep into the rivers.

Rivers have been a staple ingredient in our civilization. They still are. Correspondent Charles Kuralt said, "America is a great story, and there is a river on every page of it." Stories of river travel are as old as our presence on the land. Imagine the tales of Jacques Cartier sailing up the St. Lawrence in 1534, of revolutionary army volunteers ascending the Kennebec

River in Maine or crossing the Delaware with George Washington, of keelboaters on the Ohio River, or of John Colter poling up the Missouri. More recently, naturalist Edwin Way Teale wrote, "To the lost man, to the pioneer penetrating a new country, to the naturalist who wishes to see the wild land at its wildest, the advice is always the same—follow a river. The river is the original forest highway. It is nature's own Wilderness Road."

Musician and songwriter Mason Williams has collected more than 1,000 river songs and performs concerts in which he never strays from a riverine theme. The standards include "Shenandoah," "Deep River," "Shall We Gather at the River?" "Down by the Old Mill Stream," "Moon River," and so on. The cultural anthem of modern-day river lovers might be Loggins and Messina's "Run, River, Run."

Rushing from rivulet to riparian artery, waterways have formed our highways—the Hudson, Mohawk, Susquehanna, Tennessee, and Mississippi—all well-known routes of settlement. Now, discovered by canoeists, rafters, kayakers, and captains of anything that floats, including more than one rubber dinosaur I have seen, thousands of rivers in all corners of the countryside are routes of adventure, recreation, and escape. They offer a different way to see the land, a remarkably fitting way to enjoy the wonders of America.

Rivers offer a way to enjoy the earth, to appreciate it. Fishing, boating, swimming, hiking alongside waterways, and all forms of river recreation surge in popularity. One conservative count has Americans spending more than 550 million days a year in recreation by streams, a figure that no doubt fails to account for those times people simply stand at the water's edge to look, to think, to laugh, to cry, to reflect on the past, and to plan for the future.

Except for driving—and one could argue that time spent in a car is not really recreation but only a gas-consumptive means of getting somewhere—water-based pursuits are the most popular form of outdoor recreation. In much of the West, tourism outranks all other "industry," leaving ranching, mining, and logging far behind. The popularity of rivers can be seen explicitly in the boom in whitewater paddling, an industry at once nonpolluting, labor-intensive, and dollar-infusing to such towns as Ohiopyle, Pennsylvania; Albright, West Virginia; and Wesser, North Carolina. This is also seen at Moab, Utah; Galice, Oregon; Buena Vista, Colorado; Taos, New Mexico; and Coloma, California.

On the Gauley River in West Virginia, a rafting season of only twenty days generates $20 million of economic activity, each visitor resulting in 1.8 days of employment, giving that mountain state an alternative to the chemical-factory and strip-mine way of life. In Colorado, commercial river running accounts for $70 million in the state economy; fishing contributes a whopping $1 billion. The number of anglers nationwide doubled between 1955 and 1988. In 1985, 38.4 million anglers spent $17.8 billion, according to the U.S. Fish and Wildlife Service. Since 1960, canoeing has increased in popularity by 515 percent compared to the mere doubling of hikers, bikers, and campers. In Arkansas, canoeing contributes a generous $20 million a year to the economy.

Time spent on rivers is more than recreation; it can be re-creation in the finest sense—a renewal of the spirit, a refreshment of the mind, a reinvigoration of the body. Floating on a boat in the current, we watch a kaleidoscope of scenery drift by. Skimming through morning mist, sneaking past herons, warming our bodies with sunshine that scatters stars of reflection aross the water—all of these moments add to our understanding of what a river is. Blue depths beyond whitewater ledges, rocks colored red and black like a mosaic, and fish glinting across a green pool all add to the endless picture book of a river, a book that depicts a perfect place.

Passions run higher on rivers. Life seems more vital. On a river, it's easier to believe in the power of nature, in the water cycle, in the chain of life, in the flow of nutrients down to the sea, in the fact that we are made from earthly elements and when we die those elements go back to the ground and feed some other life. In a society that has become increasingly urban and alienated from the natural world, rivers offer an opportunity to return, to rejoin the pattern and the company of life on earth, to share in this archetype of creation. But that possibility exists only if the rivers are worth going to.

Rivers are central to heritage, history, and recreation, and they are universally visited and depended upon. To think that only anglers use a river is like thinking only hunters use the woods. Other people simply love the woods, and so it is with rivers.

William K. Reilly, before becoming administrator of the U.S. Environmental Protection Agency, testified in support of a National Park Service program that was assisting local communities in protecting rivers, and recalled the Sangamon River of his youth in Illinois: "Its mud banks and smells, the occasional snake, the mysteries of its undergrowth and its capacity to roll and rise and spread in spring rains are for me an important childhood association. On many a lazy afternoon, only the river seemed alive and in motion, always available to play with or just watch." Many people will agree: the days spent along rivers are the days of heaven.

No one, in fact, can really get away from this thing we might call riverness. Streams pass through virtually every community. More common than mountains or seashores, rivers of one size or another are one of the most universal features on the landscape.

Modern news headlines report the cutting of tropical rain forests, global warming, and ozone shrinkage, and high-profile conservation initiatives have centered on wilderness and endangered species protection—all vital concerns. Yet these issues may seem distant or abstract from daily life. This is not so for rivers and streams. How far must anyone go to find a waterway in need of care? And because a stream's health depends on its watershed—all the land in the drainage—the stewardship of rivers becomes a holistic endeavor, touching virtually every aspect of our relationship to the earth.

The difficult global environmental problems require commitments for reform that must be rooted in a love of the earth. Local features such as rivers, experienced in our day-to-day lives, engender that love, much as the warmth of a close family instills the esteem needed to deal with less friendly people in the outside world.

When we fly over the continent, rivers are the dominant features seen from 30,000 feet. My last coast-to-coast flight disclosed the claustrophobically leveed Sacramento and then the bearishly rugged American River of California; the Carson, bound for irrigation ditches in Nevada; the comprehensively diverted Sevier and then the bow-tie loops marking the

Green and Colorado rivers in Utah; the wide, shallow Platte of Colorado and Nebraska; the ponderous Missouri and Mississippi; and then, mostly obscured by clouds, the Wabash, Ohio, and Potomac.

Our highways often follow rivers, mimicking sinuous routes through hollows, valleys, and canyons. Even the interstate highway system—though striving to be as oblivious as possible to natural features—follows the lead of rivers: I-91 along the Connecticut, I-81 along the Shenandoah, I-80 following the Platte, I-5 along the Willamette and Sacramento. Virtually every time we travel, a stream or river is revealed to us.

Among our 150 largest cities, 130 are sited along rivers. Pittsburgh, Cincinnati, Memphis, St. Louis, Minneapolis, Boise, and Fairbanks are a few riverfront cities. Likewise, the coastal cities—New York, Houston, Seattle, San Francisco, and Anchorage, for example—lie at the mouths of rivers. It is to rivers that urban populations now turn for green relief. Fairmont Park along the Schuylkill in Philadelphia is the largest urban park in America. The Potomac River frontage in Washington, D.C., and the Boise River in Boise, Idaho, are urban oases. Walkers, runners, rafters, rollerbladers, horseback riders, swimmers, beachcombers, anglers, and bird watchers account for 5.1 million visitor days a year along the American River in Sacramento. The Chattahoochee River near Atlanta is used by 1.5 million people a year.

And when we travel from home to marvel at the wonders of our national parks, rivers are often the subject of our awe, from the Little River in Great Smoky Mountains National Park to the Snake in Grand Teton. The Yellowstone crashes over falls and winds through the moose-grazed Hayden Valley. The Flathead borders Glacier National Park, the Virgin flows through Zion, the Colorado creates the Grand Canyon, and the Tuolumne and Merced form highlights of the nation's scenery at Yosemite. Niagara Falls—the most visited natural tourist attraction—is first and foremost a *river*.

Beyond all this, rivers are magnets for the imagination, for conscious pondering and subconscious dreams, thrills, and fears. People stare into the moving water, captivated, as they are when gazing into a fire. What is it that draws and holds us? The rivers' reflections of our lives and experiences are endless. The water calls up our own ambitions of flowing with ease, of navigating the unknown. Streams represent constant rebirth. The waters flow in, forever new, yet forever the same; they complete a journey from beginning to end, and then they embark on the journey again. Reflecting the symbolism, the titles of hundreds of novels include the word *river*, though most of these books have nothing to do with flowing water.

Our treatment of rivers takes on extra meaning as well. When we heal our streams we may likewise heal our society. And perhaps it works the other way around. A society that truly values such principles as fairness, health, peace, freedom, and cooperation would surely find itself unwilling to treat rivers with neglect and abuse.

Increasing numbers of people view rivers as unique, essential, and sacred, and Indians have long regarded rivers with reverence. Futilely opposing a dam above his reservation in the Rocky Mountain foothills of Alberta, Canada, Peigan Blackfoot chief Leonard Bastian said that to flood the Oldman River will have the same effect on his people that the burning of all books would have on Western culture. In a landmark ruling in 1984, the federal government recognized spiritual values that the Confederated Salish and Kootenai Tribes attached to the Kootenai River in Montana and denied a permit for a power company to dam and divert the stream. To do so would infringe on religious beliefs protected by the First Amendment.

Rivers are sometimes seen as spiritual centerpieces, but too frequently they are taken for granted. How often when we drive across a bridge do we ask ourselves: What stream was that? Where does it come from? Is it healthy? How are we affecting it? Ironically, the commonness of rivers may contribute to our disregard. Consider the everywhere-presence of rivers: when we turn on the kitchen tap, it is a river of some sort that feeds the other end; and in virtually every community, it is to a stream that we relegate our human waste.

Though overlooked in much of day-to-day life, rivers are central to American geography, culture, economy, identity, and national consciousness, from Mount Vernon on the estuarine Potomac to the Oregon Trail as it treacherously crossed the Snake River and later emerged from the green-walled depths of the Columbia Gorge.

❧ Rivers of Life

Most important, rivers form lifelines, housing fisheries of eclectic diversity and riparian corridors with the richest habitat, while underpinning a wide range of ecosystems. Rivers are exquisite in their abilities to nurture life, sublime in functioning detail, impressive in contributions of global significance. They carry nutrients to estuaries and the fishes of the sea, deposit fertile soil on flood plains, mold and sculpt the earth we live on, and maintain their channels and streamsides as biological wonderlands. Their clean water and gravel beds sustain and shelter a host of invertebrate life essential to the food chain.

The rivers' flood plains absorb excess runoff and release it slowly when floods recede. Rivers generate microclimates that moderate summer's heat. They form the homes and highways for hundreds of species of fish—one of the world's great food sources.

Rivers do all of this for free if we allow them to do it. Once the waters are squandered, these services are provided only at great cost—if provided at all—and usually without the desired results. Dams destroy fisheries, for example, that we attempt to replace through hatcheries—prohibitively costly in the long run and ironically weakening the gene pool of the very fish whose numbers we seek to augment. After water quality is compromised, we purify water at great expense or, worse yet, we buy it in bottles when pollution abatement would have been cheaper. As President John F. Kennedy said, "Conservation is the highest form of national thrift."

Riparian frontage is the most critical habitat to 75 percent of all western wildlife species and to a large percentage of eastern species as well. Cottonwood groves in the West and sycamore trees in the East contain an ark of animals and birds. In the vast deserts and drylands, the rivers' value is doubly important.

The great majority of endangered species depend on waterfronts, and aquatic species are in far more peril than terrestrial ones. The enormous importance of rivers to endangered species is only beginning to be realized. If you took the rivers out of most ecosystems, not much would be left.

The ecological importance is all the more evident from a bird's-eye view. In many regions—certainly in the flatlands and farming country—

river corridors are the only areas surviving in some semblance of their original selves. Soybean fields, hayfields, and orchards lie gridded and patchworked on the landscape, but in their midst, serpentine twists of waterways endure as havens for wildlife, depleted though those havens might be.

Down there at the rivers are sturgeon that can grow to sixteen-foot lengths, tiny minnows that move eighty-eight pounds of gravel while preparing spawning beds, loons that hold their breath for five minutes when diving, freshwater ducks of thirty-four species, ospreys that pluck fish from the surface, and otters that slide in the mud for fun. There are whirligig beetles with double sets of eyes so they can see into the water and into the air at once. Beetlelike water boatmen carry a bubble of air with them so they can breathe when submerged. Caddis flies string nets to catch food, and frogs inhale oxygen through their skin while resting in mud during winter. There are clams, sponges, mayflies, snails, rotifers, protozoans, diatoms, crayfish, muskrats, herons, trout, and ninety-pound snapping turtles.

We have planned ineffectively for our rivers partly because they are so difficult to describe in all their glory and promise. Even if we could diagram the networks of lives depending on lives, the descriptions lack the fragrance of springtime cottonwoods, the chilled electricity of a splash on a summer day, the soothing hiss of the riffle in our ears at night. The scents, the sounds, and the light on the water at sunset might best trigger the impulse that a river is worth saving.

✷ The Lost Wonders of America

The first white settlers found rivers in a wild abundance that today is unknown even in protected places. In 1685 William Penn wrote, "Sturgeon play continually in our Rivers in Summer." Henry Hudson saw seven-foot-long sturgeon upstream from today's New York City. In 1779 soldiers with General John Sullivan in southern New York and northern Pennsylvania reported that fish were so plentiful that streambeds could not be seen. The abundance has diminished, and mere survival of many life forms is now the challenge. Even rivers in Alaska are plagued by the effects of mining, drilling, and logging, and by too many hunters, anglers, and floaters dropped by airplane into areas where wildlife is extremely sensitive to change.

Along the Feather River in California, a riparian belt appears healthy and vibrant and makes it easy to picture the way the Great Valley of the Golden State appeared before rivers were diverted and wetlands drained. But the Feather looks good to me only because I didn't know it before the drainage and diversions of the past fifty years. Imagine a depth of riparian forest measured not in feet but in miles! We take pleasure in watching waterfowl there today, but to envision what used to be, multiply today's qualities by ten times or more.

The changes have occurred over days and over decades, in the invisible trace of mercury and in viscous mudflows of silt. Idyllic scenes of America still invite people to paint, sketch, or photograph along some rivers, but those scenes have become scarce. It is no wonder that people are starved for a national identity beyond political clichés.

The changes have occurred in a relatively short time, most of them between 1930 and now. We have rendered biologically useless a substantial part of the river resource of America within the memory of one generation. The rivers and their water have gone to polluted channels in the industrial states, to irrigation canals with holes that leak the volume of broken fire hydrants, to the once-a-week car wash, to Kentucky bluegrass transplanted in Utah, to hayfields on irrigated acres all across the Great American Desert, to the world's tallest fountain in Arizona, and to a general attitude that water is free and limitless.

The Indiana state song, "On the Banks of the Wabash, Far Away," fails to recognize that the banks no longer in truth exist; the river is girded by levees of engineered precision and vacuous biology. Another state song, "Beautiful Ohio," tells of "drifting in the current," a possibility long lost from memory since the 981-mile-long Ohio has been back-to-back dammed for barges since before the Great Depression. Although our national symbol, the bald eagle, soars high in artistic renderings, the bird remains endangered for the simple reason that rivers are endangered.

One reason we lack roots as a culture is that places don't last long enough, and this unfortunate tragedy applies to rivers as well as neighborhoods and whole towns. In fighting Tellico Dam on the Little Tennessee

River, traditional Cherokee Indians believed that they would end as a society when their valley was flooded. We have also seen the demise of many white societies, including farming communities flooded in the Youghiogheny Valley of Pennsylvania, in the Blue Valley of Kansas, and at hundreds of other sites. The lower Susquehanna of shad and sky-clouding waterfowl is gone, as are the long reaches of the lazy-flowing Savannah, flooded by reservoirs. The Mississippi's uncompromised empire of sprawling wetlands, gone. The South Fork of the Flathead, majestic in the grizzly bear country of the northern Rockies, gone, now flooded by a reservoir instead, as is the upper Skagit, once the gem of the North Cascades.

A Nature Conservancy study found that one-third of all freshwater fish species are imperiled, as are 20 percent of freshwater shellfish and invertebrates. Two-thirds of the fish species of the Illinois River have disappeared, and this is not an unusual case. Salmon runs in the Columbia have declined by 85 percent, and by 95 percent if hatchery-raised fish are not counted. Bob Doppelt of the Pacific Rivers Council asked, "How would our society respond if our agricultural productivity declined by 85 percent?" In Arizona, thirty-two fish species existed in presettlement times; five were extirpated, and twenty-one of the twenty-seven that remain are listed as endangered or are being considered for listing. The Science Advisory Board of the Environmental Protection Agency rated habitat alteration and species extinction as the most crucial issue to humankind, matched only by global warming. In contrast to the scientists' report, surveys showed that the American public was relatively unaware of the consequences of widespread extinction. Esteemed biologist E. O. Wilson stated that 18,000 species worldwide may be going extinct each year, according to the best calculation of habitat loss.

Much of our riverine legacy was lost in an age of innocence when the myth of abundance had a more convincing ring to it, when real needs were in fact met by projects that actually made sense. That age has passed, and most new developments now pose threats disproportionate to advertised gains.

Statistics tell part of the story. The United States has 3.6 million miles of rivers and streams of all sizes (rivers of 25 miles or greater in length total about 320,000 miles). Thirty percent of that mileage does not meet clean water standards, according to the Environmental Protection Agency, and the figure would rise to 50 percent or more if biological criteria were applied rather than only chemical criteria centering on human health.

According to National Park Service data, 75,000 large dams block nearly every major river in the country outside Alaska. The Salmon River in Idaho, the Greenbrier in West Virginia, and the Delaware in Pennsylvania, New York, and New Jersey are among the few exceptions. Hundreds of thousands of miles of free-flowing rivers now lie impounded behind dams.

It is estimated that 200,000 miles have been channelized. The bulk of this serves to drain water faster in the name of flood control, incidentally aggravating floods elsewhere and leading to more channelization and dam proposals, to more flood damage, and to rivers truncated from their flood plain ecosystems.

River frontage has been developed for industry, homes, railroads, roads, and plowed fields—a clear majority of the stream frontage in most regions. In many parts of the country, a stream segment without development or farming at its edge is a rarity, a state-park-type attraction.

No one knows how much stream mileage is depleted of flows by diversions, mainly for irrigation, but nearly all western streams outside of headwaters fall into this category of biologically botched mileage, lacking water and therefore lacking life. While water can be withdrawn from many streams without noticeable effect, we exhausted that generous margin of error without even questioning what the limits were. Biologists are now considering that question at some streams.

What is left? Even the least affected rivers have their share of problems. The St. John River of Maine flows wild for 120 miles in its upper reaches but is dammed again and again down below. The Salmon River is plagued by scores of unscreened irrigation diversions that take water from the river and kill up to 80 percent of the migrating fish, by timber cutting on highly erodible soils, and by cattle and sheep, which leave their stamp on 70 percent or more of the public land in the West and on much of the private land as well. In the spacious state of Colorado, the San Miguel is one of the longest undammed rivers, but is only seventy-five miles long. Even it begins virtually in the midst of a Superfund site of hazardous mining waste. For truly natural rivers unencumbered by the gamut of effects, we are restricted to a few gems such as the Selway in Idaho, to Alaska, and to headwater streams, few of which remain untouched by human intervention outside national parks and wilderness areas. Surveying the nation's rivers, the National Park Service found 2 percent with both outstanding natural qualities and little degradation. More detailed surveys would increase the number, but not much.

Natural rivers are a scarce resource, ranking right up there with the remaining 10 percent of wilderness outside Alaska, the 12 percent of old-growth timber in the Northwest and almost none elsewhere, the 1 percent of grizzly bear habitat outside Alaska, and the 1 or 2 percent of tallgrass prairie.

The statistics are numbing after a while, but anybody can look at his or her local river and imagine some of the changes that have occurred. Where I grew up in the Appalachian foothills, the streams would surely have run higher year-round with a canopy of virgin hardwoods instead of the logged-over, mined-over, roaded and subdivided watersheds that exist today. The Beaver River in Pennsylvania would have been an ecological treasure house in that climate of hot summer humidity, with rapids where hydroelectric dams were later built, and with clean water filtered through an ecological nursery rather than the industries, strip mines, and sewage pipes of today.

Where I now sit, the Middle Fork of the Boise River in Idaho runs with exceeding beauty through the lower slopes of the Rockies; yet this river and its accompanying habitat of willows and cottonwoods are diminished by mining, logging, and cattle. Mercury, deposited in the silver boom of the last century, accumulated in the upstream sediments of a small dam that burst in 1991, spilling the silt and heavy metals. A stroll up the Roaring River tributary reveals logging on slopes of unwalkable steepness and high erodibility. Downstream, dams have eliminated the most fertile and productive habitat at lower elevations and blocked teeming numbers of salmon from migrating to the headwaters. So, while the river looks good, it retains only a fraction of the value it once had.

Rivers host an interconnectedness never imagined by most casual viewers. While the gross losses from dams, diversions, development, and pollution are apparent, other kinds of deterioration may go unnoticed. Manipulation of the flow, for example, precipitates a chain of events that can be catastrophic in the long term. Diversions, dams, and pollution often raise the temperature of the water beyond the limits of native fish and the invertebrate life on which they depend. Beyond seventy-seven degrees Fahrenheit—exceeded in the sun-warmed surface of reservoirs and in the depleted flows of agricultural regions—trout die.

Less obvious are the morphology changes—unintentional manipulation of the streambed—a tampering with the very structure of the river and thereby its ability to renew and maintain itself. Related to this is the plight of the cottonwood. Tuned to the cycles of the ages, the tree's regermination often requires a large flood carrying silt, which is deposited on the insides of bends. The seeds of the cottonwood land on the silt and sprout, a sequence occurring about once every twelve years. Lacking the floods and the silt below dams, this king of the riparian forest finds no seed beds below many dams in the West. Nothing of comparable value can replace the cottonwood, which serves as a food source for animals and bird species, as cover for scores of songbirds, and as nesting sites for bald eagles, ospreys, and great blue herons.

Troubles that plague the cottonwood also plague the commercial fishing industry at sea. Silt and organic detritus coming from rivers are needed not only for estuarine life but for fish in the oceans; 70 percent of the fish we eat begin their lives in bays that are fed directly by rivers.

While much of our river heritage has disappeared, it is not too late to save a vital remnant, nor too late to restore a meaningful share of what has been lost.

❧ Era of Awakening

Combating the losses, a river conservation movement is slowing the ruin of waterways, gaining safekeeping for some of the finest river segments, and beginning restoration on a long backlog of streams.

After two centuries of neglect, the federal government effectively adopted water quality as a goal with the Clean Water Act of 1972, ultimately solving many of the grossest sewage problems. Metropolitan agencies with federal money have restored the Potomac to the degree that people accidentally dunked in the river no longer need tetanus shots. The Willamette in Oregon, the Allegheny in Pennsylvania, and the James in Virginia—once quarantined because of industrial overloads—now glide respectably past their communities.

With its genesis in the Hetch Hetchy controversy on California's Tuolumne River in 1910, the protection of rivers from dams and large water projects was a minority concern, and only a few rivers in national parks were rescued through the first half of the century. In the 1960s and 1970s, however, dam fighting became a full-scale conservation battlefront. From an initial interest in protecting parklands, involvement blossomed to embrace fish and wildlife, wilderness, scenic areas, home sites, farmland, and ecosystems. Through effective opposition, along with the exhaustion of practicable sites and tighter purse strings, the era of big-dam building ended in the late 1970s, and only a few projects persist as threats to American rivers.

Going beyond the rear-guard battles against dams and canals, the National Wild and Scenic Rivers Act of 1968 established a positive alternative. Beginning with 12 rivers (counting designated tributaries), the system has grown to 224 in twenty-five years—portions of rivers and tributaries where federal projects or licenses damaging to the rivers are prohibited and where action to save open space and manage recreation is encouraged. More than thirty states have likewise established scenic river programs involving 13,000 miles of waterways—an amount comparable to that of the national system but not as well protected. Progress with wild and scenic river designations is impressive and has saved many important streams, but in the total picture of American rivers, it barely scratches the surface. Even a tenfold increase in the National Wild and Scenic Rivers System would protect only 3 percent of the nation's total stream mileage.

The early 1990s saw an explosion in grassroots interest in local rivers, with primary concerns being leapfrogging land developments on shorelines, water quality, and hydroelectric threats. In six New England states, 100 different river conservation groups were formed. Ohio boasted 4,000 official "creek watchers." In North Carolina, 150 stream protection groups sprang up. Idaho Rivers United drew 400 people to a conference at which a gathering of 50 would have been a reasonable goal just a few years before. More than 1,000 people attended a Friends of the River annual conference in California.

Not only river enthusiasts but corporations enlisted in the cause. An oil company advertised in *Audubon* magazine that a part of Colorado's Gunnison Gorge had been saved; this announcement was regarded as good public relations. Imploring people to visit, the state of West Virginia advertised its whitewater. A mood in the nation has changed; rivers are now *worth* something.

It is no coincidence that rivers have been central to the environmental history of America. Though he lost, John Muir's fight for the Tuolumne River in Hetch Hetchy Valley sparked initial preservation attempts and gave rise to the formation of the National Park Service. The Echo Park Dam battle on the Green and Yampa rivers in Colorado was the founding event for a new, aggressive brand of conservation in the 1960s and provided the essential impetus for the Wilderness Act in 1964. The modern-day Sierra Club was built on the fight to save the Grand Canyon from damming. The Clean Water Act stands as a milestone in advancing environmental responsibilities. Progress has been made, but the threats persist.

❧ Multiple Threats

The impressive conservation gains from 1968 to the 1990s have unfortunately not halted the tide of destruction, which overruns the conservation agenda on many fronts. Too often, the intricate workings of a river diminish, then cease, before people have mobilized to save their stream.

Although the era of big dams in the United States died, a few large dam proposals did not, and the interest in small dams for hydroelectric power grew by leaps and bounds, first with the 1973 Mideast oil embargo and then with the 1978 Public Utility Regulatory Policies Act, which established incentives for small hydroelectric development. An oil glut depressed energy prices temporarily, and with them the plans for hydrodams, but the threats linger ominously with the inevitable need for more electricity to serve an expanding population. Meanwhile, Americans consume more—not less—in a frenzy of driving and of accumulating material goods that outstrips anything that other people in the world can imagine.

Even worse than the profusion of small hydroelectric projects, the big dam era isn't really over when a continental view is taken. In the expansive open spaces of Canada—places of astonishing wilderness and home to some of the least affected indigenous people on the continent—a provincial utility constructs hydroelectric dams of science-fiction scale, obliterating entire ecosystems and cultures and already ruining a land mass the size of Switzerland. Other dams threatening major destruction have been advanced for the Stikine River in British Columbia, called a 100-mile-long Yosemite by John Muir. These are not just Canadian projects. Some of the power is to be shipped south, so they are also U.S. projects, although we fail to recognize our responsibility for supporting another government in liquidating the more remote treasures of the continent.

Water quality improvements scarcely touch the ubiquitous problems of polluted runoff coming from large areas of land—farmed fields, clearcuts, and urban streets—sources that together account for more than two-thirds of all water pollution. The effects are not just a matter of mud in streams; pesticides and herbicides chronically pollute agricultural regions and their water supplies. A study at the University of California at Davis in the late 1980s reported that 60 percent of California's creeks were in some kind of trouble, and the figure is no doubt higher in the densely developed areas of the East and the farmed Midwest.

While the stench of sewage has been abated below cities, the overflow of toxic waste appalls the most informed viewers. Laws attempt to stem the proliferation of thousands of poisons but fail to keep up with the production, consumption, and dumping of some of the more hideous substances ever to leave chemical factories.

Diversions of water throughout the West date back to white people's settlement in the mid-1800s, but the virulent effect of drying up tens of thousands of miles of streams is just becoming focused in the public eye. Many of the dewaterings are unnecessary and the problems correctable, except that the water is "free" to its takers, and the labyrinth of western water law encourages waste by letting an irrigator have any water he can "beneficially" use, a term of stupendously loose interpretation. No incentives exist to recognize streams as living entities.

More than aiding family farmers, much of the subsidized water and the desiccated riverbeds are monuments to agribusiness. The federal government lavished $20 million in subsidies on one corporation in 1986 *not* to grow surplus cotton with its already subsidized water. In the once biologically blessed rivers of the Southeast, channelization and the overcontrol of floods exterminates hardwood swamps, and wetlands are still eliminated as a "public nuisance."

Finally, land development is the most pervasive threat to riverfronts nationwide, the accumulated losses making long-term inroads on the riparian ecosystem. From the industries lining the banks of broad waterways, to the geometry of suburban subdivisions, to the seemingly innocent scattering of vacation cabins, the streamsides constituting so much of the rivers' integrity continue to be bulldozed, filled, and built on. Land-use regulations are weak, bypassed, ignored, or nonexistent along most waterways. Here, on the vulnerable private frontage of rivers from the Saluda in South Carolina to the Alsea in Oregon, is a classic confrontation of American values: the desire to conserve the environment versus the desire to sustain individual rights no matter what.

The rate of deterioration of some rivers has diminished in the latter twentieth century, making long-term protection a more plausible argument, but still, New Englanders face development on verdant banks, southerners confront ditches and drains, midwesterners grow alarmed at the agricultural residue in their taps, Rocky Mountain natives see streams degraded by logging and grazing on public land, northwesterners fight hydroelectric dams wherever the power of the river can be wired, and Californians experience new pressure to dam and divert dwindling water supplies to propagate runaway growth.

ᴥ A Bridge to the Future

Beyond the concern for specific waterways, a new urgency sweeps the country as people become aware of the importance of whole ecosystems—not just specific parks or neighborhoods, but the web of life and the greater habitat. Hal Borland wrote that a river is "the summation of a whole valley," and yet, the river stands for even more than that.

If we appreciate a clean drink of water, then shouldn't we also appreciate the banks and bed that provide the stucture for a river's health, the flood plain that purifies the flow, the headwater streams that feed it, the raindrops that coalesce to form running water, and the ground on which the raindrops fall? If we love a shaded home near a river, then shouldn't we love all these things too?

An ecological consciousness implores us to reach out beyond the waterfront and beyond the acreage where we sit. Yet progress is blocked by a kind of inertia. People do not deny the facts or doubt the legitimacy of recurrent exposés detailing environmental distress, but their reaction somehow stops there. They are not affected personally. They fail to realize that all of us must change. For many years, our choices when voting gave us political leaders who ignored the demise of the real America—not just an abstract concept represented by reverence for the flag, but America itself—the land, water, and air that make up this country. Saving the rivers and the land is perhaps the most patriotic endeavor a person can pursue.

While the need for ecosystem planning is widely accepted among scientists, public land managers, and much of the public itself, it remains extraordinarily difficult to do far less ambitious things—to stop a small hydroelectric dam, for example, or to keep a modest amount of water in a stream, or to secure a 100-foot building setback from a waterfront. Underlying our failure are ignorance, greed, and apathy. And underlying nearly all of the problems, population growth continues while nobody wants to address the issue. Bursting at the seams, California alone swells by 700,000 people a year—more than another San Francisco annually. The U.S. population is growing by about 25 million each decade. Continuing at recent rates, the nation's population will exceed 400 million by the year 2050. Even a 1 percent growth rate results in double the number of people in seventy years (in 1990 the nation was growing at 0.8 percent per year). Rivers, ecosystems, and most qualities of the earth as we know it are doomed without a leveling of this growth. Otherwise we will be tied to the sociology of the anthill, to a future that Indians have called "the end of living and the beginning of survival." Waterfronts are where the growth pressure is strongest, placing rivers on the front line of jeopardy.

States experiencing less growth than California have other, no less formidable obstacles to river protection. In Wyoming, the smallest state in population, politicians cite the lack of growth as a reason to avoid saving anything they might dam, divert, mine, cut, drill, or sell—in short, to liquidate the natural wealth of the state as fast as possible. Ironically, Wyoming's most promising economic prospects lie in tourism.

The urgency to protect our rivers increases every day as the threats increase and as the inventory of healthy waterways diminishes. Even though much has been lost, the continent may never be this good again. In the difficult leap from isolated environmental improvements to ecosystem management, rivers form a bridge or a half-step, incorporating the older motivation to save specific places such as parks but demanding a larger view of watersheds, of interrelationships among species, and of the effects of development on private land. Rivers offer an avenue of access to ecosystem protection that may prove more effective than traditional environmental efforts, which have frequently focused on wilderness, parks, or public lands without addressing the overlap and the complications of the larger picture. River protection advocates have already begun the difficult step of incorporating concerns about private land and the widening circle of factors involved in watershed management.

Because of the bridge that rivers create between specific sites and ecosystems, and because the parallel movements to establish parks and wilderness areas are maturing, river protection may become the country's foremost program of natural areas protection. When comparing the recent growth of the National Wild and Scenic Rivers System to that of parks or national wildlife refuges, rivers are found to be at the forefront of successful efforts.

Even more difficult than the transition from saving sites to saving ecosystems, the modern era requires the transition to a different way of regarding the earth—not just as capital to be consumed, but as a place to live, as a place for all creatures to live, as a place for nature to thrive. If we can treat our rivers with greater respect, then we might prove that we can live more compatibly with the rest of the earth. Jimmy Carter, one of the few environmentally conscious presidents we've had, said, "We must face the prospect of changing our basic ways of living. This change will either be made on our own initiative in a planned and rational way, or forced on us with chaos and suffering by the inexorable laws of nature." Our treatment of rivers may well be a vehicle for those changes.

Throughout the past era of water development, we considered the manipulation of rivers and asked: Can we do this—is it physically possible? Will it benefit *anyone*? Can we get somebody else to pay for it? But in the future, perhaps we will ask: Do we really need this? Can we afford it? What will be lost, and is it replaceable? Will this be a burden to future generations? Will the result be attractive or ugly, healthy or toxic?

Historian Bernard DeVoto called rivers "the conduits of national adventure." And so they remain to people who push forward with a new brand of conservation on this incomparable continent.

In swimming from the headwaters to the sea and back again, salmon signify the essential nature of rivers. Though spawning at the headwaters is not a human requirement, people need the rivers for sustenance and survival no less than the last sockeye salmon that attempts to ascend the Columbia River.

Chapter Two

The Embodiment
of Rivers

❧ A Vital Presence

A living monument to rivers, the salmon journey upstream from the sea, momentarily seeking the refuge of eddies behind rocks, then dashing forward through the current. Climbing the riffles, surmounting the rapids, leaping small waterfalls, the salmon strive always onward to a place they know, to a mountain stream of limpid water and gravel as clean as shiny new marbles. No one knows exactly how they find their way back to the rivulets where their lives began, but a reading of the earth's electromagnetic field may be important in their return from ocean waters. Once in the rivers, salmon appear to be guided by a sense of smell; the chemistry of each stream is different. A small margin of fish do not return to their birthplaces, but rather colonize new habitat, some searching for ancestral sites above dams but encountering dead ends, quite literally, to their journeys.

Mysterious, powerful, and beautiful in their appearance, in their movements, and in their habitat, salmon are the embodiment of the river itself. Hatching at the headwaters, they require clean, cold water and a healthy, silt-free streambed. Being anadromous fish, which live in the sea but migrate up rivers to spawn, the salmon grow for two to five years in the ocean and then return. The ultimate river travelers, they are as dependent on the continuity of the flow as we are on breathable air. These fish symbolize the lifeline of water, portraying the wholeness, the promise, and the problems of that common yet enigmatic feature we call "river."

The salmon were to Indians of the Northwest as buffalo were to Indians of the Plains. A staple in the diet of the tribes, storehouses of fish made possible the leisure time necessary for highly developed art forms that remain today in the Haida and Tlingit cultures. Indians revered the salmon in legend and believed that the fish lived in human form inside great rooms under the ocean, where they would dress in garments of salmon flesh to reappear in the river. If people placed the bones of the fish they had eaten in the water, the spirit of each fish would return to the sea and later ascend the river once again. However, the migration was voluntary, and the fish could refuse to return, so people had to be careful not to offend the salmon people. Under terms such as these, the fish and the Indians coexisted to the people's great advantage for 10,000 years.

Though the Northwest is better known for its salmon today, the rivers of the Northeast are also vital to these fish. At the mouth of the Machias River, Atlantic salmon (*Salmo salar*) still swarm in from the chilled, foggy waters of the ocean and enter the fresh flow of their New England birthplace. Ascending the river, these great sea travelers will spawn in streams draining the forests of Maine, sustaining their species by a narrow margin.

Once teeming in Northeast rivers, Atlantic salmon were decimated by dams, the first of which was erected in 1623. Hundreds of other dams followed, blocking the salmon's upstream paths. In the late 1700s, Hadley Falls Dam eliminated 300 miles of the Connecticut River from spawning salmon and shad. Once populating the Aroostook River in numbers "equal to any waters on the continent" according to an 1894 *Maine Sportsman* article, the fish have since disappeared from that river, with seventy dams now blocking the main stem and its tributaries. When the river developers expunged this species, 433 state laws about fisheries were on the books, but they were not enforced. Some fish ladders were built around dams, but many of those didn't work.

With only ten sections of river in the United States still supporting natural populations of Atlantic salmon, federal and state agencies accelerated efforts to restore runs in several New England rivers with the Anadromous Fish Restoration Act of 1965. Fish and wildlife agencies finally prevailed in their fight to require the Holyoke Water Power Company to build effective lifts and ladders at its Connecticut River dam in 1976. Increased commercial harvest at sea continued to prevent salmon recovery, but after public acquisition of some critical fishing rights, the Atlantic salmon have begun to return to the Connecticut, migrating as far as the White River in Vermont. In 1993, 486 salmon ascended the river. On the

Merrimack River of Massachusetts, where salmon were halted by dams and by pollution that may as well have been a solid wall, a nominal run has been reintroduced. On Maine's Penobscot River, the second-largest river in New England, catches of 25,000 fish a year before the turn of the century declined to nothing by the mid-twentieth century. With a tentative recovery of salmon, anglers are flocking back to that once-great waterway of the East, resulting in a boon to local economies.

On the other side of the continent, chinook salmon still venture into San Francisco Bay as they have done for thousands of years. Seeking clean gravel in the upper reaches of rivers, the female chinook will sweep pebbles into a nest, or "redd," with her tail and then lay up to 5,000 eggs, which are immediately fertilized by the male, who hovers nearby.

Once an extraordinary population that fanned out to tributaries of the Sacramento and San Joaquin rivers as if ascending the trunk and branches of a tree, the California chinook were the first commercial salmon fishery on the West Coast. Pillaged like other resources during the Gold Rush, salmon populations crashed to the point that fishermen moved north to the Columbia by the time of the Civil War.

The remaining chinook populations could have recovered with runs that would be remarkable today, except that the Sacramento River Basin salmon are now stopped by dams on all major tributaries, including the country's tallest dam on the Feather River at Oroville, and by 300 large diversions for irrigation. The Glenn-Colusa diversion alone has killed 7 million fish a year. State and federal water agencies massively compound these problems by sucking Sacramento water out of its delta near San Francisco Bay and pumping full-size rivers of it to farmers of the San Joaquin Valley and to southern California.

Until recently, the Sacramento River represented 70 percent of California's commercial salmon catch; now there *is* no commercial catch on the Sacramento. The winter chinook are threatened, and the run of giant spring chinook, facing a 92 percent mortality rate owing to overly warm waters, is even more threatened. The fall run of chinook decreased from 140,000 in 1988 to about 20,000 in 1992. In addition to salmon fatalities, problems exacerbated by the 1986–1992 drought nearly eradicated ocean-going striped bass. Steelhead—the most popular anadromous game fish—once spawned from Alaska to Baja California, but have been eliminated from much of their California range owing to habitat loss.

Moving northward, we see that a clutch of rivers rising in the coastal forests of California survive as salmon and steelhead streams. This is one of the premier wild river regions of America—our greatest concentration of undeveloped waterways outside Alaska. Protected as state and national wild and scenic rivers, the Smith, Klamath, Trinity, Eel, and Van Duzen rivers host the annual return of salmon. The Smith is one of the nation's outstanding undammed and largely undeveloped watersheds. The Klamath has been one of the finest large steelhead rivers in America. But dams on its principal tributary—the Trinity—have cut salmon populations there by 70 percent and more. Logging on fragile soils has ruined tributary basins by the dozen when the resulting erosion of disturbed soil blankets spawning beds with silt. A once-abundant run on the isolated, sixty-four-mile-long Mattole River of northern California enjoys determined restoration efforts by local people who have banded together to repair eroded slopes and reestablish spawning sites to welcome wild fish.

Farther north, in Oregon, the Elk River epitomizes the finer remaining aspects of the coastal rivers of the Northwest and is one reason that the Siskiyou National Forest is the leading producer of native salmon in the region. But damaging logging in the Elk River Basin was averted only by citizen action. The Chetco, Umpqua, and other Oregon streams continue to produce salmon and steelhead, though many runs are seriously depleted by habitat loss to logging. On the legendary Rogue River of southern Oregon, four runs of salmon are so small that they will likely be added to the federal Endangered Species List. Along the Northwest coast, twenty-five coho salmon runs were the subjects of petitions for endangered species listing in the mid-1990s.

At the Oregon-Washington boundary of the Columbia River, the Northwest Power Planning Council calls the attempt to halt a decline of salmon "perhaps the greatest effort anywhere to save a biological resource." The Council's success has been remarkably limited.

On the Olympic Peninsula of Washington, in 1899, Richard Rathbun of the Smithsonian Institution wrote, "The quantity of salmon which frequent these waters is beyond calculation, and seems to be so great as to challenge human ingenuity to affect it in any way." With clearcut logging on 97 percent of the lowlands of these rich river basins, the runs today are sad remnants of what Rathbun saw.

Puget Sound rivers of northern Washington have accommodated prodigious runs of fish, the Skagit River system being a centerpiece, but logging has decimated many populations and threatens additional runs. In the 1980s the timber industry accelerated the cut, anticipating tight restrictions on logging in the 1990s. Meanwhile, land development damaging to watersheds radiates from booming Seattle.

In British Columbia, the Fraser River shines as a virtual Columbia with no dams. North of the Fraser, the province remains a riverine paradise of big, wild water, dozens of rivers scarcely known even to Canadians. But an apocalypse of logging threatens hundreds of streams, and battles are waged over some of these.

Along the Copper River, an Alaskan resident can still haul in forty huge salmon a day by dipping a net into the rapids. Farther north and west, at Bristol Bay, the Kvichak River feeds some of the richest sockeye salmon runs on earth. Only recently recognized as a commercial opportunity, the bay is now dragged by fleets of fishing boats as San Francisco Bay was 120 years ago.

Chinook salmon ascend the Yukon River for 2,000 miles in one of the longest river migrations of any fish on earth. With Rampart Dam and its reservoir the size of Lake Erie, the Army Corps of Engineers would have blocked runs of 270,00 fish. Fortunately, conservationists and U.S. Department of Interior officials stopped the project in one of the major dam fights of the 1960s. But now Yukon salmon have declined radically because of increasingly efficient fishing by commercial operators and sport anglers. Chum salmon still ascend the Porcupine and Sheenjek rivers at the eastern end of the Brooks Range where grizzly bears amble down to the riverfront to dine. Many Alaskan rivers likewise remain prime salmon streams and models of ecological integrity, but survive only because of remoteness.

❧ A Cast of Endangered Characters

Six salmon species inhabit the rivers of North America, five of them in the genus *Oncorhynchus*, meaning "hooked snout," a characteristic that the fish develop after they enter fresh water and begin the long swim upstream, which is done without eating. Their abundant energy derives from reserves of oil. Fish undertaking the longer runs need higher oil reserves than coastal river spawners; one run cannot replace another.

Sockeye (*Oncorhynchus nerka*), called red salmon in Alaska, are the most common salmon in the Pacific, though now rare south of British Columbia. They spawn in lakes or in streams with lakes at their headwaters. Young sockeye smolts live a year or more in the lakes before going out to sea for several years. Then they return to the rivers to spawn from July through October. A smaller, landlocked form called kokanee lives in some lakes and reservoirs as far south as the Sierra Nevada.

Chinook (*Oncorhynchus tshawytscha*), also known as king salmon, are the mainstay of the genus on the West Coast south of Canada. They occur from the Bering Sea to Monterey Bay and were also introduced to the Great Lakes. With weights sometimes exceeding 100 pounds, chinook are the largest salmon and live up to seven years. Different runs of chinook migrate long distances up rivers in spring, summer, and fall, with some fish in the rivers during most months of the year.

Chum salmon (*Oncorhynchus keta*) are the "dog" salmon; Alaskan natives feed this less tasty fish to their dog teams. Though most spawn in the far north, chum are the second most common salmon in the Pacific. Once abundant in the Columbia River Basin, chum have declined there owing to habitat destruction, but small runs continue to migrate to lower tributaries.

Coho (*Oncorhynchus kisutch*), also called silver salmon, were originally found from the Bering Strait to the Sacramento River and stayed mostly in coastal streams, making them somewhat less vulnerable to the dams that eliminated fish on some longer rivers.

Pink salmon (*Oncorhynchus gorbuscha*), nicknamed "humpies" for the humped back of the male, are the smallest salmon and occur mostly in Alaska, British Columbia, and Puget Sound.

Atlantic salmon (*Salmo salar*) spawn in rivers, but unlike the Pacific species, they return to the sea to survive for another cycle, spawning two or three times in their lives.

While these are the major species of salmon, hundreds of stocks, or runs, are each unique, and many are irreplaceable, adapted to spawning in specific streams. Each of these is, in effect, a separate species.

Other important anadromous fish include the steelhead trout (*Oncorhynchus mykiss*), one of the most prized game fish in the world. These fish are virtually identical to rainbow trout except that they migrate to the ocean and therefore grow larger, some up to forty pounds. Unlike other Pacific salmon, not all steelhead die after spawning; some return upriver several times. Winter runs migrate in November through June, summer runs from June to October. The Columbia continues to produce more steelhead than any river in the world.

The anadromous shad migrate up rivers of the East Coast and also some western rivers where they've been introduced. Sturgeon, the largest freshwater fish in North America and the source of caviar, are normally an anadromous species but when landlocked can sometimes survive and breed entirely in fresh water, such as in the Snake River above Hells Canyon. Striped bass, alewife, smelt, blueback herring, and sea-run cutthroat trout also migrate between rivers and the sea.

Anglers, river watchers, and biologists had known for years that Pacific salmon were in serious trouble, but the appraisal by biologists Willa Nehlsen, Jack E. Williams, and James A. Lichatowich in the March/April 1991 bulletin of the American Fisheries Society alarmed everybody who cared about fish. Already extinct were 106 stocks of Pacific salmon and steelhead. Among 214 naturally spawning stocks of salmon, steelhead, and sea-run cutthroat trout that are at risk, 102 faced a high chance of extinction, 58 were at moderate risk, and 54 were of special concern. At the time of the article, only one species was listed on the federal Endangered Species List. The authors reported that 18 of the stocks on their high-risk list may already be extinct. Describing his impressions of the sorry state of affairs, Bill Bakke of Oregon Trout said, "I look at Oregon like a natural history book. When Europeans settled this region, we had a complete book. Each time a population of plants or animals goes extinct, another page is ripped out."

❧ A Legacy in Ruins at the Columbia

The story of salmon is the story of rivers in America: commercial overharvest, spawning bed destruction by logging, depleted flows from diversion, and total annihilation at the concrete walls of dams. Once the largest salmon population in the world, the Columbia River runs now occupy the front line of threats and are the center of regional and national attention.

Arriving on the scene after a run of salmon had spawned nearly 200 years ago, William Clark wrote, "The number of dead salmon on the shore and floating in the river is incredible." Commercial fishermen began netting these fish in 1866 and soon established the first great industry of the Northwest following the fur trade. In 1883, canneries packed 43 million pounds of salmon from the Columbia under no fishing regulations at all. With the best fishing soon ruined, much of the industry moved on to Alaska, where the process that had begun on the Sacramento River would be repeated. Attempts to manage the Columbia fishery eventually resulted in a ridiculously modest ban on fish wheels as traps at the late date of 1926. In 1946, Congress passed the Columbia River Fishery Development Program, emphasizing not corrections to the problems, but hatcheries.

Meanwhile, logging and grazing nullified vast areas of habitat in Columbia tributaries. One of the more catastrophic examples was the 1960s clearcutting along the South Fork of the Salmon River—the finest spawning area anywhere for chinook salmon. Subsequent landslides in 1964 and 1965 devastated the entire river with a smothering blanket of silt. A painfully slow recovery of the scarred basin evolved during the following twenty-five years, only to have the U.S. Forest Service propose new logging of that fragile watershed in the early 1990s. Additionally, along spawning streams in many basins, herds of cows trample the banks, resulting in shallow, silted excuses for mountain streams, impossible for fish to spawn in.

Even worse, thousands of young salmon find themselves swept into irrigation ditches to flop up waterless in hayfields. With ranching reigning supreme in the West, no law requires ranchers to screen their own ditches, so the Idaho Department of Fish and Game and the Northwest Power Planning Council do it for them at a cost of more than $400,000 a year in the upper Salmon River Basin alone. Many ditches remain unscreened and unattended. Other spawning streams as notable as the Umatilla in Oregon and the Yakima in Washington were completely dried up by irrigation diversions.

Furthermore, the original method of decimating salmon continues:

the commercial harvest. The endangered runs of salmon swim in the ocean alongside other fish as far away as Alaska, and all are caught together. In 1990 the commercial catch took 74 percent of Idaho's nearly extinct fall chinook. The salmon is the only endangered species that can be bought in a can from a grocery store shelf.

Swimming from headwaters to the sea and back again, salmon encounter just about everything that people can throw in their way as trouble. Recognizing this in 1967, biologist Wesley Marx wrote, "A program of anadromous conservation thus runs up against every conceivable political and economic obstacle in modern life."

The big losses in the Columbia River Basin, however, come from the dams. First, Puget Sound Power and Light Company built Rock Island Dam on the Columbia in 1932, followed by the Army Corps of Engineers' Bonneville Dam in 1938. The latter Depression-era edifice rises sixty-five feet above the water for the eye-straining width of this fourth-largest river in North America. The dam was originally planned without fish ladders. The chief engineer of the Corps had stated, "We do not intend to play nursemaid to the fish," but the ladders were finally built.

To form a reservoir 151 miles long on the upper Columbia, the Bureau of Reclamation built Grand Coulee Dam, fifty stories high, with no passage facilities for fish. One thousand miles of choice salmon habitat was the casualty in Washington and British Columbia, including the giant "June hog" run of five-foot-long fish. Today, the Bureau of Reclamation's tour guides are totally mum about the fish at Grand Coulee Dam. Rather, the first message encountered at the Bureau's visitors' center exclaims, "In the Columbia River Basin man and nature work closely together to redistribute nature's gifts." The dam site is a landscape transformed, with wires and pipes leading off in all directions, the shores below the dam riprapped with rocks, the reservoir above the dam a flooded tomb, and the dam itself nearly a mile across—an Art Deco monument massive in its river-destroying design. Downstream from Grand Coulee, other dams followed, with surviving runs of Columbia River salmon required to climb 900 feet over ladders.

On the Snake River, with a length almost equal to that of the Columbia where the two join, the Idaho Power Company constructed three dams without fish passages in the 1960s in upper Hells Canyon. Company executives claimed they could save the fish, when in fact they knew almost nothing about the problem. Salmon were blocked from 3,000 miles of streams, some of which had already been cut off by earlier dams on tributaries and by older dams farther up the Snake. The Corps then erected four back-to-back dams on the lower Snake in the 1960s and 1970s, ostensibly justified by making Lewiston, Idaho, a seaport, for which the local establishment gladly traded the region's status as a world-class fishing destination for that of a third-class barge depot of profound ugliness.

Without the extraordinary expenses now being incurred, some semblance of sustainability on the Snake might have been possible until the Corps' Lower Granite Dam was completed in 1976—the uppermost obstacle to the salmon, the eighth dam in a row. All of this put *Oncorhynchus* at the brink of extinction. Yet the threats kept coming.

The worst dam proposal in American history would have barricaded the Salmon River as well as the lower Hells Canyon of the Snake. The dam, insultingly named Nez Percé after the Indian tribe, was beaten in the 1960s by fishing interests and competing utilities. The newly born conservation movement in Idaho then defeated the alternate site, High Mountain Sheep Dam, in Hells Canyon. Yet another Snake River dam was planned at Asotin, just above Lower Granite. It was deauthorized in 1974, only to be reproposed by private hydroelectric developers in 1988. Surely the doom of vestigial salmon runs, Asotin Dam would have been prohibited by a proposed wild and scenic river designation, but that idea got nowhere under the anticonservation disposition of the Idaho congressional delegation. Congress did grant a dam-building moratorium on that reach of river while a new wild and scenic study proceeded.

Finally, after eighteen dams that blocked or hindered the fishes' passage on the Columbia and Snake, the orgy of building was stopped, but only remnants of a natural system remain. Thirty percent or more of the salmon habitat of the Columbia River Basin has been blocked by dams, and much of the remainder is under extreme stress. Back-to-back dams of the lower Snake and lower Columbia incorporate fish ladders for upstream migration, but the return rates of salmon continue to plummet, and the dams are the reason for 95 to 98 percent of the human-caused deaths of these species. The runs continue to decline into the 1990s, and the worst seems yet to come.

All the time, the dams' builders, utilities, agencies, fisheries interests, and Indian tribes relied on the chimera of human-made hatcheries to fix the declining salmon runs. Since 1936, artificial propagation was regarded as a panacea to deep-seated problems, masking the gravity of salmon eradication. An infusion of $300 million in federal money and about $75 million from states and utilities by the 1970s bought a lot of fish but did nothing to prevent escalating percentages from being killed. The hatcheries augmented some runs while allowing others to go extinct—it depended on what crops were grown at the fish farms. Decisions were made to stock steelhead since they sold lots of fishing licenses but to neglect coho because they were not "worth" much.

But worse than all that, hatchery stocks lack the genetic integrity of wild fish and deplete the native fishes' genetic vigor by interbreeding. Prone to diseases in their rearing-pond feed lots, hatchery fish need to be innoculated repeatedly, and even then, they disseminate their diseases out into the wild. One thousand hatchery fish are needed to produce one pair that returns from the ocean; wild fish survive two to nine times better. Biologists Nehlsen, Williams, and Lichatowich reported in 1991, "A new paradigm that advances habitat restoration and ecosystem function rather than hatchery production is needed for many of these stocks to survive and prosper into the next century."

If this costly exercise of aquaculture—not to be confused with ecosystems—is successful, the hatchery stocks will displace wild fish. Ninety percent of the returning salmon and steelhead in the Columbia River Basin now emanate from hatcheries, and perhaps half of the upper river runs are artificially bred. But only the wild fish have endured for the centuries. Only the wild fish show the ability to sustain themselves without genetic erosion and a disease-ridden plunge to extinction. "Without the wild stocks to provide genetic vigor, it may be economically impossible to keep hatchery fish in the system," said Ed Chaney, director of the Northwest Resource Information Center and a champion of the salmon for twenty-five years. Only the wild fish hold religious significance to the Shoshone and Bannock tribes of Idaho. Losing the wild salmon would be like losing the bald eagle or the last blue whale, and stocked fish are no more a substitute than would be sickly bald eagles raised in chicken coops.

Meanwhile, total anadromous runs in the Columbia River Basin declined from historical levels of 10 to 16 million fish to 2.5 million annually, with only about 250,000 being wild fish. Even those levels were reached in only two years since 1960. Idaho's last sport season for salmon was in 1978. The chum were mostly exterminated by the 1960s. The coho of the Grande Ronde River—a Snake tributary—went extinct in 1987. The sockeye neared extinction except in the Okanogan River system and Wenatchee Lake in Washington and Osoyoos Lake in British Columbia. Only 700 chinook returned in the fall of 1989—the lowest returns to that date.

⅋ The Last of a Magnificent Fish

The signals of crisis were strong, the evidence clear. Fisheries managers, elected officials, and the public were aware of the threats to the remaining runs of salmon. People knew that our society was willfully and knowingly allowing these creatures to approach the abyss of extinction. Even back in 1979, the Department of Interior had begun studies to determine if the Columbia River salmon should be added to the Endangered Species List, but Reagan administration officials quashed the effort, a spokesman saying that "enough conservation programs already exist." Herman McDevitt, an Idahoan serving on the Pacific Fishery Management Council, threatened to file an endangered species petition for the salmon, but federal officials apparently talked him out of it. Flawed, but perhaps not fatally, efforts to save the salmon were escalated. Utilities and government agencies in the Northwest "spent" about $1 billion in the 1980s, though much of the amount is calculated as "foregone power sales"—money that the utilities did not receive because of reservoir releases for the fish. Unfortunately, much of the funds that in fact were spent were still being poured into artificial hatcheries with little consideration to adjusting the hydroelectric system at the heart of the problem.

Substantial efforts on behalf of the fish contributed to the Northwest Power Planning Act of 1980, originally designed to deal with power production concerns but broadened with unambiguous mandates to protect the fish and to give "equal" consideration to fisheries and power production. Salmon advocates thought they had done their job and optimistically awaited results from the agencies charged with restoration responsibilities, but the decline of the species continued.

Finally, shocking the Northwest, though it should have been expected for twenty years, the Shoshone and Bannock tribes of Idaho took the initiative when no one else did and petitioned for the Snake River sockeye as an endangered species in 1990. Two months later, Oregon Trout, the Oregon Natural Resources Council, the Northwest Environmental Center, American Rivers, and the Idaho and Oregon chapters of the American Fisheries Society petitioned to list three other salmon runs.

Before the dams, millions of sockeye had spawned in the majestic lakes of the Sawtooth Mountains. An unenlightened Idaho Department of Fish and Game had poisoned sockeye to make room for the more catchable trout and had devised barriers to the salmon's upstream return. The fish somehow survived. But by 1976, Lower Granite Dam was completed and only 771 sockeye returned to Idaho's rivers. In 1979 there were 30; in 1989 just 2. None were seen in 1990, followed by 4 in 1991. Those 3 males and 1 female, named Eve, were all trapped for controlled spawning in a hatchery, though the fish cannot be raised in captivity for more than one generation without risking genetic change or damaging the ability to complete the river-to-ocean life cycle. One fish was captured in 1992, and 8 were trapped in 1993.

Larry Echohawk, former lawyer for the Shoshone and Bannocks, and the attorney general of Idaho, watched at Redfish Lake Creek, waiting for the last sockeye. He questioned, "In ten years, will we be standing along some other stream waiting for the last spring chinook? We cannot let this happen to this magnificent fish."

Though people can enter the Army Corps' visitors' centers at the lower Snake River dams and gaze through windows as they do at an aquarium and watch salmon swimming through the fish ladders, the problems of upstream migration have not been solved. Thirty-four to 57 percent of the adult spawners die at the dams. Far worse is the record for the juvenile downstream migrants. Betwen 77 and 96 percent of the smolts from Idaho die on their way to the ocean because of two hazards: the dams and the reservoirs.

By the thousands, fish are sucked through the hydroelectric turbines and pulverized. Others are swept over the dams to die. But the biggest killer is the flatwater of the reservoirs. The smolts seek to drift downstream at the edge of the current, facing upstream while being pushed seaward. In 350 miles of reservoir pools they aren't pushed anymore, so they float aimlessly and too slowly downriver. The juveniles historically completed the downriver journey in as little as five days; now it takes seventeen to thirty days or more, which is often too long to match the physiological conversion from a freshwater to saltwater species. With no choice but to maunder in slack water, smolts are preyed upon by voracious squawfish, whose numbers have exploded with the flatwater advantage. While the rivers traditionally delivered two-thirds of their water in spring and summer—when the fish most need it—the dams now deliver high flows in winter, when electricity is in greater demand.

The Army Corps of Engineers' approach to these formidable problems was to construct screens to trap downriver migrants at three of the dams, funnel the fish into a pipeline, dump them like so much coal slurry onto a barge, and then motor the fish down to the base of the last dam.

With this solution of astounding management intensity, the Corps barges up to 20 million fish through the reservoirs. Compared to the fishes' survival under the lethal conditions of the reservoirs, the program works reasonably well for stocked steelhead, but not for wild steelhead or salmon. Significant numbers die at dams that lack screening devices, and even where screens exist, 45 percent of the fish fail to make the prescribed turn onto the barge. But beyond these problems is the big problem: most of the salmon that board the barges fail to return to spawn. Salmon cannot tolerate the handling, and they contract diseases when confined to crowds of 400,000 per boat, just like a lot of people crammed into one small room during the flu season. Many salmon lose the ability to find their spawning grounds. The barges, in effect, become death traps.

In 1993 the Columbia Basin Fish and Wildlife Authority reported that the barging of salmon smolts offered no benefit to many stocks and may be detrimental to some. This corroborated a U.S. Fish and Wildlife Service conclusion that the barging is no substitute for safe migration within the river.

The alternative solution, advocated by Indian tribes, fish and wildlife agencies, and the Northwest Power Planning Council, would install new and better screens allowing fish to pass the dams and float to sea, avoiding the 55 percent cumulative turbine mortality that now looms over every young smolt's head. The Army Corps of Engineers refused to do this and spent money instead on the barges until ordered otherwise by Congress in 1988. In 1994 the screening devices remain inadequate.

The second, more vital part of the solution speaks to an elegant simplicity: lower the water level in the reservoirs to better approximate the flow of an undammed river. The Corps could drain some of the water in the lower four dams on the Snake, each about 100 feet high. Reservoirs would be dropped below the normal operating levels (but not the whole way), reinstating a current for two and a half months through part of the dam-created flatwater. This involves a capital cost of $65 million to $90 million at Lower Granite Dam—the most troublesome structure—as spillways and fish ladders would have to be modified. Governor Cecil Andrus championed this "Idaho" plan for salmon restoration, which appears to be the only feasible way to reverse the plunge of all Snake River salmon runs toward extinction.

The Idaho Department of Fish and Game responded to opposition by barge companies that ply the 100 percent subsidized system of dams and locks, by downstream irrigators in Washington who consume the federally subsidized water, and by power interests that still offer the lowest rates in the country thanks to the federal dams. It was made clear that power losses would not occur during the peak season of Northwest demand, which is winter, when the reservoirs would be full.

After initially promulgating a scare that electric bills would double, the Bonneville Power Administration (BPA) was forced to actually study the Idaho plan for lowering the reservoirs and reported that power rates would rise by 50 cents to $1.50 for a $50 monthly power bill. While power rates may increase by 5 percent, the residential rate would have to increase by 47 percent simply to reach the national average. With this cheap, subsidized power, BPA customers consume 200 percent of the average power use nationwide. About one-third of the federal hydropower goes to the aluminum industry at even cheaper rates below market value. Under contract with the Northwest Conservation Act Coalition, economist Jim Lazar estimated in 1992 that if the BPA renewed its aluminum industry contracts in the year 2001 under present terms, the rate-payers of the BPA would be subsidizing the industry at $100,000 to $150,000 annually for each job in the aluminum plants. Furthermore, the lower four Snake River dams produce only 4 percent of the BPA's power—far less than the amount now exported to California. The BPA meanwhile argued in the early 1990s that it spent more than $100 million per year for the fish, mostly in foregone power sales. That may sound like a lot, but only 2.4 percent of the agency's budget goes to fish recovery. This occurs while the Northwest Power Planning Act mandates "equal" consideration to fisheries and power.

Grain slated for barging to foreign markets could be stored while the reservoirs are drawn down, or the grain could be moved easily by rail, the way it used to be. The 3.6 million tons of products shipped by barge down the Snake account for only 8 percent of the Columbia River shipping below Bonneville Dam—hardly a resource of national importance when compared to the endangered salmon.

Only one of the four reservoirs serves irrigators, and it serves only sixteen farmers. They would still have plenty of water and would simply need to attach extensions to their pipes in order to reach the lowered levels of the reservoirs. The government would bear the expense. In spite of all this, Al Wright, representing power companies in the Pacific Northwest Utilities Conference Committee, told the U.S. Senate in 1991 that the drawdown would "rip the Northwest's economy apart."

The Northwest Power Planning Council, caving in to utility and aluminum industry demands, called for only a tentative approval of the drawdown by 1995. The BPA claimed more time was needed to study the issue.

Witnessing the failure of the public institution charged with saving the fish, salmon advocate Ed Chaney led the formation of a coalition of forty groups called Save Our Wild Salmon. Arguing against the alleged need for further study, he said, "We already have 10,000 years of data. That's how long the rivers served those fish. We know what works. We know that those fish need to be washed downstream by a current. The closer we return the existing system to a naturally functioning river, the closer we will be to avoiding extinction." Not believing that the BPA has overcome its compulsion to manage the river one-sidedly for hydropower, he added, "We've set our governments up to take care of the long-term issues, but the governments have become a captive of the special interests. The Columbia River system can be fixed in a businesslike fashion, but there is nothing that vested interests fear more than change. It appears that lawsuits will be the only answer."

❧ Beyond Endangered

After the required procedural steps, the National Marine Fisheries Service (NMFS) in fact listed the sockeye as endangered in 1991. It *had* to list the sockeye; *four* fish were left. The fall and spring-summer chinook were listed as threatened, and the lower Columbia coho was declared extinct.

Endangered status means that federal agencies cannot take actions that jeopardize the species or modify critical habitats. Yet everyone knows that the Army Corps of Engineers and the BPA are killing more than 90 percent of the fish. Forced to confront this dilemma, the NMFS prepared a recovery plan for the salmon with the goal of improving stocks to the point that the fish can be removed from the Endangered Species List.

Though the process began with high hopes, overt political pressure on the agency resulted in a 1992 NMFS ruling that hydroelectric operations at the federal dams posed "no jeopardy" to the endangered and threatened species. The ruling was widely considered an outrage and was appealed. Summing up the complaints, Lorraine Bodi of American Rivers' Northwest office said that the decision "denies reality." An October 1993 draft recovery plan reaffirmed the status quo with the reservoirs.

Ed Chaney continued to argue on behalf of the salmon: "Those fish are a perpetual food source that just keeps coming back. All we have to do is get out of the way." Politically, Chaney saw no hope within the Northwest. "We tried. The utilities simply buy the region. Our only chance is to go to the federal courts, and then to Congress." His hope is that people in the rest of the nation will recognize the tragedy of extinction being allowed to occur day by day, year by year, with very few years left to go.

In 1992 Idaho conservationist Pat Ford wrote to vice-president-elect Al Gore, asking for help: "The BPA and the Corps have been lawless. In the 1960s, Congress told the Corps to build its Snake River dams with safe passage for salmon; it did not. In 1980, Congress told the agencies to give salmon equal treatment in hydrosystem operation; they have not. Now, the Endangered Species Act requires the agencies to restore Snake River salmon; so far they have rolled up the act's enforcer, the National Marine Fisheries Service, and stuffed it in their back pockets. All with the support and connivance of recent administrations."

Unmoved by such criticism, the Army Corps of Engineers in 1993 rejected a limited drawdown proposal for Lower Granite Dam submitted by the Idaho and Oregon fish and wildlife agencies, the U.S. Fish and Wildlife Service, and the Columbia River Intertribal Fish Commission. The Corps claimed the proposal was not received in time for analysis, and the agency planned to operate the dams nearly the same as it did in 1992. The only thing that saved the fish in 1993 was an act of God—it rained enough for higher flows. Meanwhile, the Idaho Department of Fish and Game filed a lawsuit in District Court to order federal agencies to improve salmon survival.

While it's business as usual at the dams, shoppers in the Northwest can browse through stores and find a booming industry in the icons of salmon: salmon plates, stuffed salmon toys, salmon balloons, salmon earrings, and salmon key rings. A popular item is a can bearing the artful, old-fashioned label of the salmon canneries along the Columbia River. Inside is not the pink flesh of the chinook, sockeye, or coho, but a tee shirt with the charismatic portrait of a hooked-jaw fish. Are tee shirts celebrating this symbol of the great Northwest all that we will have left when the current debate is over? If salmon are so popular, why do we continue to kill all of them for the sake of slightly lower electricity bills?

Is it too late when four sockeye are left? Maybe it is or maybe it isn't, but in any event, the same fate for the stronger runs of chinook could be averted. At stake are these unique species, beginning life in the headwaters, journeying to sea, swimming 10,000 miles as far as the Gulf of Alaska, evading the commercial fishermen, evading the natural predators and hazards, finding the mouth of the Columbia, and swimming upstream 800 miles over eight high dams. These creatures are unlike any the earth has ever seen.

Biologists expect that effective screens, reservoir drawdowns, and augmented flows would work well, that the salmon could be saved if we would just take the necessary actions. And beyond survival lies the possibility of again having a robust fishery that would mean food for millions of people, spiritual sustenance for Indian tribes and others who see a power in this fish, and a recreation industry that is needed as the underpinning of dozens of rural economies. In the Northwest, commercial and recreational fishing for anadromous species has provided 62,000 jobs and generated $1.25 billion as recently as 1968. According to the Pacific Fisheries Management Council, direct and indirect income from commercial and sport fishing for salmon in Washington and Oregon generated $135 million in 1988. With restoration to even 50 percent of historic levels, the economic potential is extraordinary.

✌ The Lessons of the Salmon

At great expense and effort, we might save some of the Columbia River salmon. The survival of these species depends on solutions contrived to the extreme: screens across dams, and reservoir levels dropped for two and a half months and then raised again like an oversized bathtub. An unusual aspect of the Columbia River salmon problem is that, while a river has been lost to reservoirs and manipulated flows, important tributaries remain. The Columbia and Snake are needed by the salmon principally as conduits to reach the headwaters. The Selway, Lochsa, Clearwater, Grande Ronde, Imnaha, Middle Fork Salmon, Salmon, and other tributaries can still carry on in that inimitable process so nourishing to the fish. If Columbia River Basin salmon are lost, even more money might be expended in efforts to bring them back, based on recent experience with the manipulated reintroductions of the California condor and the Atlantic salmon. In Massachusetts, for example, $22 million was spent just on the Merrimack River to establish a run of several hundred fish that do not sustain themselves. On the Penobscot River of Maine—the model for re-introduction of Atlantic salmon—$4,000 is spent on each returning adult fish in a program that remains popular.

What is the meaning of all this in the larger arena of river protection? The Columbia case is not so much river protection as river management, but it shows that attempts can be made to accommodate the life of the river along with the lives of the people. The funds spent on attempts to save these species make abundantly clear the need to avoid the problem in the first place by sustaining healthy rivers elsewhere. While we spend billions to restore remnant runs of fish, we lose entire fisheries and entire rivers owing to neglect and a failure to take relatively simple and inexpensive preventative action. Logging in the watersheds of the Imnaha, Elk, Chetco, and Umpqua in Oregon, clearcutting at the Skagit, Cascade, and Sauk in Washington, international fishing disputes at the Stikine in Alaska and British Columbia, and commercial salmon harvest within Glacier Bay National Preserve at the mouth of the Alsek River in Alaska are just a few examples of threats to salmon elsewhere. All of these illustrate the importance of the lesson of the Columbia. The lesson is to protect rivers before it's too late.

Two recent stories instill some hope: pushed into action by Indian tribes and fisheries agencies, the Northwest Power Planning Council saw the foolishness of spending billions on the correction of past mistakes while still allowing new destruction to proceed. Developers had proposed hundreds of new hydroelectric dams on tributary streams in the Columbia River Basin, nearly all of them to generate small amounts of power but nonetheless harmful to fish. In a landmark decision, the Council adopted rules in 1988 making it unlikely that new dams will be built where prime fisheries exist. Hundreds of streams and thousands of miles were safeguarded—the largest single action ever taken to protect specific rivers. And on the other side of the continent, Maine's governor in 1983 designated many of the remaining salmon rivers for state protection, an action supported by bills in the state legislature.

Much more needs to be done to prevent the catastrophe of the Columbia River salmon from happening elsewhere. Most undeveloped rivers in Oregon and Washington, and the vast wilderness rivers of British Columbia and Alaska, lack protection and are vulnerable to overharvest, new dams, and watershed damage through logging. The few unspoiled streams remaining in New England are also vulnerable.

❧ A New Promise of Life

On the upper reaches of the Salmon River, high in the Sawtooth Valley, ranchers had diverted water from the main stem of the river and from other streams since early in this century. A concrete structure, four feet high and spanning the width of the waterway, was the only blockage on the entire Salmon, otherwise the longest river in forty-nine states without a dam. But at this site the river was totally diverted for pasture, resulting in a bone-dry streambed in the landmark waterway, more appropriately called the Cow River than the Salmon River. Nine acre-feet of water was spread onto grass that actually needed only two acre-feet. Habitat for 7,600 chinook salmon was destroyed while water ran in the riffles of overflow down the ruts of tire tracks made by a rancher's pickup trucks.

In 1992, with negotiation by Idaho Nature Conservancy director Guy Bonnivier, the land and water rights of that ranch were sold to the Forest Service for inclusion in the Sawtooth National Recreation Area. The Forest Service planned to destroy the dam and return the upper Salmon River to the fish for which it was named. Expressing hope for the species, Charlie Ray of Idaho Rivers United reflected, "The salmon are so incredibly strong, fertile, and determined to survive that all we have to do is give them back a little of the river. They'll do the rest."

Downstream, draining into the Columbia, the Umatilla River of northeastern Oregon likewise became an example of reform when three runs of salmon were brought back by reinstating flows to the depleted river.

Across the country in New England, half a million shad passed a Connecticut River dam at Holyoke, and 196 salmon returned to spawn in 1991. The state of Maine dismantled the East Machias Dam to restore Atlantic salmon runs in the Machias River. And at Maine's capital of Augusta, the license for Edwards Dam, built illegally in 1837 on the Kennebec River, expired. Outdated, dilapidated, and inefficient, the 3.5 megawatt dam was supplying only 0.1 percent of Maine's electricity and was in need of major reconstruction, proposed by its owner but opposed by a river conservation lobby that argued the dam had served its purpose. Its owners had reaped their profits for 150 years. Now it was time to turn a seventeen-mile section of river back to the salmon, and also to the sturgeon, striped bass, and herring—ten species in all that once migrated upstream. The American shad, rainbow smelt, and alewife alone totaled 3 million pounds of catch annually before the dam's construction. The Kennebec's striped bass, rainbow smelt, Atlantic sturgeon, and shortnose sturgeon cannot use fish ladders, even when they are properly designed for salmon. The Natural Resources Council of Maine argued, "A restored river is not a luxury. The Edwards Dam is not a necessity." The governor of the state sought an agreement to buy the dam and raze it and in 1990 asked the federal government to deny a request for relicensing the dam. By 1994, action had not yet been taken on the license, but support continued for elimination of the 157-year-old dam; perhaps the Kennebec will be restored.

These are only minor success stories in a century of losses, but they could mark a turning point for the survival of wild salmon and wild rivers everywhere.

Chapter Three

Breaking the Concrete Fix

❧ The Passing of an Era

On the night of May 21, 1979, in the Sierra Nevada foothills of California, a man walked in the darkened canyon of the Stanislaus River without knowing if he would ever return. Mark Dubois and thousands of other members of Friends of the River had fought the construction of New Melones Dam for nearly a decade. Among other efforts, they had lost a state initiative after contractors working on the project funded a blitz of pro-dam advertising. The dam builders' slogan was "Vote no, save the river," when in fact that was a vote to construct the dam. The strategy worked; after the election, a survey revealed that 60 percent of the voters had intended to cast their ballot against the dam but were confused by the advertising.

The Army Corps of Engineers then completed New Melones, and the gates slammed shut on America's fourth-tallest dam. Each day, rising levels of flatwater invaded farther into the canyon that had inspired perhaps more supporters to work for the protection of a river than any other single threat anywhere.

Few people who had seen the wild Stanislaus walked away with ambivalence regarding its fate. After coursing down from the peaks of the northern Sierra, brilliant water plunged through nine miles of spellbinding rapids and reflective pools as deep as the imagination could go. Gray and marbled walls veered from river's edge to rocky ridge, guarding sandy beaches, luxuriant riparian oases, and artifacts of native people who had lived in the West Coast's deepest limestone canyon for 9,000 years.

Perhaps more than any other river, this one was being flooded in full view of the American public. What was at stake had been well publicized.

As the most popular whitewater in the West, the Stanislaus had carried tens of thousands of people down its gleaming surface on a path of joy and wonder in a world elsewhere being stripped of those emotions.

Supported by the administration of Governor Jerry Brown, Friends of the River bolstered its case with hard data and the analytical view of economists and hydrologists. The State Water Resource Control Board had ordered that the dam not be filled until the need for it could be proven. Ample evidence indicated that flood control could be provided more effectively by a partly filled reservoir having extra available storage space, that no market existed for the irrigation water, and that the hydroelectric power was inconsequential to the state's appetite for energy. All these findings were verified in the years that followed, yet Friends of the River could not stop the dam builders, whose project had been authorized fourteen years earlier and who rode the breaking wave of a monolithic power base of industrial agriculture that gripped California and dominated its congressional delegation.

In May 1979, Mark Dubois resorted to a new form of persuasion. By a limestone ledge in the tangled undergrowth where the rising reservoir lapped against shores of chaparral, he chained himself to a rock, snapping shut a lock whose key he had hidden beyond reach. He had notified Colonel Donald O'Shei of the Army Corps of Engineers about his plans by letter. "The life of the 9 million year old Stanislaus Canyon is far more significant than my short tenure on this planet," he wrote. "I plan to have my feet permanently anchored to a rock in the canyon at the elevation of Parrot's Ferry the day the water reaches that elevation. I urge you to do all in your power to prevent flooding of the canyon above Parrot's Ferry."

Dubois always insisted that this action was only one in a long series of actions he had taken to save the river, and that it was certainly not the most significant. His efforts to work "through the system" and his untiring attempts to communicate with all of his fellow Californians about the values of the river and the costs of the dam had dominated his life for eight years; yet publicity concerning his new commitment now spread nationwide in a day, and the Stanislaus became a household word. As a result, the Corps stabilized the water level. With help from a secret informant who could reach Dubois by raft, and thus retrieve the key to the chain's lock, Dubois emerged from the canyon a week after his dark entry. By means of an action unmatched in personal dedication and drama, Dubois had brought the Stanislaus, and rivers in general, to the attention of many people.

A reprieve had been won, but subsequent efforts to gain protection failed by a narrow political margin, and in 1982 New Melones Dam immersed the canyon under the gloom of hundreds of feet of flatwater. Ironically, the Reclamation Reform Act was passed that same year, setting new federal standards for construction and water efficiency, officially distancing federal policy from the dams-everywhere approach of the past.

The Stanislaus struggle ranks as a landmark in the history of river protection because New Melones was the last enormous dam project to destroy such significant river assets. Two years after New Melones was filled, proposed hydroelectric dams on the nearby Tuolumne River were defeated in a difficult contest that proved the river conservation movement sustained momentum after the loss of the Stanislaus.

The tide had been turning for twenty years with a list of battles now embedded in the lore of river conservation: Bridge Canyon Dam on the Colorado in Arizona, Gilbert on the Buffalo in Arkansas, Tocks Island on the Delaware in Pennsylvania, Oakley on the Sangamon in Illinois, Blue Ridge on the New in North Carolina, Dickey-Lincoln on the St. John in Maine, and dozens of other sites where dams were stopped. The opponents of destructive water projects gained strength while the builders had exhausted the most practical sites and as Congress tightened public purse strings to the exclusion of projects with transparently trumped-up benefits and obviously concealed costs. Though the Stanislaus was lost, its death marked the end of an era.

More and more people realized that in winning a battle against nature by stopping floods, irrigating the desert, or generating electricity, we were losing another opportunity for a better life on earth—indeed, for the life *of* the earth. About 75,000 large dams have been built in America, with 3,000 in Pennsylvania alone, 1,450 in California, 136 in the Columbia River Basin, and 15 in the Stanislaus River Basin. Only forty-two rivers in the United States outside Alaska are judged to have outstanding qualitites and also flow for more than 120 miles with no dams.

In their day, some dams made sense and yielded significant benefits at acceptable costs. But many projects, especially in the later years of the development era, were simply boondoggles. The true costs in lost canyons, extinct species, drowned farmland and home sites, stilled whitewater, and dullness imposed on a previously diverse landscape had not been charged to those who benefited from speculative development on the flood plain or from subsidized irrigation of the desert. Nor had anyone entered the real costs in the ledger of the government, which on many rivers had eliminated one source of perpetual wealth in natural ecosystems in favor of commerce and short-term economic gain for constituents with political pull.

While tens of thousands of dams had blocked rivers without a whimper of dissent at most of the sites prior to 1960, virtually nothing could be built by 1975 without opposition. The history of environmental conservation shows that the opposition to destructive dams—following the loss of the Stanislaus—stands out as a preeminent success.

ﯨ The Proof of Transition

One hundred twenty miles south of the Stanislaus, in the heart of the western agribusiness empire near Fresno, California, the Kings River Conservation District contracted for engineering studies of the Rogers Crossing dam site in a canyon that John Muir had wanted included in Kings Canyon National Park. A recurring phenomenon, the proposal for the 640-foot-high dam had been found uneconomical in previous studies, but surfaced as a serious undertaking once again in 1985.

The structure would have flooded eleven miles of the Kings, including California's finest large wild-trout fishery, the second-closest whitewater rafting to the megalopolis of southern California, and winter range of important but declining deer herds. The entire section ran through national forest land and diverse habitat of pines, oak savannah, grasslands, and riparian flats. The Kings flowed with the largest undammed vertical drop of any river on the continent and carved the deepest canyon—even deeper than Hells Canyon of the Snake River.

Planned for damming by a group of men that included some of the corporate giants of American agribusiness, the waters would augment the already available supply from Pine Flat Reservoir, below the Rogers Crossing site. New deliveries would go to cotton farms, one of which was a multibillion-dollar enterprise that received $20 million in 1986 from the federal government not to grow cotton with already subsidized water. (The corporation was then allowed to profit from other crops on the same acreage.) With essentially unlimited funds owing to their membership and taxing structure, the Kings River Conservation District contracted with the Bechtel Corporation to plan the dam and hired the nation's largest advertising agency to sell it to the public.

Opposing Rogers Crossing, trout anglers reactivated the Committee to Save the Kings River and hired a staff of two. Led by Donn Furman, the Committee had the unstinting support of one local congressman, Richard Lehman, but the virulent opposition of another, Chip Pashayan. Furman's ingeniously crafted campaign included documentation of river values and dam liabilities, promotion of alternatives to supply water more economically, and endorsements from newspapers, civic organizations, and local governments. Representative Lehman secured sponsorship from more than a hundred congressional members. Even here in the San Joaquin Valley, where big agriculture had run the economy for generations, people realized the folly of one more dam to serve the same old subsidized consumers of water. In only one year, the Committee to Save the Kings River turned the tables and legislation banned the dam while designating a national wild and scenic river in the sections immediately upstream. Celebrating victory, conservationists reasoned that if river destruction could be thwarted in the agribusiness capital of Fresno, big dams could be stopped anywhere.

The acid test of this sentiment was undertaken on the South Fork of the Platte in Colorado, where the Denver Water Board—widely considered the most powerful political entity in the state—had planned Two Forks Dam and spent $30 million just on environmental studies so that the final proposal would fly. Fought for several decades by Trout Unlimited, the Environmental Defense Fund, and other groups, the contest reached a rolling boil by 1987 when the Water Board sought approval from the U.S. Environmental Protection Agency (EPA) under the Clean Water Act.

The 615-foot-high dam would have flooded thirty miles of river, eliminating one of the finest trout streams in Colorado. With the additional storage that would result, the Denver Water Board intended to divert more streams from the west slope of the Rockies by tunneling them eastward to urban areas. Reduced flows below Two Forks would plague endangered whooping cranes, sandhill cranes, and water use in Nebraska, leading politicians in that state to oppose the dam when the Colorado delegation wouldn't budge to protect its own river.

Charlie Russell, a public relations man who spent several years worth of pro bono time helping Trout Unlimited, devised the campaign slogan "Why Two Forks?" Simply but ingeniously crafted, the question raised awareness of the issue, offended few people, and put the Water Board on the defensive. And the defense became more and more difficult. The Board had based its rationale on boomtown growth rates of the 1970s, which were over. River conservationists showed that the water industry could pursue efficiency alternatives in lieu of new development and still serve the city's suburbanizing fringe.

In what has become a model case of Clean Water Act requirements stopping a dam, the EPA in 1989 refused to approve Denver's proposal because of its effects on water quality, fish, wildlife, and recreation. The threat of west-slope diversions increasing the salinity of the Colorado River was one reason the federal agency was able to base its action on the Clean Water Act. EPA director William Reilly upheld the veto under intense political pressure to reverse it.

Unlike the Kings, the South Fork of the Platte enjoys no assurance of long-term protection. Two Forks Dam appears to be dead, but a building boom in suburban Denver in the early 1990s may again test the waters and may point out the need for long-term protection.

While the South Platte controversy raged and caught most of the media's attention, water suppliers in Rhode Island promoted a dam site on the Big River that would destroy hundreds of acres of wetland and thousands of acres of forest. The state's governor announced plans to proceed with the project in 1988, but a coalition of local groups organized support for the stream. As it had with the Two Forks proposal, the EPA denied a permit for the dam in 1990.

The dynamics of river use had been evolving since the defeat of a dam at Dinosaur National Monument on Colorado's Green River in 1956, but a new era of regard had conclusively arrived in the 1980s. The Kings and South Fork Platte had survived against the archetypal agents of power in water development and were not substituted with damaging alternatives. These cases confirmed that America's new regard for rivers was profound and lasting. Conservation leaders estimated that citizens stopped more than 150 unnecessary dam, channelization, and canal projects between 1975 and 1985. Several projects were halted even after many millions of dollars had been spent on construction. But not everything was halted.

At the North Fork of the Stanislaus in California, a large hydroelectric project was built in the mid-1980s. At the Dolores River in southern Colorado, McPhee Dam was built, flooding a valley and robbing the river of healthy flows. This left the Yampa as the last major Colorado River tributary without an impoundment, but then Stagecoach Dam was completed on the Yampa in 1988. Jordanelle Dam was built in the early 1990s on the upper Provo River in Utah.

Though opposed for a decade, Elk Creek Dam in Oregon slipped through the new nets of water reform, and construction began in 1985. Blocking a small tributary to the Rogue, one of the nation's first designated wild and scenic rivers, the dam would eliminate twenty-five miles of salmon spawning and diminish riparian corridors, a superb fishery, and downstream flows affecting the Rogue all the way to the sea.

Following a lawsuit by the Oregon Natural Resources Council and other groups for failure to comply with the National Environmental Policy Act, a judge ordered the Army Corps of Engineers to stop construction in 1987, a decision upheld by the U.S. Supreme Court. In 1992 the Corps recommended that the dam be completed for $85 million but that it be used as a dry dam, filled only in times of flood. Unsatisfied with a project considered fundamentally flawed and unnecessary, Oregon Governor Barbara Roberts called for complete removal of the structure, which would cost $15 million to $20 million. Andy Kerr of the Oregon Natural Resources Council maintained that the benefits of finishing the dam—including speculative development on flood plains—don't exist. "What you have is simply the Corps trying to justify a project which probably didn't make sense in 1962 and certainly doesn't today."

In 1993 one could visit Elk Creek and walk on the skeletal hulk of a dam rising eighty-three feet—only one-third its planned height. Crushed stone, meant for mixing into cement, lay waiting in cone-top piles stacked across the valley floor that had been a riparian garden of willows the last time I visited the site in 1977. Scraps of rusting reinforcement bars now litter the landscape, and the dam itself rises as an ineffectual wall of concrete while Elk Creek gurgles through a grated outlet pipe. Voices echo against the concrete walls with all the emptiness of ancient ruins, except that these ruins are modern, perhaps the type that would be seen everywhere if our civilization suddenly collapsed in the midst of this age of extravagance. Elk Creek Dam rises as a monument to a plan that outlasted its era of acceptance, only to be stopped after $100 million was wasted. The final outcome is uncertain.

‎❧ Concentrated Conflicts

As if Rogers Crossing and Two Forks dams had never been defeated, as if twenty years of reform eliminating nearly every big project proposal had not marked a changing of the times, a few proposals for large dams remained. Political pressure both in support and opposition in the mid-1990s became concentrated at these sites, and in particular, at Auburn, California.

Auburn Dam, on the American River thirty miles upstream from Sacramento, had once been designed in the grand style. The Bureau of Reclamation intended it to be the largest dam of its kind in the world—a thin, concrete arch rising 685 feet, curved in an upstream arc from one canyon wall to the other and also curved from bottom to top, somewhat resembling the side of a teacup. Instead of reflecting the end of the era, which in fact was occurring, this design of engineering elegance symbolized dam building triumphant—not a final gasp but a final glory. Unfortunately, the Auburn design represented more style than substance.

Designed to subsidize irrigators of California's San Joaquin Valley, who were pumping out far more groundwater than flowed in and counting on the government to bail them out, the dam would have flooded forty-eight miles of wild canyons and cut flows in the lower American to a trickle where 5.1 million people a year now paddle, hike, bike, fish, and otherwise enjoy the river in Sacramento.

Prudence and public outrage forced the Bureau to halt construction in 1975 after a nearby earthquake of 5.7 on the Richter scale triggered alarm that 250,000 people or more would be flooded if the gracefully designed dam failed. Auburn held the potential to be the worst dam disaster in American history by a factor of perhaps a hundred.

Seismic studies undertaken at that late date revealed old fractures crossing the dam site like broken glass. The Bureau redesigned with safety in mind, though how safe was "safe" remained in dispute among experts and government agencies. More important to the political process, the concrete monolith now cost so much that Interior Secretary Cecil Andrus ruled that Congress must reconsider it.

While those circumstances had detained Auburn on the drawing boards, the metamorphosis of water development policy had continued its process of shedding one skin and growing another. It was no longer politically tenable for the Bureau to propose selling the reservoir's water to irrigators for as low as $3.50 an acre-foot when it cost taxpayers $350 to $900 an acre-foot to provide. Those kinds of economics were now a liability, along with almost everything else about Auburn. More than $200 million had been spent on a foundation that most resembled a Kentucky strip mine of scars and dirt piles, a scene still evident from the Auburn Dam "scenic overlook" twenty years later. Counterproposals to designate the American as a wild and scenic river or a national recreation area fell victim to a political standoff at the canyon. As with Two Forks and some other dam proposals, the Auburn fight became emblematic of movements stopping blatant river destruction but falling short of long-term protection.

The American became our finest example of a river as a resource on hold, neither exploited nor preserved, a purgatory of the American landscape. Historically, water developers at other sites had dealt with identical problems with a code of patience: "If all else fails, just sit and wait."

In February 1986, seven days of rain prompted one of the larger flows ever to rise in the American River Basin. The existing Folsom Reservoir, just downstream from the Auburn site and immediately upstream from Sacramento, swelled from drought-induced mudflats to full in a matter of days. Seeking to store water for the summer irrigation season, the Bureau of Reclamation failed to spill water from Folsom early enough to sustain some breathing room for storage even when it was apparent that the reservoir would rise further.

Meanwhile, the temporary dam built to allow construction at the Auburn site overflowed. When waters ripped away the armor of loose rock rubble, the coffer dam exploded into a roiling torrent of stone and mud slurry, a multistory wall of water pushing solid chunks as big as cars and pounding though the narrow channel of the American that funneled into the backwater of Folsom Reservoir. Folsom Dam was instantly jeopardized by the unexpected surge the size of the Mississippi, requiring emergency releases beyond the design capacity for downstream levees guarding large neighborhoods in the state capital. Evacuation was considered while the flood waters crept nearly to the brim of the Sacramento levee, then slowly subsided without causing much damage. It was just the kind of event that resurrects water projects from dusty shelves of neglect.

Though the chief hazard had been the result of risky management of Folsom Dam, Auburn Dam boosters propped up their sagging proposal, designed a new dam dressed as a flood control panacea, and sent it off to Congress.

Annoying to the project enthusiasts, two reforms regarding flood control had been instituted since the old political era of pork barrel and log rolling for dams: local beneficiaries had to share the cost so that the federal government no longer paid the entire bill, and flood insurance was required for new construction on the flood plain, theoretically to avoid the need for disaster relief payments.

The insurance program provides highly subsidized insurance to existing structures provided local governments control new development by keeping it off the flood plain or by "flood-proofing" it. Federally backed mortgages—essentially all mortgages—are banned for development that fails to meet insurance requirements. When officials factored the 1986 flood into the hydrologic history of the American River, they found that Folsom Dam and the city's levees did not provide adequate protection from a flood likely to visit the area once each 100 years. Thus, low-lying farmland coveted by speculators and developers in the Sacramento area of Natomis was now off limits to new construction, as were other areas in the city.

Real estate investors who intended to develop cheap, flood-prone land convinced their congressional representative to sponsor a bill flatly exempting their areas from flood insurance rules. The bill passed. Meanwhile, any new development would increase the jeopardy posed by floods and thus the justification for Auburn Dam. The free ride, however, expired in 1992. Once flood plain maps were completed, the Sacramento developers—entrenched by this time—would have to meet requirements that apply so routinely to the rest of the nation.

With the rationale that a dam at Auburn would reduce downstream flood risk and exempt developers forever from the flood-proofing requirement, real estate interests pushed hard in a revitalized campaign for the dam. This appealed to many Sacramento residents who would also receive better flood protection.

Congressmen Vic Fazio and Robert Matsui introduced a bill in 1992 to reauthorize Auburn as a flood control project to be built for $700 million by the Army Corps of Engineers, with 75 percent of the cost paid by federal taxpayers.

A far cry from the elegant monolith once planned by the Bureau of Reclamation, the Corps designed a concrete gravity structure—squat in design—that appeared more fitting to a dying area of big dams. Further detracting from its grace, the 434-foot-high plug would be used as a dry dam, filled only during floods. While avoiding some of the problems that the old Auburn Dam had posed, the new one was far from benign. Reservoir water would periodically inundate thirty-four miles of the forks of the American, killing riparian vegetation. The subsequent drawdown of water could cause erosion and landslides on a scale more appropriate to geologic time; the water would repeatedly be pulled away from saturated soils of the canyonsides, likely causing them to slump.

But the main reason that groups including the statewide Friends of the River and the local Protect American River Canyons opposed the dam was that it could readily be converted into a 700-foot-high structure for year-round storage and hydropower; the new compromise could simply yield in increments what the Bureau of Reclamation had wished for twenty years earlier. Facing controversy, the Sacramento Area Flood Control Agency hired an independent consulting firm to consider the options. Engineers found that changes to the levee system along with revised operation of the existing Folsom Dam and other upstream dams could provide protection from the 150-year-frequency flood without building Auburn, still allowing develoment to continue on the flood plain. Those nonstructural alternatives, costing half of what the Auburn Dam would, were not pursued because the Flood Control Agency insisted on the biggest dam possible.

In 1992 the national organization American Rivers included the American River on its "most endangered rivers list" for the fifth year in a row—the only waterway with that unfortunate status every year since inception of the list in 1987. Calling the project a $700 million subsidy for developers of flood plains, Ed Osann of the National Wildlife Federation said, "It is irresponsible for local officials to sanction the placement of homes, buildings, commercial establishments and people's lives in areas that have a significant statistical probability of flooding and then expect taxpayers in Maine and Iowa to come forward and supply them with money for a flood control project."

Congressmen Fazio and Matsui pushed for passage of the Auburn bill, but Friends of the River lobbied successfully to defeat reauthorization by a 2 to 1 vote in 1992. Vic Fazio then told a reporter, "We may have learned something, and that is that there is no way you are going to get a dam through Congress, maybe in my lifetime." Congress authorized another $5 million for restudy of the dam, and the danger remains that the Army Corps will spend the money on the same old proposals.

In 1993 the city of Sacramento proceeded with plans to develop the low-lying rice fields of the Natomis area into a residential agglomeration with only a thin levee between 300,000 potential new residents and fifteen feet of flood water. With hydrologic data backing him up, Ron Stork of Friends of the River argued that "the Natomis Basin was, is, and will remain subject to catastrophic flooding."

While river groups have lobbied against the dam, the American River canyons have continued to be enjoyed by half a million people a year, offering choice habitat to fish, otters, and mountain lions. This river of the Sierra Nevada, dropping through spectacular whitewater gorges of the North Fork and Middle Fork, may yet survive as it does today. With California encumbered by state deficits of up to $14 billion a year and with the national debt sprinting ever upward, public funding for Auburn appears less likely than ever. Political pressure persists, however, despite the lessons learned from other water projects that have been consistently defeated following the loss of the Stanislaus.

In 1993, with a policy direction that should eliminate the Bureau of Reclamation's threat to the American River once and for all, Interior Secretary Bruce Babbitt called for "the transforming of the Bureau of Reclamation from a civil works agency into a preeminent water management agency that is cost effective in serving its customers."

ᴥ Appalachian River at Stake

In spite of changes in the West, where the big-dam era had achieved its fullest force, an extraordinary eastern river remained threatened. The Greenbrier—the longest free-flowing stream in the Appalachians and one of the longest unimpounded rivers in the country—winds for 199 miles through a green splendor of hardwood forests and mountain farms in West Virginia. Most Appalachian rivers flow quickly out of the mountains by running east or west and thus lack the rugged mileage of the Greenbrier as it flows south, set between high paralleling ridges of our oldest mountain range. Other Appalachian rivers are also dammed, principally for flood control, and along the reaches that survive, railroads crowd many of the steep shorelines. But the Greenbrier, named for a thorny vine growing in the area, is the great exception, even lacking roads along much of its mileage. Popular for fishing, the clear water washes through mile after mile of gentle riffles. Sycamores, willows, maples, and hemlocks shade shorelines of rare riparian quality. Without major rapids, the stream is popular for canoeing, and hikers come here as well.

In 1985, after the highest flood on record for the river, some Greenbrier residents pushed for a large flood control dam above Marlinton, which would impound one of the finest and least developed reaches of the river. However, much of the Greenbrier's length has also been found eligible for national wild and scenic river designation, and the West Virginia Highlands Conservancy and the Sierra Club led local efforts to protect 144 miles of the waterway. This would constitute one of the landmark additions to the National Wild and Scenic Rivers System.

As with the Auburn Dam, the Greenbrier project is not likely to be funded in austere times. The challenge of river conservationists is to gain long-term protection for these two outstanding streams before the dam proposals are revived.

❧ Like Going Back in Time

With today's scientific knowledge and political values, we may not have dammed the Stanislaus or decimated the Columbia River salmon. Using insight and hindsight gained from a half-century that included regrettable decisions about natural resources, there remains an opportunity to avoid the errors of the past.

In Canada, many rivers retain the free-flowing splendor once known throughout the United States. Northern North America holds a large portion of the world's remaining wilderness, and many of the accessible waterways have likewise survived as functioning ecosystems. The Oldman River of Alberta was one of these.

Flowing from peaks of the Canadian Rockies just north of Waterton National Park, the river curved through the foothills of that great range. Cottonwood forests rustled in warm chinook winds while the snowy, eastern escarpment of the Rockies loomed behind. Some of Alberta's finer trout habitat lay in the main stem and two tributaries, the Castle and Crowsnest rivers.

Questioning the justification for Three Rivers Dam to be built across the Oldman, river supporters found this irrigation project to be a cog in a grand scheme devised in the 1960s for a linked chain of reservoirs on rivers of the Rockies' eastern slope, accompanied by canals sluicing runoff southward to the United States for export. Though the memos indicating the interbasin transfer scheme were leaked from the government in 1982, provincial officials avowed that the export strategy had been abandoned. The dam sites, however, remained.

After lengthy hearings, the province's Environmental Council of Alberta found in 1979 that "a dam on the Oldman River is not required now or in the foreseeable future . . . the Three Rivers site would be the worst possible location from environmental and social perspectives." Three Rivers Dam would benefit about 150 farmers at a taxpayer cost of several million dollars each.

If the estate of natural rivers of Alberta has survived longer than that of the United States, the unreformed determination of its provincial government to dam and develop at all costs has survived just as well. Alberta's environmental minister, Ken Kowalski, in sponsoring the dam, dismissed as "social anarchists" the Friends of the Oldman River, who had advanced a formidable anti-dam case from economic, biological, and cultural points of view. Kowalski and his deputies sought to insult and then ignore pleas of the river conservation group, the Peigan Indians whose reservation and waters were grossly affected, and a lengthening list of prestigious river supporters, including newspaper editorial boards, journalists, and civic leaders.

In 1988 the province faced the requirement that the reservoir be licensed for a specified use, but lacked plans and cost estimates for irrigation facilities. Alberta thereby licensed its dam for the ludicrous purpose of evaporating water.

Courts meanwhile ruled that Canadian national agencies had a legitimate role in the project owing to impacts on fisheries and native people. But while lawsuits and protests continued, the provincial government finished construction at a breakneck schedule to stay ahead of opponents, though the reservoir was not entirely filled.

With the natives' lawsuit reduced to procedural and economic haggling in 1990, an activist Indian group known as the Lonefighters Society diverted flows away from the white farmers' irrigation canal, which lay within the reservation. After an armed confrontation with Royal Canadian Mounted Police, who retreated, the diversion was restored. Arrested in the protest, Milton Born With a Tooth vowed to die if necessary in order to destroy Three Rivers Dam. The case was clearly the foremost river conservation battle in Alberta history and one of the greatest ever in Canada.

In 1992 a federally appointed panel of nonpartisan members found that the dam was difficult to justify economically, the environmental effects were severe, and the Peigan Nation had been treated unfairly. The panel made the extraordinary recommendation that the dam be decommissioned and the river restored. Lacking that action, the panel insisted on significant measures to mitigate losses and meet Indian claims. Ken Kowalski, then serving as Minister of Public Works, called the panel's report "technically adolescent," and the Alberta provincial government under Premier Don Getty unhesitatingly vowed for business as usual without federal approvals. On May 22, 1992, editors of the *Calgary Herald* called on the provincial government to "apologize for the affront to fair play, honesty, and good judgment it showed in pig-headedly plowing ahead with the dam in spite of legitimate environmental and jurisdictional concerns." *Herald* columnist William Gold called Alberta's action "an illegal act by an outlaw government." Friends of the Oldman River appealed in court, arguing in 1993 that the province was operating the dam contrary to federal law.

The attitude of provincial officials can be traced to a deep tradition of authority that runs back to England and draws on a Canadian heritage of "respect" for government and a presumption of obedience from the citizenry, which is expected to be easily intimidated. River conservationists such as Martha Kostuch and biologist Cliff Wallis, who have fought the Oldman Dam for a decade, are breaking that mold by opposing a government that pushes ahead with the kind of public works destruction that routinely occurred in the United States thirty years ago but is rare in the 1990s.

If nothing else, the Oldman fight, like the Stanislaus in the United States a decade earlier, marked a turning point. Never again will a river be destroyed with disregard for native and natural values without encountering intense conflict. Alberta conservationist Kevin Van Tighem organized conferences on Alberta rivers in 1988 and 1990, advancing the movement to protect rivers province-wide. A dam proposal on the Milk River, south of the Oldman, was stopped. Environmental assessments throughout Canada are now being prepared where they had never been required prior to the challenges by Friends of the Oldman River.

Worldwide, the prospects for rivers are not so bright. Especially in the developing countries, new dam construction continues, in many cases owing to the export of American technology, engineers, and money. The International Rivers Network, founded by Mark Dubois after the loss of the Stanislaus, established a worldwide organization of people committed to protecting the threatened rivers of the globe.

❧ The Response to Scarcity

Droughts of the latter 1980s and early 1990s elevated the need for water to a paramount concern in many regions of the United States. A drought in the Southeast in 1986 ranked as the century's worst in that region. In 1988 a drought emergency was declared in 40 percent of the nation's counties and was most severe in the Midwest. The Mississippi, Columbia, and Saint Lawrence—together carrying more than half the flow of forty-eight contiguous states—ran at 55 percent of normal. Concentrations of toxic wastes in the Mississippi River grew dangerously high with less dilution.

A prolonged drought hit California hardest, where the old-time fervor for building dams had given way to political standoffs—a balance tested by seven dry years. Sun-baked reservoirs spawned widespread concern not only about the adequacy of the most complex and costly water delivery system in the world, but about the vitality of this fastest-growing state.

A difficult situation only worsened in the early 1990s. After voluntary efforts fell short, the Metropolitan Water Board, with jurisdiction over much of southern California, cut deliveries in its service area in 1991 and forced some mandatory conservation measures. Federal and state deliveries to Central Valley irrigators were sharply reduced, though these did not result in an overall loss in production, nor in a significant retirement of marginal lands, of which there are great tracts owing to salinity, toxic selenium, and drainage problems. While 500,000 to 800,000 acres were temporarily fallowed, the cutbacks in water did not stimulate a marked change in cropping patterns to reduce commodities in chronic surplus or those that consume the most water, such as rice, cotton, alfalfa, and pasture. Nor did they prompt a plausible revolution of efficiency improvements, such as drip irrigation investments and pumped return of wastewater. Instead, the reduced supplies from dams resulted in intensified pumping of groundwater, already being overdrawn in the agriculturally rich San Joaquin Valley by several million acre-feet per year, an extraction operation with a life as finite as that of a coal mine. The drought led to farmers' concern that urban areas would infringe on the irrigators' long-established rights to 83 percent of California's water for an agricultural industry contributing 2.5 percent to the state's economy.

In 1992 the drought extended north to Seattle, where a lawn-watering ban affected 1.2 million people. Half of the counties in Washington developing water supply plans reported that they needed more water to serve anticipated growth—some of it a result of Californians fleeing the growth-induced problems of their old state.

In Idaho the drought was considered the worst since the 1930s. While fear of being stranded amid cultivated fields and suburbanizing cities on an arid Snake River plain struck to the hearts of many people, irrigation deliveries were nearly unaffected in most areas except for a shutoff of late-season waterings. Boise homeowners continued to receive water from canals for flood-irrigating their lawns, a process that requires far more water than just sprinkling.

Prospects looked even worse with the long-term predictions for global warming. While hotter temperatures will result in greater water needs and higher evaporation rates, a drier climate will likely bake many middle-latitude zones encompassing much of the American West. According to the National Aeronautics and Space Administration, flows in the upper Colorado River could drop by 40 percent. A similar decline in rainfall in the American breadbasket could convert whole clusters of counties into dust bowls.

Facing scarcity, some people were bound to cling to the dam-building response. In Utah, for example, the town of St. George boomed in population, so it proposed dams on the Virgin River, identifying fifteen sites, including some in wilderness areas and others at the borders of Zion National Park. Las Vegas proposed water supply projects on the Virgin River and as far away as Colorado. In water-rich Alabama, the Locust Fork of the Warrior River remains as a free-flowing gem, ninety miles long, one of the state's finest recreation rivers with an unusual diversity of life, but in

1992 the city of Birmingham prepared to apply for permits for dams and diversions. Friends of the Locust River argued instead for a comprehensive water plan, believing that adequate supplies already exist.

Yet throughout all the drought-induced anguish, serious proposals for big, new dams went nowhere. The agencies in charge of delivering water had earlier built empires on constructing more dams and plumbing systems to distribute the water and were reluctant to change, but now people began to see enormous opportunities to stretch the supplies they had and avoid the expense and hostility resulting from new proposals such as Two Forks Dam. More and more, citizens and water managers saw the crisis to be one of management rather than absolute supply. As David Kennedy, director of California's Department of Water Resources, said in 1993, "We're not going to simply build our way out of this urban growth situation."

Seattle proposed a diversion from the North Folk of the Tolt River but dropped older, destructive projects on the North and Middle forks of the Snoqualmie River. Later, the city launched a program to distribute water-efficient plumbing fixtures, which were expected to save 12 million gallons a day at one-third the cost of the North Tolt diversion. With equally bright prospects for new supplies from benign sources, the Metropolitan Water District of southern California entered into a path-breaking agreement with irrigation districts of the Imperial Valley to fund water conservation measures and then receive the saved water for urban use.

Hartford, Connecticut, hoped to tap the Farmington River but encountered opponents who pushed for water conservation and wild and scenic river status instead. Columbus, Ohio, planned to dam the biologically unique Upper Darby Creek and the Scioto River but later dropped the proposals when faced with a determined rivers constituency that included Ohio Rivers Unlimited, led since its founding by one of the great river conservationists of the Midwest, Mike Fremont.

More and more, efficiency improvements were seen as the most economical way to meet new residential water demands, which the U.S. Geological Survey estimated will increase by 31 percent between 1985 and 2005. That's a large increase, but 40 percent of urban water in the West goes to lawns and thirsty shrubbery, much of which are nonnative varieties from the East. Toilets requiring five gallons per flush and accounting for one-third of the water use in an average home can be replaced with ones that use one and a half gallons.

In the Denver area, the cost of recycling water was $800 an acre-foot, while new diversions from the west slope of the Rockies would cost $3,000 per acre-foot in the early 1990s. Distributing efficient toilets, shower heads, faucet aerators, and outdoor watering improvements to all Denver residents could supply as much water as Two Forks Dam but at one-fifth the cost according to Andrew Jones of the Rocky Mountain Institute. The California Department of Water Resources found that residential consumption can be cut by 55 percent in new homes and by 43 percent in existing ones. New York City, where water use climbed 25 percent even when the city lost 12 percent of its population, has no metering of water, resulting in less efficient use. Sacramento, which boasts one of the highest growth rates in the nation, has had no water meters, though these are now required in new construction. Municipal water systems generally lose an average of 12 percent of their water to leaks. Boston loses 35 percent; Houston loses 20 to 30 percent.

Irrigation accounts for 81 percent of water use nationwide, but 50 to 80 percent of that supply leaks or evaporates before reaching the crops. Conversion to drip irrigation, whereby plants are watered through small hoses set in the ground, can save more than 50 percent of the water that is otherwise wasted. With this technique, productivity frequently goes up, and weeds—not receiving the water they need—can be eliminated without herbicides. University of California resource economists Henry Vaux, Jr., and Richad Howitt reported that a 10 percent cutback in farm use would meet California's urban needs for twenty years without serious harm to the agricultural community.

As commissioner of the Bureau of Reclamation in the Clinton administration, Daniel Beard said that "water conservation is the most important part of our program. You hear that we're out of water, but what we're running out of is *cheap* water."

A plethora of conservation measures are not only feasible but automatically implemented when the economics of water more effectively reflect the scarcity. Instead of spending $28 billion a year on current farm subsidy programs that frequently fail to achieve the desired results, the federal money could be used to subsidize the efficient use of water. In California, irrigators paid an average of $.04 per 1,000 gallons of federally supplied water while residential customers paid $1.04. With both groups—but especially irrigators—the low cost of water offered little incentive to conserve.

Efficiency improvements and a revamping of water costs can carry our cities and farms far into the future, but until the American population is stabilized at a sustainable level—meaning one at which environmental destruction stops and the fundamental sources of wealth are sustained—even the abundant opportunities for efficiency may some day be exhausted. Then the West will see widespread conversion from agricultural water to city supplies—a process already under way with some cities buying ranch and farm supplies.

In Colorado, where agriculture accounts for 2 percent of the population but uses 92 percent of the water, farmers' sale of water to the cities has retired 60,000 acres of formerly irrigated land. The amount of water used by a typical farm or ranch can supply 1,136 city-dwellers. Enormous supplies could be gained without loss of important agricultural capability if farmlands of marginal value are retired. In areas with poor soil types, irrigation on millions of acres now results in salinization, erosion of topsoil, and pollution of downstream water supplies. Regarding water use in the Rockies, Colorado College economist Mark Smith said, "It's a lot more efficient to take marginal land out of production than to build new mountain reservoirs."

The health of the land and the economy may well be served by retiring marginal lands—those underlain by selenium and salts, along with soils of high erodibility. Instead of irrigating those troublesome areas, the water can instead support urban populations committed to more efficient water use. Perhaps such action can buy time until population growth comes to a halt and we learn to live within a balanced resource budget whereby we no longer consume the wealth of the earth faster than that wealth can be generated.

❧ Revisionist Development

After several years of drought in California, the level of New Melones Reservoir on the Stanislaus River had slowly receded in the late 1980s. Flatwater drained from the upper canyon between Camp Nine and Parrot's Ferry, once again exposing a riverbed with glistening runoff from the Sierra.

In 1990 and 1991 the backwater receded even farther down the canyon, exposing one magnificent rapid after another. Newly sprouted willows shot up to heights of ten and twenty feet. Maidenhair ferns sprouted again from the same shaded cliffside where they had grown before. People likewise returned to the sinuous canyon—first a few Stanislaus veterans, then visitors by the hundreds. In 1992 thirteen commercial rafting outfitters once again operated in that limestone canyon, and thousands of people again experienced the wonders of a once-enchanted place.

The canyon had changed, certainly. The "dead zone" of skeleton trees and discolored cliffs marred the view, but the river had returned to its old patterns of rapids and sandbars, pools and eddies. From the water, the remarkable impression was not one of loss but one of recovery.

And, of course, the times had changed. The Stanislaus had been dammed in the final throes of construction of the Central Valley Project—a large collection of Bureau of Reclamation dams and canals. Now, only twelve years after New Melones construction, a congressional bill sought to reform the Central Valley Project to require remedies for the damage wreaked on fisheries and wildlife. Led by board chairman Richard Roos-Collins, who had worked on the original campaign, Friends of the River successfully lobbied for a study of New Melones reauthorization. The dam will be evaluated for maintenance of water quality in the Sacramento and San Joaquin delta. This downstream estuary urgently needs freshwater flushes to sustain a municipal water supply for millions of Californians, for aquatic life, including endangered salmon, and for the health of San Francisco Bay. Releases from New Melones Dam to save the delta could keep New Melones Reservoir low enough most of the time to spare the upper nine miles of the Stanislaus Canyon. The encroachment of development on the lower river's flood plain makes large releases from New Melones unlikely, and so the canyon would still be flooded periodically, preventing full restoration. Yet by using New Melones to correct one of the worst problems resulting from the diversion of northern California water to the southern part of state, the Bureau of Reclamation could also reduce the losses of one of the most damaging projects the federal government has ever built.

❧ Old Gains and New Losses

While the sacrifice of natural rivers behind large dams can only be described as extreme, and while a few such threats persist, the transformation of water development and management away from big, destructive projects marks one of the clearest accomplishments of the modern environmental movement in America. While the opposition to new dams grew, inflation made proposed projects more expensive. Federal purse strings were tightened, and as a part of fiscal reform, cost sharing by the states was required. The combined effects made it apparent that the most logical dam sites had already been built on.

Yet the effectiveness of river conservationists should not be underestimated. The new economic imperatives were in part a result of environmental concerns. The federal budget for dams was cut because dams had lost their popularity due to effective opposition. In contrast, concern for cutting federal expenditures did not stop runaway increases in funding for the military in the 1980s. Cost-sharing requirements were also a result of environmental opposition to new water projects during the Carter years of 1977 through 1980. Various dam-building entities showed little inclination to pursue nonstructural alternatives—even when they could save money—until the resistance to new dams became insurmountable. Even with federal budget cuts, nonfederal projects such as Two Forks in Colorado, Blue Ridge in North Carolina, Clavey–Wards Ferry on the Tuolumne in California, and many others would have been built had they not been effectively opposed.

In summary, a seemingly hopeless array of new dam proposals in the mid-1970s has given way to an age of management and efficiency with few proposals advanced for massive projects. Nuclear power plants were similarly halted after concerns for safety and waste disposal eventually caused nuclear power to become uneconomical, but few other environmental pursuits can claim such success.

Yet other threats to rivers abound, multiply, and worsen. Losses that had been ignored previously are now recognized. Dried-up riverbeds below diversions for irrigation and cities, the razing of riparian habitat, and rampant watershed destruction eliminating entire ecosystems pose challenges for the future. Some of these go more to the heart of social, political, and economic change than did the abandonment of big water projects. And while the likelihood of large dams faded along most rivers, a new age of hydroelectric development began, posing proliferated threats at far more streams than river conservationists had ever imagined.

Chapter Four

The Myth of Hydropower

❧ Hidden Truths and Hidden Costs

Strange and delusive myths have surrounded our use of rivers ever since Alexander Mackenzie and Henry Hudson sought the Northwest Passage and explorers wandered the Great Basin deserts in the early 1800s looking for the River Bonaventura. This "River of the West" was said to link interior America with the Pacific, but it existed only on maps and in wishful minds. Myths about rivers continue to abound, the most troublesome being those with some basis in fact.

People widely believed that rivers would purify themselves, given just a few riffles for aeration of the water, but many rivers are hopelessly overloaded by pollutants and by chemicals that don't break down at all. The "miracle of irrigation" indeed yields bountiful harvests, but not without costs that often dwarf crop values. Enthusiasts failed to recognize grim prospects for soil, water, and desert societies in the long term—the total effect being something far less than a miracle.

One of the greater myths is that rivers can generate clean and cheap electricity to fuel a growing population while avoiding environmental pitfalls. In fact, the energy is not cheap and clean but costly and damaging on a scale rarely recognized, and the amount of power to be gained by damming additional rivers is small.

Inundation of thousands of farms in the Appalachians, incessant erosion of beaches in the Grand Canyon, and the extinction of salmon runs in the Northwest and New England are only a few examples of the hidden costs of hydropower. Though massive new dams have been defeated, as described in Chapter 3, there remain a multitude of smaller hydroelectric proposals in the United States and modern megaprojects in Canada.

Less than one-tenth of U.S. electricity comes from hydropower, and while maximized hydro development in this country would not boost that figure substantially, the specter looms that new dams could block hundreds of rivers. As supplies of oil and natural gas dwindle, as we awaken to the reality of global warming and acid rain emanating from fossil fuel use, and as our foray into nuclear reactors fails ever more decisively, hydropower, by comparison, will be painted as a benign bargain. Yet the sacrifice of aquatic ecosystems for electricity is one of the most troubling prospects ever faced by people who value rivers as they are.

Hydropower is produced when the force of falling water turns the wheels of a turbine, making electricity. Some small hydropower projects don't require dams but simply divert a stream's flow through a pipe, which runs steeply downhill to turbines in a generating plant. But to avoid low wattage in dry seasons, power brokers build dams to store water. With schemes of great complexity, engineers have designed tunnels to divert one river into another, and whole series of reservoirs release runoff to networks of canals, penstocks, and turbines, the river having been pressed by pipefitters into an outsized schematic of plumbing.

Hydro projects can require large initial investments but yield exceptionally long service lives and low operating costs, which means low rates on consumers' monthly bills, all of this owing substantially to environmental losses not paid for by the customers.

☙ Multiple Losses

The most obvious environmental cost of hydroelectric dams is that the reservoirs flood portions of rivers, causing them and their landscapes to utterly disappear. Hundreds of projects decimate resident fisheries by flooding habitat and blocking migration routes. Back-to-back dams on the Susquehanna in Maryland and Pennsylvania flooded a wealth of river-bottom life and wetlands where the largest source of water neared Chesapeake Bay. Choice valley lands of the Little Tennessee, held sacred by Cherokee Indians and productively used for 200 years by mountain farmers, were flooded as recently as 1979 by Tellico Dam, though it contributes only 23 megawatts of power—0.1 percent of the Tennessee Valley Authority's supply. The Skagit River once ran as one of the most spectacular wild rivers of America, bursting with runoff from the alpine heights of Washington's North Cascades and plunging through rocky canyons shadowed by ancient trees of enormous girth. Even to the Skagit's headwaters in British Columbia, Seattle City Light impounded the upper river behind Gorge, Diablo, and Ross dams. Half of Hells Canyon—the celebrated second-deepest canyon in our country—lies beneath water dammed for hydroelectricity, interring what senior boatman Martin Litton described as a whitewater journey comparable to the Grand Canyon itself.

In an additional agenda of river loss, hydro projects divert water so that it bypasses its channel altogether, creating the ecological absurdity of a river in a pipe. Presumably the water is only borrowed from the stream. But in fact the diversion leaves the intervening bed dry and as conducive to aquatic and riparian life as corrugated conduit. Rivers such as the Sierra Nevada's Yuba and South Fork of the Stanislaus host complex schemes of piping, ditching, and tunneling from one valley to another to maximize the vertical drop, or hydraulic head, in the process reducing the integrity of the river that is left behind.

Finally, the flow regimes below hydroelectric dams are often given as little concern as a bathtub drain. Power companies cut off flows entirely as they recharge reservoirs; then they release torrents that scour riverbeds for peaking power two hours each afternoon. The results are degraded riverbeds and bulk losses of habitat caused by dam-induced erosion.

No one has calculated the losses of rivers and river life to power dams already built, yet hydro projects have been a source of destruction to America's native landscape dating back to the nation's first power plant, which was located on the Fox River in Wisconsin and lit 250 light bulbs in 1882. One of the initial efforts at natural areas protection in the nation was at Niagara Falls, with establishment of a New York State Reservation in 1885, but limitations on power development at the site were not recognized until later. Many of New England's 11,000 dams remain relics of a hydropower era that ignored everything else that rivers were good for. Nine dams on the Tennessee and forty-two on its tributaries constitute the most completely dammed large river system in America and flooded 635,400 acres—much of it productive farmland. Hydro dams in the upper Midwest block the Manistee, Pine, Middle Branch of the Ontonagon, St. Croix, and Namekagon—all outstanding rivers in other respects.

Gross reductions in natural rivers occurred up through the 1960s, and serious losses owing to hydroelectric development continue. One of the few big water projects to be built since the 1970s, a complex of four dams and diversions on California's North Fork of the Stanislaus and its tributaries Beaver Creek and Highland Creek, erased the singular beauty of Gabbot Meadow and one of the oldest structural remains found by archaeologists in North America. During construction of a project planned to provide a scant 7.5 megawatts of power, a diversion from the Fall River, below Yellowstone National Park in eastern Idaho, eroded through an embankment in 1992. A roiling, uncontrolled avalanche of water, rocks, and mud resulted in one of the worst water-quality disasters in recent Idaho history, ruining twelve miles of the pristine river and dumping debris into the Henrys Fork of the Snake.

No one can stand at the base of a hydroelectric monolith and deny that some projects produce a lot of power. Capable of generating 3,492 megawatts, Grand Coulee Dam ranks as one of the largest single sources of electricity in the world. A typical large hydro dam might produce 200 megawatts. To many people, that amount of power may be worth the cost. And, stirring little complaint, some small hydroelectric generators are innocuous. Fewer than 3 percent of the large dams in America produce power, and at many of these sites the harm has already been done; adding generators may cause little further loss. Ninety-three percent of the licensed or authorized hydro developments in 1989 occurred at existing dam sites. But, unfortunately, many of the retrofits depended on drying up new sections of river; half of the proposals in New England involved diversions causing dryways, some of them as long as 1,000 feet. Many projects can be engineered for minimal impact, but developers tend to resist compromises that forego kilowatts.

Most hydropower plans go unopposed. In the 1980s the Federal Energy Regulatory Commission (FERC), the licensing agency for nonfederal power dams, permitted about 200 new projects annually. Only a few of the approvals each year met with strong objections by a broad-based river conservation community. Among thousands of hydroelectric projects in the nation's history, several score have been subject to concerted opposition. Several dozen serious proposals have been stopped by conservationists, and several hundred vaguely feasible sites have been precluded by protection measures. But many threats to rivers continue.

◆ The Current Threats

Combing the topographic maps of the nation, hydroelectric developers propose new projects for rivers wherever substantial gradient carries water on its downhill journey. Just when the Penobscot River in Maine is becoming a national model for Atlantic salmon restoration, the Basin Mills Dam would create a 3.6-mile-long reservoir and a new impediment for migration. The dam would reduce the likelihood of a self-sustaining run of salmon at the same time that Maine and the U.S. Fish and Wildlife Service are spending $800,000 a year to reestablish the run. Here and elsewhere, developers press for new barriers in the fishes' way, canceling the hard-earned gains from taking old barriers out.

At the Black River near Watertown, New York, a hydropower proposal threatens one of only four year-round "adventure class" whitewater rivers in the Northeast; another project at Hawkinsville could eliminate a small town and an excellent fishery. Other Northeast projects have been proposed on the Sacandaga and Salmon rivers in New York, the Dead River in Maine, and the Pemigewassett in New Hampshire.

On the mile-wide Susquehanna River in the Pennsylvania state capital of Harrisburg, the Dock Street Dam proposal, with a reservoir eight miles long, has been fought by the state. The U.S. EPA found "unacceptable adverse effects" with the dam, which would inhibit long-standing efforts to reestablish American shad in the huge river. On the Savage River in Maryland, a new hydro project would eliminate much of the whitewater where world championship races are held. The developer was first foiled in seeking an exemption from the normal permitting process, but resubmitted another, more complete application.

In the South, hydro projects are proposed on the James, Shenandoah, and New in Virginia; the Green in North Carolina; the Talloosa in Alabama; and the Chattahoochee and Tugaloo in Georgia. Hundreds of additional proposals are on the books to dam or divert little-known rivers of common appeal—the swimming holes, waterfalls, fishing spots, and centerpieces of local culture.

Near the top of the list of river controversies in the 1990s, the Salt Caves Project on the Klamath River in Oregon would cut flows by 80 percent in ten miles of prime trout fishery, also considered one of the finer whitewater paddling runs on the West Coast and habitat to fourteen protected species. The federal Bureau of Land Management (BLM) recommends wild and scenic river protection for the threatened reach. FERC intended to approve diversions even after voters passed a statewide initiative to safeguard the Klamath in the Oregon scenic rivers system. The state government proceeded to block the diversion because of water quality concerns despite appeals by the hydroelectric sponsor—the city of Klamath Falls. In 1993 Oregon Governor Barbara Roberts requested federal protection of the Klamath in the National Wild and Scenic Rivers System, which would stop the project.

Dozens of hydroelectric diversions are plotted for the brilliant waters of the eastern Sierra Nevada, including Rock and Virginia creeks, superb trout streams that would be piped to turbines for a pittance of power in a region that depends on tourism, not electricity, for its economy. On the Clavey, Mokelumne, and Kern of the Sierra Nevada, new hydro dams are proposed but fought by Friends of the River and other groups. These throwbacks to the big-dam era include plans for a 430-foot-high dam on the Clavey, where the Turlock Irrigation District and Tuolumne County proposed to spend $707 million, in the process dewatering nineteen miles of the remarkably remote and scenic river, home to thirteen species nominated for the federal Endangered Species List. More than 600 hydropower applications posted in the 1980s could some day affect 2,000 miles of California streams.

In Washington, where seventeen new hydroelectric projects could affect outstanding waters, the Rivers Council of Washington works to guard Sunset Falls on the South Fork of the Skykomish and the gemlike Cispus River, which flows from the glaciated volcanic mass of Mount Adams.

In Colorado, 41 percent of the waters of a spellbinding gorge just below the Black Canyon of the Gunnison National Monument could be diverted in the A-B Lateral Project. The affected waters constitute some of the finest trout habitat in the state. A minimum flow of 300 cubic feet per second—now occurring only several days a year—would handicap the river 60 percent of the time. According to Colorado State University biologists, the change could endanger a riparian ecosystem critical to eagles, otters, and ospreys. The project would tunnel flows to the neighboring Uncompahgre River, bolstering its level to a near-flood stage that would chew away banks, bury some of the finest wetlands in western Colorado, and drain others as the channel, which would be riprapped, erodes deeper into its bed. The power is not needed by local utilities; the largest one recently went bankrupt because of overcapacity. The objective, rather, is to reduce water rates for farmers of the sponsoring Uncompahgre Valley Water Users Association, which has already reaped considerable benefits from multiple Bureau of Reclamation dams as infamous as the Dallas Divide Project, which was on President Jimmy Carter's hit list of uneconomic boondoggles in 1977 but was built anyway. Seeking to protect the Gunnison, which was recommended for national wild and scenic river status after a decade-long study, the National Park Service and Bureau of Land Management lost a struggle within the Interior Department to the Bureau of Reclamation, which saw the A-B Lateral diversion as a way for waters users to squeeze elusive revenues out of existing federal development schemes that don't pay their way. Activist and journalist Steve Hinchman of nearby Paonia, Colorado, summarized the threat: "The project would dry up one river and flood another to produce expensive electricity that utilities don't need." In a major setback for the project in 1993, the Army Corps of Engineers rejected the applicant's request for a "404" permit to modify the rivers, though the Gunnison Gorge remains unprotected.

For sheer scale and magnitude of destruction, however, nothing matches the new hydroelectric ambitions in Canada. In the magnificent wilds of British Columbia, the Stikine River, one of the wilderness wonders of North America, flows hundreds of miles through the moss-clad forests and mountains of that far western frontier. Its headwaters offer an extraordinarily wildlife-rich section of river, then a wilderness gorge serves up one of the continent's most thundering complexes of rapids, followed by a reach of 100 miles winding out to sea by way of glaciated peaks, virgin forests, and teeming schools of salmon. A power dam built for sale of electricity to the United States would ruin this hemispheric masterpiece. Plans of the 1970s were put on hold, but with new power needs in the Northwest and California, the threat to the Stikine could return. Elsewhere in Canada, Ontario planned to develop twelve projects in the Moose River Basin, and Manitoba proposed the $6 billion Canawopa Dam on the Nelson River.

❧ Rearranging the Waters of the Continent

It is no exaggeration to say that the James Bay Project in Quebec is causing the most draconian effects on rivers since the Columbia was dammed. Twenty rivers in an area the size of New York and New England combined are to be impounded and the drainage manipulated in 60,000 square miles of wilderness to create one of the largest hydroelectric complexes in the world. The province-owned utility, Hydro-Quebec, is developing one of the last great wildernesses on earth and, in the process, is destroying globally significant waterfowl habitat and the traditional way of life for native Cree and Inuit peoples, whose patterns of hunting and trapping near Hudson Bay have amazingly survived until today.

Many of the region's rivers still exist as huge, untouched Susquehannas, Wabashes, and Colorados cutting across unblemished forests, over dozens of waterfalls, and through miles of boiling rapids, some of them 400 miles from the nearest road. The largest woodland caribou herd anywhere roams here, and birds of both the Atlantic and Mississippi flyways converge in the region. The fisheries, including anadromous species, have sustained native peoples for thousands of years.

After first hearing about the provincial government's proposed dams from surveyors and on the radio, Indians opposed the initial phase of the James Bay Project. In 1971 the Crees drafted a resolution opposing the project, stating that "We believe that only the beavers had the right to build dams in our territory."

The Crees fought celebrated court cases in the 1970s but lost in their efforts to sustain an independent and isolated culture. They were given money as compensation for losses and have been returning to court since

1977 demanding that Hydro-Quebec live up to agreements made with them regarding Phase 1 and future plans.

Dams on the La Grande and Eastmain rivers have flooded an area larger than Connecticut and diverted water so that the flows of five different rivers were all channeled into one. Below the dam-released waters on the Caniapiscau River in 1984, 10,000 caribou were killed as the herd, on its annual migration, attempted to cross the river. The La Grande dams drowned soil and vegetation that was naturally high in mercury, infusing the aquatic food chain with the toxic metal and poisoning the fish on which the Cree depend. That was Phase 1 of the James Bay Project.

Thousands of Crees feel the effects of the new road access, which brings white anglers and hunters, the influence of a massive construction industry, alcoholism, junk food, and a pervasive undermining of cultural integrity. Hydro-Quebec is quick to point out that new goods and services are available to the Crees, that infant mortality has decreased, and that the natives have money with which to assimilate into white culture. But drug abuse, sexually transmitted diseases, family violence, and suicides are on the rise, problems that the Crees say scarcely existed a generation ago. Asked about progress stemming from the project, Sappa Fleming, the former Inuit mayor at Great Whale, said, "Well, my children can choose from six different kinds of potato chips." Cree spokesman Matthew Mukash said succinctly, "Enough is enough. We do not want Quebec's dams and roads and everything else that comes with them."

A future phase of the project involves damming the Great Whale River, a 219-mile-long artery named for the beluga whales that once lived at the river's mouth on Hudson Bay and still congregate at the mouth of the Little Whale River, whose flow would be cut off. Five dams would inundate an area the size of Delaware, displacing thousands of Crees from their hunting grounds. Bird life, fur bearers, and rare freshwater seals would be decimated at the mouth of the Great Whale River with drastically altered flows. John Petagumscum said that the project "will mean the end of us as a people." The Nottaway, Broadback, and Rupert watersheds would also be developed.

The almost incomprehensible final phase of the project would add yet more dams on more rivers, and the $100 billion Grand Canal Project would dike the mouth of James Bay for 100 miles so that Hydro-Quebec could pump fresh water to the U.S. Great Lakes, Midwest, and Southwest. The altered river flows and fresh and salt water balance would eliminate estuarine areas and marine mammals, including seals, polar bears, and whales.

If the hydro project is completed, it will produce 28,000 megawatts of electricity—13,000 more than the entire Columbia River system. The ensuing environmental disaster has been called the northern equivalent of cutting the Amazon rain forests.

This rearrangement of North American waters, fought by the Crees with all the resources they can muster, depends on the sale of electricity to the United States via a 950-mile-long transmission line connecting wires from the Crees' rivers to appliances of every useful and trivial sort in homes in New York and New England. Cree Chief Robbie Dick said, "They are telling the Americans this is cheap and clean. But it's not cheap for us. When you turn on your switch, you're killing us." Hydro-Quebec contracted with the New England Power Pool for 2,000 megawatts, with 45 percent of the power to go to Massachusetts, though a bill in that state's legislature could require a full environmental impact statement—something Hydro-Quebec has not prepared. Maine declined to accept contracts with Hydro-Quebec. Vermont approved the acquisition of 340 megawatts with the agreement that the power not come from James Bay.

According to Ihor Kots, managing director of the largest credit-rating service in Canada, "The whole essence of James Bay 2 depends on export sales. The electricity demand in Quebec won't be sufficient to take up the capacity for years to come. If there is not demand from elsewhere, it would add considerably to the financial risk." In 1993 Hydro-Quebec's development plan called for an additional investment of $52.5 billion throughout the province. Up to 75 percent of the money was to be borrowed.

Seeking support for the Crees' cause, Grand Chief Matthew Coon-Come spoke at Times Square on Earth Day, 1990: "Hydroelectric development is flooding the land, destroying wildlife and killing our people, and eventually we will all be victims." In 1992 New York State canceled its

$17 billion contract to buy James Bay power but did not rule out a reversal of the decision after the state's current energy surplus is gone. Hydro-Quebec proceeded with Phase 2 anyway.

In January 1993 the Grand Council of the Crees signed an agreement to let much of Phase 2 of the La Grande project proceed. Matthew Coon-Come stated that his "hands were tied" because the dams were already three-quarters built. The Indians will receive $125 million in settlement, including $500,000 a year to encourage Cree hunters and trappers to continue their traditional hunting activities in other areas. The Crees remain opposed to the Great Whale dams and further developments.

And now, just as the Bureau of Reclamation, Army Corps of Engineers, and American consultants have done, the Hydro-Quebec engineers are exporting their expertise, aiding the Chinese government, which has announced that it will build Three Gorges Dam on the Yangtze River. For electricity, that reservoir will displace up to 1 million people.

❧ The Power Profile

Of the nation's total energy use, 36 percent is electricity. Fifty-six percent of that electricity comes from coal, 17.7 percent from nuclear power, 10.6 percent from natural gas, 9.7 percent from hydroelectric projects, and 4.6 percent from oil. Hydropower generating capacity was 88,000 megawatts in 1987.

Hydropower accounts for about 12 percent of electric "capacity," a measurement of maximum generating ability but not actual power use. The hydropower share of the total is down from 57 percent of electricity use in 1900 and 40 percent in 1930. Half of America's hydroelectricity comes from just two river systems: the Columbia and Tennessee.

Many of the largest hydropower projects are owned by American taxpayers. These are federal facilities on dams built by the Army Corps of Engineers, Bureau of Reclamation, or Tennessee Valley Authority, with the dams being operated and power being sold by those agencies or by two power brokers in the West—the Bonneville Power Administration in the Columbia River Basin and the Western Area Power Administration in the Missouri, Colorado, and Rio Grande basins.

About 2,000 hydropower projects owned by private and public entities are operating in the United States. Some projects consist of several dams, and many dams have escaped licensing and regulation altogether through loopholes and grandfather clauses allowing old developments to continue unaffected. There are thirty-eight unlicensed projects in Wisconsin, for example. Unlicensed dams cause impacts as serious as a Saco River project that lacks facilities for fish passage and undermines efforts to restore Atlantic salmon in Maine. In Michigan 2,200 dams were built mostly in the early 1900s by logging companies or utilities. Of the 113 that produced power in 1992, only 71 had federal licenses; the others escaped the process, ostensibly because of their age or small size.

The number of operating projects increased by nearly 50 percent between 1984 and 1988, indicating a lot of new, small facilities. Forty percent of the growth in capacity since 1972 has been in pumped storage. With this technique, water is pumped uphill to reservoirs by consuming electricity from coal or nuclear power plants during nighttime hours of low demand. During hours of peak energy use, the water is dropped through turbines, increasing capacity but netting more energy consumption than production—sometimes three times as much.

Enormous amounts of electricity—one-third of the Columbia River generation, for example—go to produce aluminum, which requires twelve times the energy needed to make the same amount of iron. One aluminum plant might consume 300 megawatts—enough for a city of more than 175,000 people.

Power rates where hydroelectricity predominates are among the lowest rates in the nation. The Idaho Power Company, for instance, charges half the national average. Per capita use in that state, not surprisingly, is four times that of New York.

Major controversies ensue over projects that generate even small amounts of electricity. The average capacity of hydro plants in 1980 was 50 megawatts (a shopping mall of a hundred stores uses about 3 megawatts). One of the more heated river protection battles of the 1980s, for example, was over Big Ambejackmockamus Falls on the West Branch of the Penobscot in Maine. Though it was eventually defeated, the "Big A" dam would have generated only 40 megawatts. Some of the projects attracting opposition will produce as little as 2 megawatts—a drop in the bucket of distribution. Though the power to be produced may be insignificant to society or even to a single town, the entrepreneur building the dam can often earn a profit.

While many hydro plans in the 1980s failed owing to a lack of need, a surplus of electricity may be running out. The Pacific Northwest and California predict possible shortages by the year 2000, and deficits soon thereafter could occur elsewhere in the nation. Between 1978 and 1990, about 7,500 dam proposals appeared on the books at FERC. The agency reported that about half the nation's available hydropower sites had been built upon. Of the 95,000 potential megawatts remaining, one-third is at existing dam sites.

In 1988 FERC estimated that 1,500 new dams may eventually be built for hydroelectric power. Only 13,000 megawatts were likely to be developed by the year 2030 due to low energy prices and "regulatory constraints."

Regarding the small projects most likely to be built, American Rivers stated that the new development "could not have any discernible impact on global warming or the serious national problems of acid rain, dependence on foreign sources of energy, or the negative balance of trade." Yet hundreds of miles of rivers are threatened by the belief that increasing our electric capacity by a percentage point or two is of vital importance to American society.

A system of regulation theoretically exists to weigh the choices and protect public values. How well that system has functioned is a good question.

⋟ The Guardian of Public Assets

The Federal Energy Regulatory Commission, formerly the Federal Power Commission, was created by the Federal Power Act in 1920 as a result of compromises between legislators who advocated hydropower development only by public agencies versus those who backed an uncontrolled private market. The resolution, like others in our history of resource management, dealt with the conflicting choices by calling for development by all of the entities in question. Regulations, however, were imposed on private industry in an effort to guarantee protection of public values. Five members, appointed by the president with approval of the Senate, govern FERC. Regarding hydropower, FERC has seen its primary mission as the licensing of new projects.

Both the FERC and state-level public utility commissions weed out some projects if there is a "lack of need." Public utility commissions, along with the occasional reform-minded state water board, can temper the pro-dam inclinations of FERC but in the final analysis cannot overrule it. FERC may approve power developments even over objections of state legislatures, governors, and dissenting federal agencies. In the U.S. Supreme Court, California took FERC to task over jurisdiction. Impressively supported by every other state in its Rock Creek case, California lost an appeal in 1990 to require a higher minimum flow from a project. The only way to reverse or prevent a FERC license has been to override the agency by designating national wild and scenic rivers, as was done at Hells Canyon of the Snake in Idaho, the New River in North Carolina, and the Tuolumne in California. The power lobby has resisted repeated efforts to amend the Federal Power Act to allow states the right to veto new dams, which would put state-designated scenic rivers off limits to development.

Opposition to a preliminary FERC permit is never effective because only a "study" is being approved. Later, opposition to construction licenses is often ineffective because the sponsor has invested millions of dollars and gained unstoppable momentum. In all cases, citizen participation in the FERC process is tightly governed by rules of intervention, deadlines, and frequently the need for lawyers simply to gain access. FERC is notorious for its courtlike demeanor in its dealings with the public, down to every neighborhood group that wants to have a say about its local creek. "The purpose of the Federal Power Act was to protect the public from wholesale private development," said John Echeverria of American Rivers in 1991, "but FERC has become a captive of the industry that was to be regulated, and it regards public groups as interlopers and strangers."

In all of its history, FERC has denied only several hydroelectric licenses because of environmental concerns. Among the notable few: a 1953 decision not to dam the Namekagon River in Wisconsin because of fishery values; a 1987 denial of a Kootenai River project in Montana because of Indian spiritual beliefs, fisheries, and aesthetics; and a 1988 rejection of four projects in the Owens River Basin of California. This environmental record is not getting much longer in spite of the fact that, under the Electric Consumers Protection Act of 1986, FERC is required to give equal consideration to environmental values and power needs.

Ed Crouse, an environmental specialist on FERC's staff, disagreed that the agency gives the environment short shrift. He argued that the review process alone eliminates many damaging projects and that many other "economic" failures occur because of the FERC-required cost of mitigating environmental damage. Many of the requirements killing new dams stem from reviews by the U.S. Fish and Wildlife Service, though that agency is underfunded and understaffed to do the job. The National Park Service reviews applications for recreational impacts, but the law does not obligate FERC to abide by National Park Service conditions.

The federal Clean Water Act adds some balance to FERC's development orientation. The act requires the Army Corps of Engineers to certify that water quality standards can be met. The Corps in turn counts on the EPA to make the decision. Ironically, the Corps—the biggest dam builder of them all—has blocked some hydroelectric plans, such as one at Canaan Valley on the Blackwater River in West Virginia, where Clean Water Act requirements could not be met. Section 401 of the act also mandates that developers secure approvals from state water-quality agencies prior to receiving a FERC license, though state authority has often been limited to narrow criteria.

In granting licenses, FERC must consider any comprehensive river plans by states or other federal agencies, but "consider" is the key word here. More than 440 different plans have been recognized, and though conflicts are plentiful, they have never been the sole basis for license denial. The Northwest Power Planning Council's Protected Areas List included the Klamath River, thereby recommending against hydro development, but FERC intended to approve the project anyway. A hydro development on the Ompompanoosuc River in Vermont conflicted with an official state waterfall study. FERC's own judgment was that no problem existed: "Since we have concluded that Project No. 9085 would not have an unacceptable adverse impact on the visual resource . . . licensing of the project is not in conflict with the Waterfall Study." FERC has, however, rejected proposals because of conflicts with some comprehensive plans, including a development on Lena Creek, in Washington, where the U.S. Forest Service identified problems.

Though none of these review procedures offers firm protection for rivers that deserve it, the complications—when combined with marginal economics—yield a high casualty rate for new hydroelectric dam proposals. California's South Yuba River is a case in point; regulatory constraints and appeals by the South Yuba River Citizens League delayed proposals long enough that the sponsor's contracts to sell the power expired, and the projects became uneconomic. Many dam plans die quiet deaths even after receiving FERC licenses. And John Echeverria recognized improved environmental reviews at FERC in the 1990s: "The agency is better than it was ten years ago. There was a feeling after the Electric Consumers Protection Act that things *had* to change. But a new national energy strategy such as the one proposed by the Bush Administration in 1991 could rescind much of the progress and grant new powers to FERC." More important and more likely, a sharp increase in the value of the power produced could eventually resurrect plans for new dams from the Olympic Peninsula to the tidal zone of Maine.

ఊ Subsidized Destruction

In an era of government budget cuts and deregulation across the land, subsidies and incentives to plunder yet more rivers through private hydropower development anachronistically abounded. Without subsidies and government props, much of hydropower's appeal to energy developers would have vanished.

While a real demand for electricity accounted for the construction of many dams in the past and will account for proposals at most conceivable sites in the future, the surge of applications in the 1980s was due largely to economic incentives legislated in the Public Utility Regulatory Policies Act (PURPA) of 1978. Congress gave an impressive advantage to new developers of small projects by forcing utility companies to buy the power, typically produced by private entrepreneurs or municipal governments, and to pay the price required for alternative supplies, which was frequently as high as the cost of oil. The utilities thus had to pay top dollar for new hydropower whether or not the market demanded it and, indeed, whether or not they wanted the power at all. The Electric Consumers Protection Act of 1986 eliminated the PURPA requirement where states have designated scenic rivers, and the new law placed a temporary ban on other PURPA benefits at some other sites.

In the early 1980s developers also received 21 percent of their expenses back in tax breaks the first year they built new hydroelectric dams, amounting to a taxpayer subsidy of hundreds of millions of dollars. Those incentives have expired, but others remain, including the availability of public land. In the North Fork of the Stanislaus Basin, forests, meadows, and canyons were sacrificed for a hydropower complex without Forest Service opposition. The court case of *Escondido Mutual Water Company v. La Jolla Band of Mission Indians* confirmed the ability of federal land-managing agencies to impose conditions on projects, such as mitigation for fish and wildlife losses; yet the agencies have been loathe to take aggressive stands for their rivers, freely yielding the controversial decisions to FERC with its consistent history of backing development.

Private entrepreneurs, with FERC licenses in hand, have the authority to condemn land owned by private citizens. In the mid-1980s, a corporation based in France planned to condemn a portion of a state park along the South Yuba River in California before the project was stopped. The 1992 Energy Security Act later banned condemnation of state or local parkland but did not affect private land. While even the most limited proposals for new wild and scenic river designations arouse a militant citizenry fearful of condemnation of private land—a fear without basis in fact—the hydropower industry escapes unscathed with its condemnation privileges.

Topping the list of subsidies to hydropower developers, a private company secured a permit to install hydro facilities at Island Park Dam on the Henrys Fork of the Snake River in Idaho over the objections of the Henrys Fork Foundation, which was concerned about the country's finest dry fly trout fishery and the safety record of the sponsor. Senator James McClure of Idaho devised a $1 million federal appropriation to be given to the developer of the 4.8-megawatt project with the rationale that the application was not processed in time to take advantage of tax breaks that had expired in 1988.

Finally, in what Matthew Huntington of American Rivers calls "the largest subsidy issue," the waterways belong to the public but dam operators pay virtually nothing for their use of the rivers, which yield millions of dollars in profits annually.

ɜ Ample Alternatives

Already effective in meeting the energy needs of the 1980s and early 1990s, energy efficiency improvements without new hydropower dams can economically extend the reach of existing sources. The growth of innovative, renewable supplies is possible, feasible, and inevitable.

An industrial trade group, the Electric Power Research Institute of Palo Alto, predicted that new energy conservation programs will save the nation 25,000 megawatts in the 1990s, surpassing the 20,000 megawatts saved in the 1970s and 1980s. That is enough to eliminate twenty-five large coal or nuclear power plants. California's utilities forecast that 70 to 100 percent of their new demands in the next twenty years can be provided by efficiency improvements at up to one-seventh the cost of new construction. Enticements in the 1980s came not from the federal government, which was entrenched in development policies of the past, but from state public utililty commissions and the utilities themselves, which realized the economic sense of efficiency.

Energy analyst Amory Lovins of the Rocky Mountain Institute in Snowmass, Colorado, said that the nation can easily cut production of gases causing global warming by 20 percent through efficiency, without hardship or inconvenience, and in the process save $200 billion. Simply converting to new, efficient light bulbs and lighting facilities could save 25 percent of U.S. electricity use according to Lovins and the Electric Power Research Institute. Equivalent savings are possible with more efficient electric motors, which in 1991 accounted for half the electricity use. More efficient refrigerators and freezers can consume 80 to 90 percent less electricity than they do now. An Electric Power Research Institute study found it technically feasible to cut electricity use by 24 to 44 percent by the year 2000, and Lovins predicted that use can eventually be cut by 75 percent.

Pointing out the sensible alternatives to new hydropower, the California Resources Agency under Huey Johnson found that the hotly contested New Melones Dam would yield only one-sixteenth the amount of energy that would be saved if Californians properly inflated their tires, or one-eleventh the energy saved if they tuned their car engines, or one-thirteenth the energy saved if they slowed down to fifty-five miles per hour—and this was in 1979, when traffic was far less.

The peaking demands that hydropower accommodates are among the easiest demands to reduce. Peak load management devices that alternately shut down air conditioners for ten minutes at a time have cut loads by 10 to 20 percent in some California cities.

Aluminum production, accounting for much of the hydropower use in the Northwest, can be cut by 90 percent through recycling. For steel, recycling uses only 14 percent of the energy it takes to produce the metal from raw materials.

There are ample reasons for limiting new hydroelectric sources to the less harmful options. The U.S. Department of Energy estimated that 12,500 megawatts of power can be developed with free-flow turbines, set into rivers without dams, and potentially with minimal impacts. Another 5,000 megawatts may be available by tapping irrigation canals, domestic water systems, and very small sites of less than 1 megawatt. And benign sources of other kinds can be tapped to increase energy supplies. A study for the Department of Energy found that wind could supply 20 percent of our electricity needs. Even more promising, photovoltaic technology to convert solar power to electricity is nearing commercial success in the 1990s. Many experts predict that it will compete economically with coal by the year 2005 and that photovoltaic energy sources will be built on the rooftops of many houses.

Any one of these opportunities represents more power than would be provided by even the most ambitious growth of hydroelectricity. Even greater energy savings will result when the larger culture no longer considers an electric appliance, no matter how frivolous or impractical, to be the ideal gift at Christmas, and when laundry drying on a clothesline is no longer seen as some kind of social stigma in suburban neighborhoods.

❧ Facing the Ultimate Limits

Even with efficiency improvements, the inevitable, ultimate realization is that we cannot sustain a way of life in which 6 percent of the world's population—that is, Americans—consumes one-third of the energy. The rest of the world wants to emulate our nation's consumptive pattern, and if they do, planetary destruction will be far worse than even the current projections for global warming, acid rain, toxic poisoning, soil loss, species extinction, and unraveled ecosystems.

The prospects for benign energy are great in the short term, but even those may ultimately prove futile unless the population level is stabilized. The U.S. Census Bureau reported in the early 1990s that the possibility for a steady state of population actually exists in the United States. Countering this trend, immigration has increased markedly with the liberalized quotas of the 1990s. Birth rates are high among many new immigrant populations, and illegal immigration results in an unknown number of new residents, though authorities agree the number is huge.

Casting uncertainty and pessimism over the energy issue, the world's most powerful nation has had no national policy save the implicit one of fighting wars over oil, seeking to extract fossil fuel supplies at all ends of the earth, including the biological wonderland of the Arctic National Wildlife Refuge, and presidential vetoes in the 1980s of congressional attempts to improve appliance and auto efficiency. A national energy policy based on efficiency, conservation, and truly renewable sources could be the first major step toward the reforms that are essential if we are to have an environment much worth living in. The energy tax proposed by the Clinton administration in 1993 would be an important step.

Depressed energy prices in the 1980s and early 1990s rendered many hydroelectric plans uneconomical. In constant dollar values, energy cost less in 1993 than anytime in the past sixty years. But this is a short-term phenomenon fed by our heavy reliance on cheap, imported oil and our government's willingness to guard Middle East supplies even by shipping American troops off to war. In the twenty years following 1973, the nation has operated under the illusion of plenty while in fact living in the midst of scarcity. The United States has grown ever more dependent on foreign fuel, and its low prices have eliminated any chance of gradual market adjustments to the inevitable hard times ahead and of financial incentives to invest in alternative and benign energy sources.

Being finite resources, our supplies of oil and natural gas will run out; estimates by the Complex Systems Research Center at the University of New Hampshire predicted that the United States could exhaust its oil and gas by the year 2020 and that world reserves may be effectively spent by 2050. Coal supplies will last much longer, but burning coal grossly aggravates acid rain and air pollution, and its extraction has become synonymous with landscape wreckage and mine drainage, turning thousands of miles of streams to Day-Glo orange. Even after the scrubbing of pollutants such as sulfur, the release of carbon into the atmosphere—the principal cause of global warming—will increase with each shovel of coal burned. Some people regard nuclear power as an alternative, but in fact that industry's waste disposal problems are insolvable. The industry presumes with an arrogance unique to world history that thirty years of power production for today's particular lifestyle is worth chronic expenses and hazards for thousands of years to come. Future generations will not have used a single kilowatt of the troublesome power but will have to maintain our nuclear waste dumps for up to 250,000 years, let alone endure the risks of another Three Mile Island or worse.

Within this energy climate and moral morass, developers advertise hydroelectric generation as the clean and harmless source, only one step removed from the ideal of power from the sun itself. In the desperate search for energy to promulgate the consumptive culture held so dear, hydropower promoters will turn up the pressure for new dams and diversions. Their arguments will appear sound to many people regardless of how small an amount of energy is really produced and regardless of the loss of rivers and riparian ecosystems.

New hydro schemes will eventually surface and eclipse the proposals of the past. Any stream with a healthy flow, noticeable gradient, and lack of protection, such as national wild and scenic river status, will be considered fair game. Where will it all end?

Now, before insurmountable pressures build, long-term protection for quality streams is needed. Efficiency improvements and benign sources can supply our energy appetite for years, but to avoid new power development beyond those years, our culture must evolve into one that consumes and burns less in pursuit of happiness. And the ultimate need is for a stable population that no longer grows as if the earth were unlimited in its resources.

ஐ Overcoming the Hydroelectric Threat

Many of the landmark cases in river conservation involved stopping hydroelectric dams. Historic opposition blocked dams at Ramparts on the Yukon River, where a reservoir the size of Lake Erie was planned; at the Allagash River in Maine, where one of the wildest streams in the East was to be flooded; and at the Blackwater River in West Virginia, where pumped storage projects could have ruined a spectacular Appalachian valley. The Storm King case, involving a pumped storage plant along the Hudson River in the 1960s, led to a landmark court ruling allowing a citizens' group to bring suit because of aesthetic, conservation, and recreational interests. Wild and scenic river status halted projects posing imminent threats on a handful of rivers.

Hydro developers would have depleted flows along sixteen miles of the North Fork of the Payette—a reach of rapids considered the Mount McKinley of whitewater. Wendy Wilson and other Idaho river conservationists organized a statewide movement to save the Payette, and in 1990 they convinced the State Water Resource Board to deny water rights for the diversion and then to designate the Payette as a state scenic river. This killed the hydro project, at least until the developer challenges the state's authority.

In West Virginia, an Army Corps of Engineers proposal to divert flows from the Gauley River in the early 1980s threatened one of the finest of the difficult whitewater runs in the country. Stressing the economic value of recreation, river supporters convinced local Congressman Nick Joe Rahall to introduce legislation that expanded the authorized uses of the existing Summersville Dam—just upstream from the threatened reach—to include the use of reservoir water for recreation in the river below. A new water release schedule was written into law, effectively stopping the diversion. The Gauley was then designated a national recreation area to foster protection and recreation use.

Operating with unusual authority, the Northwest Power Planning Council adopted a Protected Areas List as a model of river recognition. The four-state agency designated outstanding fish and wildlife streams accounting for 44,000 out of 250,000 total miles of streams in the Northwest as off limits to new hydro development. The Bonneville Power Administration denies intertie privileges on its power lines to any nonconforming project. Planning Council biologist Peter Pacquet described the list as a way of letting hydroelectric entrepreneurs know that they will be throwing money down the drain if they pursue development on the designated rivers.

Many projects will continue to be fought by citizens' groups through the permitting process with FERC. An entire book on the subject, *Rivers at Risk*, produced by American Rivers, clearly outlines the procedures for stopping hydroelectric dams once they are proposed.

Expansion of state wild and scenic river systems can fill some of the gap that national wild and scenic river designation will never touch. A new Federal Power Act amendment, pushed by river conservation groups, could give state governments veto authority over FERC.

Beyond opposing destructive dams and diversions in the United States, it is essential that Americans consider the extraordinary but imperiled rivers of Canada as the unique and irreplaceable wonders that they are. Our appetite for energy could result in the demise of the remaining wilderness of James Bay, the Stikine River, and other continental jewels.

Resistance to river protection comes from congressional members who support hydroelectric developers and from the National Hydropower Association. In a 1991 interview the Association's director, Elaine Evans, said, "There is a lot of confusion over what we, as a society, want to have. We want to drive half a block to the store and buy electric tinker toys and yet still preserve the environment for a very limited number of users. Look at whitewater rafting. You folks are not driving out of the middle of Watts to go rafting. You're basically young urban professionals." She called the plan to eliminate an antiquated dam on the Kennebec River "utterly stupid," and added, "The issue is fishing. People are very worried about turbines killing fish, but what is fishing about? It's about killing fish."

When FERC licenses new hydro dams, safeguards can extend protection far beyond the dismal record of the past by requiring adequate flows below the dams and by attempting to secure protection elsewhere to compensate partially for new losses. On the Cowlitz River in Washington, for example, a power developer will flood several miles of river that lack exceptional values, but he will spend $275,000 for acquisition of easements to save open space on other waterways qualifying for national wild and scenic river status.

❧ Correcting Past Mistakes

Beyond the possibility of halting the worst new dams proposed for hydropower, real opportunities exist to correct some of the damage of the past.

The FERC licenses are temporary. After a period of time—usually forty or fifty years—the agency must reconsider the licenses because it is recognized that the definition of "public good" can change over time. And it has. River conservationists now consider the relicensing of hydroelectric dams to be the best opportunity in decades to restore damaged rivers.

Before the end of the century, 366 hydroelectric plants with 3,700 megawatts of capacity will be subject to FERC relicensing. By the end of 1993 alone, 167 licenses covering more than 230 dams came up for renewal, one-third of them in New England. The greatest number of relicense applications by the year 2000 lie in New York, Wisconsin, Maine, Michigan, Massachusetts, and California. According to Fred Springer, director of FERC's Office of Hydropower Licensing, "Virtually every project we are reviewing will require changes to reduce their effect on the environment."

After the federal agency licensed a plethora of dams in the 1950s and 1960s, nearly every environmental law was added to the books. The mandates of renewal are clear—sponsors must comply with the new laws, not the old ones. The owner is assumed to have amortized the capital investment over the term of the original license; the government does not "owe" the developer a renewed license or additional profits. Corporations that have profited for fifty years and plan to do so for another fifty can be required to compensate for some of what was lost with the original license. Matthew Huntington, the director of hydropower policy programs at American Rivers, called relicensing "the once-in-fifty-years opportunity to bring dammed rivers back to life."

Without draining the reservoirs, no one can replace lost wildlife habitat, but threatened habitat elsewhere can be protected as part of the bargain. Known as "mitigation," this process has commonly failed in the past; its effectiveness depends on new commitments. Improved flows can be guaranteed for fish and recreation, fish passage facilities can be added, and public access to the rivers can be improved. Huntington stated that many of the modifications being sought cost no more than 1 percent of revenues from the dams and would have virtually no effect on the amount of electricity produced. In 1989, pushed by American Rivers and other groups, FERC required the addition of fishways at the Cataracts Project—four dams on Maine's Saco River. In Massachusetts and Vermont, new licenses for nine dams on the Deerfield River could yield improved flows for fishing and boating, and thus boost the local economy. In New York, the American Whitewater Affiliation surveyed the renewal applications and found reaches with fine whitewater potential on the Beaver, Raquette, and St. Regis rivers. These had been ignored for decades because old hydro projects so severely depleted the streams. Pete Skinner of the Affiliation wrote that "relicensing offers the first substantial opportunity to actually recreate whitewater long lost to dams." Relicensing of the Bend Project on the Deschutes River in Oregon could include provisions to stop the killing of rainbow and brown trout in the project's turbines. The dam produces 1.1 megawatts—enough for just thirty-five homes. On the Skokomish River in Washington, the city of Tacoma built Upper Cushman Dam in 1930 without fish ladders. The diverted flows left a nearly dry riverbed below, and fishing ended as a way of life for native people. In 1992 the tribe urged FERC to require fishery releases for coho salmon when relicensing the project. Facing a coalition of groups, including the Michigan United Conservation Clubs, the Consumers Power

Company agreed as part of its relicensing process to provide up to $30 million to address river flows, bank erosion, and fish passage at eleven dams on the Manistee, Muskegon, and Au Sable rivers.

FERC or another federal agency can go further and recommend a "takeover" of a project for operation by the government with compensation to the owner, or can recommend a "nonpower license" under which the project can be used for other purposes or removed. These provisions could reasonably be applied to dozens of dams now lying in disrepair. Many of them generate negligible power but continue to destroy the life of the rivers. Dozens of these dams would never have been built with today's laws and public sentiment. Though a 1990 Department of Energy publication stated that "some of these projects may cease operation," FERC has seldom considered the option of eliminating dams, and other agencies cannot require a comparison of the no-dam option. American Rivers has proposed that FERC require applicants to participate in a fund for the eventual removal of outmoded projects.

In 1993 FERC's chair, Elizabeth Moler, announced to a conference on river protection that she advocated a "brand new view" regarding relicensing, that decommissioning of appropriate projects would be addressed in detail, and that public participation in FERC's decisions will be sought. Though she would not commit to refusing permits where state governments seek to protect specific rivers, she announced that she was "glad to be talking here today about bringing the commission into the twentieth century."

⊱ A Place for Hope

The Elwha River on the Olympic Peninsula in Washington once ran as a stronghold of all five species of Pacific salmon that swam in masses of swarming life. To local Indians, the river is legendary for once supporting spring chinook salmon weighing more than 100 pounds. The river drains the largest watershed in Olympic National Park—a World Heritage Site and International Biosphere Reserve.

In violation of state law, power developers erected the 105-foot-high Elwha Dam in 1914 without fish ladders. The project never received an operating license from FERC. Upriver, Glines Canyon Dam, 210 feet high, followed in 1927 without fish passage; it lies entirely within the national park, which was established in 1938. In 1990 federal officials estimated the economic loss of the fishery as a result of the dams at $500,000 a year. Olympic National Park Superintendent Maureen Finnerty compared the historic chinook of the Elwha to the bison in Yellowstone and pointed out that at least twenty-two species of birds and mammals utilizing the salmon had been reduced in numbers due to loss of salmon stocks.

The Glines Canyon license expired in 1976, but the dam continued in operation with annual permits. Both the Elwha and Glines Canyon dams generate a total of 19 megawatts of electricity, which contributes only one-third of the power needed by one nearby pulp mill owned by Daishowa America, a subsidiary of Japan's second-largest paper producer with receipts of $2 billion in 1989 and a history of environmental conflict elsewhere, including the wholesale cutting of the boreal forests of northern Alberta. The Lower Elwha S'Klallam tribe at the river's mouth challenged the application for a new license in 1976 and pressed for removal of both dams.

Also seeking removal, environmental groups in the state of Washington intervened in the FERC relicensing process in 1986. They proposed that the Bonneville Power Administration fund a pilot project of industrial energy conservation at the mill to provide up to 20 megawatts of electricity through efficiency and recycling. The pulp mill could receive the power it needs, the government agencies could meet legal obligations to the fishery that had long been ignored, the region's economy could be enhanced by a superlative fishery, the Indians could regain aboriginal fishing rights now lost because the power goes to the Japanese pulp mill, and the American public could be returned a resource of singular value.

State, federal, and tribal biologists concluded in 1990 that the only way to restore the fishery was to remove the dams, and tribal consultants found that the structures could be torn down economically and without undue sedimentation. The National Park Service, U.S. Fish and Wildlife Service, and National Marine Fisheries Service joined the Elwha tribe and environmental groups in support of dam removal. All groups advocated negotiation with the dam owners and power users, who refused to enter into talks.

Support from Daishowa and the James River Corporation, which owns the dams, was forthcoming with a federal agreement to replace the power, accompanied by a proposed $29.5 million in federal dollars to buy the dams, and with proposed authorization of public funds for dam removal and mitigation, which could cost $160 million. The dam owners will walk away with adequate power, no liability for damages, and a lot of money—a generous offer, to say the least. If Congress does not appropriate the needed funds, the case could be referred back to FERC, where progress had been at a stalemate for years.

In 1992 Congress took a step toward eliminating the dams with the Elwha River Ecosystem and Fisheries Restoration Act, directing the Interior Secretary to submit a plan for "fish restoration of the Elwha River ecosystems and the anadromous fisheries." In April 1993, Interior Secretary Bruce Babbitt told a House committee that he would relish the opportunity to be "the first secretary to preside over not building a dam, but blowing up a dam."

It is difficult to imagine a case where so much of value has been so tragically lost and where so much could feasibly be restored. If successful, the campaign to restore the Elwha will be the most significant effort ever to remove unnecessary and destructive dams and restore river values. Many other dams of marginal or nonexistent value could likewise be eliminated. In national advertising, the Patagonia Corporation, owned by wild rivers and wild fisheries enthusiast Yvon Chouinard, pushed for removal of additional dams that provide little benefit to people but harm wild fish.

At the Elwha and at other rivers across America, people are exposing the myth of hydropower and looking forward to a time when rivers will once again be valued and used for their intrinsic worth.

Chapter Five

The Elusive Goal
of Quality

❧ A Foul Rain

Not long after dawn, the raspy drone of a low-flying airplane caught my attention. No other noise broke the stillness on that balmy morning at my riverside camp, a sandbar remarkable for its riparian microsystem amid a valley gridded by agriculture. The yellow biplane crossed the river upstream from me, curved, and dropped elevation as if to land, though the pilot now throttled his craft into a roar.

He approached his target as if to drop a hand-held bomb of World War I vintage, and I found something quaint and adventurous in this use of technology, in being able to fly with such skill, to master the normally transparent medium of the sky. But the fascination ended with the acrobatics of this piston-driven machine; the pilot was about to reveal his workaday purpose.

Only 20 feet off the ground and just 200 yards from the bank of the river where I stood and watched alongside my beached canoe, the plane disgorged a gray plume of mist. Billowing behind, thick and smoky, it puffed out at the sides in response to the aircraft's turbulence. The pilot pulled up at the end of the quarter-mile length of crops, fluffed the tops of cottonwoods with his windy wake, banked overhead, and circled to spew another load, this one thoroughly fogging the atmosphere and even obscuring the plane from my sideways view.

By now the air smelled as if somebody had taken a baseball bat to all the yellow and red bottles in the lawn-and-garden section of an Agway store. The crop duster had reduced sunrise to a yellow pesticide dawn. Over by the river, the poison mist suddenly hit me in the face. I stuffed my food into bags, but oily droplets splattered my tent and camping gear. As

I hurriedly paddled away, the river lay immersed in the acrid odor of the chemical cloud. Limited only by the volume its tank contained, the plane passed again, again, and again in its schedule of saturation bombing. Then I noticed the water.

The Sacramento River suffered from what seemed to be a clinical case of dandruff, white flakes dappling the surface. They adhered to my paddle, where I saw their greasiness. They congealed on eddy lines as a white, lenticular plume. The dry, toxic odor clung to me for hours. When I reached the confluence with the clean-running American River, I paddled up it, bathed, and washed my gear, but found that the slimy poison gripped tenaciously to everything it had touched.

For four days I had been paddling on the Sacramento River with the idea that I should know more about the streams where I was living during that summer of 1991 while I edited a book about California's environment. Even twenty years after a concerted national commitment to clean up the water had been launched, one can look at the local river and find a broth of pesticides, PCBs, oils, sewage, mine acid, hot water from power plants, mercury and other metals, nitrates, foam caused by phosphates, and the sludge of farmland residue. And crop dusting along rivers happens all the time. The biplanes fly up and down the 400-mile-long Central Valley of California throughout the growing season.

The type of pollution I had experienced represented the two foremost plagues to water quality everywhere—contamination from large areas rather than single-piped sources, and poisoning by toxic chemicals, in this case an air drop of poison intended for the crops we eat but distributed recklessly on our land and streams, infusing our air, infiltrating our workplaces, contaminating our homes. The double jeopardy of polluted runoff and toxins represents the greatest challenge ever faced by people who would clean up the nation's waterways.

❧ Comeback Rivers

Cholera and typhoid outbreaks of the 1800s announced that water pollution posed dangers. Tens of thousands of people died. The approach to the problem—damming clean streams for drinking water and piping sewage straight to rivers—accomplished little to solve the problems of the waterways and of downstream communities. In 1860, when 136 cities had public water systems, only 10 had sewage systems, and these consisted of pipes to the nearest river, lake, or ocean. Laden with the offal of the city, the Chicago River emptied into Lake Michigan, from which water was drawn. When 80,000 people died of typhoid, diphtheria, and cholera in 1887, the river's flow was simply reversed, sparing Chicago by exporting its waste down the Illinois River to the Mississippi instead.

A growing sense of government responsibility for wastewater led to primary treatment plants and a modicum of control, but action for water quality in streams lacked motivation to go beyond the prevention of sewage-borne epidemics, and the federal government acted as though the pollution problem didn't exist. The Merrimack River in Massachusetts vomited a rainbow of colors depending on the daily dye at the textile mills. In the 1960s, analysts rated that river, once eulogized by Henry David Thoreau, as one of the ten dirtiest in America. The Juniata at Tyrone, Pennsylvania, carried chunks of foam the size of bushel baskets below a pulp mill, as did the Androscoggin at Berlin, New Hampshire, the Pigeon in Waterville, North Carolina, and nearly every river below every pulp mill. Anaerobic waters pernicious to any desirable form of life created just the right backdrop for coliform bacteria, sludge worms, and a freak show of crawling pathogens.

In 1899 the federal Refuse Act sought to stop the dumping of oil and other contaminants, but was largely ignored. In 1948 a federal water pollution law called for action at the local level. Legislation in 1956 went further by authorizing $50 million a year for ten years in matching grants for sewage treatment. The law was amended four times through 1970, with no dramatic improvement in overall water quality and no discernible effect in much of the country.

Championed by Senator Edmund Muskie of Maine, the Clean Water Act of 1972 eclipsed all former legislation and set out to "restore and maintain the chemical, physical, and biological integrity of the Nation's waters." A "fishable and swimmable goal" was set for all waterways. Impressive progress ensued during the following twelve years, when $310 billion was spent to clean up water, one-third of it by government. The U.S. EPA reported that $37.5 billion was spent by all public and private entities on water pollution in 1987. In 1992 the EPA alone spent $2.9 billion on the Clean Water Act, most of it as grants to states for sewage treatment plants. The population served by treatment facilities increased by 72 percent in the 1980s, a result of the economic and infrastructure commitments of the previous decade. Public treatment has reduced sewage in the nation's rivers by 90 percent since 1970.

After $600 million was spent to clean up the 116-mile-long Merrimack, this birthplace of the industrial revolution ran respectably clear and was tapped as a public water supply, a repulsive idea just one generation before. Likewise, the nearby Nashua River was transformed from a technicolor sewer to a community asset. The Potomac—once a sewage lagoon stagnating irreverently at the Jefferson Memorial—is no longer the health threat it was in the 1960s. After $1.6 billion was spent on wastewater treatment in the 1970s, largemouth bass returned and the river became one of the most popular recreation areas in the mid-Atlantic region.

Observers had called the Connecticut River "the best landscaped sewer in America," alluding to fetid water wending its way through postcard landscapes of bucolic America. The Connecticut cleanup worked to the degree that real estate along this New England artery appreciated sharply, ironically spawning waterfront building pressures where people had not encroached much on open space since farmers first broke ground.

In the 1960s, pulp mill waste, sewage, and acid mine drainage indelibly tarnished the otherwise comely Clarion River of northwestern Pennsylvania. An annual canoe regatta, begun by a student group in 1970, highlighted possibilities for the river, and the problems were substantially solved over the next fifteen years. Once considered ineligible as a national wild and scenic river because of pollution, the Clarion in 1992 became the nation's first stream to be restudied for wild and scenic status.

The Ohio River—arterial conduit of the interior East—has gone from a septic behemoth to an inland waterway hosting bass, pike, and muskellunge, though heavy metal contamination persists. The Willamette River in Oregon became a model of water quality improvement, and in 1993 water agencies in Texas reported that the Colorado River flowing through Austin and the Trinity River in Dallas–Fort Worth had improved dramatically with regional sewage-treatment facilities.

☙ The Current Assessment

Considering how bad things had become, the cleanup of sewage and industrial outfalls between 1972 and 1985 marks one of the more remarkable achievements of a society otherwise burdened by an oppressive list of ills that mostly seem to get worse. But as the EPA admitted in its 1990 water quality assessment, the point sources were the most "blatant and easily controlled sources of pollution."

We have celebrated the cleanup of some rivers, as we should, but other rivers now run worse than they did. Ironically, during the same period that many pathetic waterways were made tolerable, others became worse, so that the whole picture was one of growing mediocrity, neither good nor horrible. In 1988 scientist Barry Commoner pointed out surveys showing no gain in water quality at four-fifths of the tested sites, and more overall deterioration than improvement.

In an important analysis by Richard Smith, Richard Alexander, and M. Gordon Wolman in *Science* magazine in March 1987, the authors compared nationwide data between 1974 and 1981. Fecal bacteria and biological oxygen demand had decreased with new sewage treatment plants. Reductions in lead reflected less leaded gasoline. But a "striking" increase in salts was noticed, much of it stemming from wintertime use of road salt, which increased by twelve times between 1950 and 1980. Nitrates also accumulated from fertilizer as application rates on farms grew by 68 percent between 1970 and 1981. Increases in nitrate, arsenic, and cadmium resulted from various factors, but chief among them was air pollution from the burning of fossil fuels. The analysis made clear the effects of air pollution on water quality. Acid rain emanating from sulfur and other air pollution affects the otherwise chaste lakes of the Adirondack Mountains in New York, the Hudson's source at Lake Tear of the Clouds, and the St. Lawrence's source at the Boundary Waters of Minnesota and Canada. According to the U.S. Office of Technology Assessment, 117,000 miles of streams are vulnerable to acid rain.

We failed to meet the 1985 target date of the Clean Water Act to establish fishable and swimmable waters everywhere. We have not even come close. In 1991 David Dickson of the Izaak Walton League succinctly stated, "The Clean Water Act has yet to achieve its goals." The League lobbied for reauthorization of the act to make it more effective.

Fish kills reported by states in 1990 totaled 600 incidents involving 13 million fish according to the EPA's biannual water quality report. Texas and West Virginia registered 80 percent of the kills, which may say more about inadequate reporting from the other states than about the severity of pollution in just those two. In 1990, 998 water bodies had fish advisories in effect; fishing bans were imposed on 50 water bodies because of pollution.

Thirty percent of the nation's surveyed river miles still fail to meet water quality criteria, which don't include anything approaching drinkable water but are based on minimum standards for swimming, fishing, chemically treated water supplies, and other less demanding uses. Also, the fact that 70 percent of the tested sites meet standards doesn't necessarily mean healthy streams; biological criteria, involving a waterway's ability to support native organisms in the long term, are not included. Agencies estimate that only half the nation's stream mileage is of tolerable biological quality. Sturgeon, for example, depend on mussels—bivalves with high susceptibility to pollution and depleted flows. If the mussel population crashes, the sturgeon may not survive. Mayflies—the favorite food of trout—may be wiped out in a stream that normally tests well for traditional chemical criteria. Dr. James Karr, one of the foremost authorities on river ecosystems, has argued that "we need to shift the societal focus from water quality to a broader concept: the ecological health of the water resource system." He has written that a biological system can be considered healthy when "its inherent potential is realized," its "condition is stable," its "capacity for self-repair when perturbed is preserved," and when "minimal external support for management is needed."

Alabama's Cahaba, one of the nation's most biologically diverse rivers, provides a good example of the failure of current water quality programs to achieve the Clean Water Act's goal of restoration and maintenance of the biological integrity of aquatic ecosystems. In the twenty years since passage of the act, the Cahaba has suffered unprecedented decline. The numbers and range of many plants and animals have decreased by more than 75 percent since 1972. Most who have studied the Cahaba's endangered ecosystem agree that a shortage of dissolved oxygen associated with sewage discharges has been responsible for the losses. Despite the fact that hundreds of millions of dollars have been spent on treatment, and despite the fact that the standards are individually high, the cumulative effects of increasing sewage discharges are felt farther and farther downstream of the populous Birmingham area each year. The U.S. Fish and Wildlife Service has stated that problems associated with sewage facilities have been largely responsible for the need to add eleven Cahaba species to the lists of endangered and threatened species from 1990 to 1993.

Without considering the more stringent biological criteria, the U.S. EPA reported in 1990 that 15 percent of large municipalities remain in "significant noncompliance" for their sewage discharges. The Ohio EPA found that 35 percent of its waterways did not meet chemical criteria of water quality standards; the figure rose to 70 percent when biological criteria were used. Thirty-nine percent of municipalities nationwide lacked adequate "pretreatment" programs to screen for toxic wastes. In the 1988–1990 period, 13 percent of industrial discharges failed to meet legal discharge requirements. This figure was on the rise from past years when it hovered in the 6 percent range.

One of the more substantial and unaddressed problems in water quality is that of renovating the multibillion-dollar investment in sewage plants that was funded by the federal government in the 1970s. Hundreds of the plants will become inadequate over the coming decades. Many economically strapped municipalities have no apparent means of rebuilding or upgrading their sewage plants, and the problem of bankrupt communities unable to afford waste treatment could be back in our laps as it was before 1972. The solution calls for a resurgence of federal involvement, for much higher user fees for water and sewer service (which will result in water conservation), and for ecologically oriented remedies, such as the system of wetlands created by the city of Arcata, California, where sewage is naturally processed by growing aquatic life and waterfowl. Water conservation can likewise reduce the amount of effluent that requires treatment, extending both the population to be served and the life of the facilities.

In 1987 the federal government replaced the construction grant program, responsible for the dramatic gains of the 1970s, with a "revolving fund" whereby money is given to the states, which in turn loan it to local governments. The Bush administration EPA termed this a "major step in restoring the responsibility for financing wastewater treatment to states and municipalities." The word "restoring" is of curious usage here: even a cursory view of the past reminds one that states and municipalities never took adequate financial responsibility for building new treatment plants. A hopeful Congress authorized $900 million for the program.

While the ambient quality has improved in some rivers—especially the large, urban ones—catastrophic spills still alter the face of North America. In 1988 a thirty-foot tidal wave of 4 million gallons of diesel fuel ruptured from a storage tank, washed over a dike as though it were a whitewater rapid, and entered the Monongahela River in southwestern Pennsylvania. The 100-mile-long toxic slick contaminated the water supplies of 750,000 people. In 1991 a broken pipeline spilled 1.7 million gallons of oil into the upper Mississippi River. While requirements for precautionary measures have helped, we fail to eliminate those kinds of calamitous accidents.

≥ The Toxic Legacy of Our Age

Widespread contamination by toxins ranks as one of the darker environmental nightmares ever to come to life. The pollution and cleanup challenges of this modern scourge make the continental cleanup of sewage seem as easy as sweeping the kitchen floor. Varieties of substances causing birth defects, cancers, and other diseases have fouled hundreds of rivers and thousands of underground aquifers, setting up an ecological chain of death that will last for generations and even longer in some basins.

Agencies typically test for only a few among thousands of chemical products and wastes. A National Academy of Sciences report concluded that sufficient information for an adequate health hazard assessment was available for less than 2 percent of 65,000 commercial substances being marketed. Trial and error is the dominant approach, whereby substances are regulated after problems occur. These problems include worker poisonings, birth defects, and wildlife losses, and we have only begun to scratch the irritable surface of the Chemical Age.

Each year, 71 billion gallons of hazardous waste are generated in the United States, posing health risks to people and ecosystems. In 1990 the EPA reported that toxins created problems in 15 percent of the nation's river miles. Out of every 100 miles of waterway, these tend to be the 15 miles flowing past the most people.

More alarming, a 1992 EPA study of freshwater fish found cancer-causing DDT in nearly all of the 388 sites tested nationwide. Though banned twenty years ago, the pesticide remains in sediment and accumulates in fish tissue, which raises an even more troubling question: How long will the unrealized effects of *today's* toxins accompany us? Each year, 20,000 new chemical compounds are introduced with relatively little testing for their effects on the environment. The EPA study found that PCBs represented the highest cancer risk to people eating freshwater fish regularly. Though this extremely toxic chemical used in the electronics industry has not been sold in the United States since 1971, 91 percent of the sampled fish were contaminated with it. Elevated levels of mercury were found in 92 percent of the sampled fish. Few streams in urban or agrarian America have survived without some ominous additives contributed by the chemical, mining, manufacturing, and agricultural industries. Evidence grows that cancer is not the most serious problem. Reproductive dysfunction, developmental anomalies, and deficiencies in the immune system are receiving increasing attention. Not only human health, but that of organisms throughout aquatic ecosystems, is of growing concern.

Barry Commoner pointed out that 30 percent of toxic wastes are emitted to the environment. He took little comfort from the fact that most of the remainder is "disposed" at waste facilities. This includes underground injection, which results in substances accumulating as long-term threats to land, groundwater, and rivers. Only 1 percent of the waste is destroyed. Commoner called America's chemical industry "the major threat to environmental quality." Citing lackluster attempts to control the flow and disposal of toxins, he argued, with statistical evidence, that real progress results only when the "production or use of the offending substances is halted." In other words, we must get rid of the entire toxic product and substitute it with something benign, which in many cases worked quite well before the explosion of chemical production in recent decades. Commoner's conclusion may be the most important realization in the entire analysis of water quality problems.

In Florida, mercury was found in the fish of Everglades National Park, and "advisories" for twenty-five streams and lakes statewide were issued in 1989. West Virginia issued warnings about PCBs and dioxin in the Kanawha River, which was expected, but also in the idolized Shenandoah and the nation's Potomac. The state toxicologist in Maine warned pregnant women to avoid eating fish from the Androscoggin River and from the lower reaches of the Kennebec, Penobscot, and other streams flowing from one of the East's least spoiled regions, but one in which paper mills have dumped effluent for nearly a century. Sediment in the Illinois River in Illinois was found to contain toxic metals at levels several orders of magnitude greater than in the water. The fact that the poisons had settled to the bottom is no real consolation; sediment-living organisms, including clams, continue to absorb toxins long after the news-making spills are over, remobilizing the wastes through the ecosystem. The EPA estimated that 300 to 600 organic chemicals infest the Ohio River, where 1,800 companies dump wastewater and twenty large cities tap drinking water.

The Mississippi River, which is 2,350 miles long and drains nearly one-third of the nation, is the flyway for 40 percent of the country's waterfowl, but it is plagued by pesticides and all kinds of water pollution, including twenty-seven federal Superfund sites of toxic waste along the river. These rank among America's worst toxic dumps, qualifying for cleanup money under the EPA's Superfund program. Ten tons of trichlorobenzene and twelve tons of the solvent TCA pass New Orleans daily. Too many people know the lower Mississippi Valley as "Cancer Alley," the high incidence of disease being directly related to 150 petrochemical plants lining the riverbanks and another 591 industries discharging wastes into the water. The EPA officially recognized the problems in a publication ominously titled "The Implication of Cancer-Causing Substances in Mississippi River Water." The relationship between water quality, toxins, and human health is clear to anyone with the stomach to look at epidemiology along this largest and most toxified of American rivers, the "Father of Waters" as the Indians called it.

Above St. Louis, the upper Mississippi is bordered by a national wildlife refuge that continues off and on for 260 miles, attracting 3.2 million visitors a year and a sport fishery worth $100 million, but spills from single-hulled barges alone dump 200 million gallons of oil or hazardous material into the water annually.

The Hudson River, with a legacy of breathtaking beauty that inspired an entire school of American painting, carries some of the nation's highest levels of PCBs. Also in New York, America's first great tourist attraction, the Niagara River, carries 3,000 pounds of toxins over its falls per day, leading to concern for the 4.5 million Canadians drinking from Lake Ontario, downstream. Many toxins are easily vaporized into the surrounding atmosphere; inhaling the mist at Niagara Falls viewpoints is no longer invigorating to the well-informed. At the nation's southern border, the Rio Grande is so heavily polluted by toxins that it may be the cause of birth defects that include massive brain damage. Unregulated pollution in Mexico—much of it owing to the export of American wastes, chemicals, and industrial processes—is among the problems.

Few sites inspire more outrage than the Butler Mine Tunnel in Pittston, Pennsylvania, where authorities jailed the owners of a local service station for dumping whole tankers of waste down a drain leading to an abandoned mine that promptly discharged into the Susquehanna River. The toxic plume extended sixty miles in 1979 and reappeared in 1985 when heavy rains flushed out the mine.

Can the most affluent nation on the globe afford to allow such abuses to multiply and burden future generations? While cutting sewage outfalls from our cities, we have allowed a proliferation of pollution that no more nurtures fish life or human life than do the black and oily drainings of a crankcase.

Among the foremost water quality problems of our age are pesticides, with the United States accounting for half the world's total use. The simplest of logic—if it kills boll weevils it can kill fish—was long overlooked. Toxic substances intended to kill pests are responsible for 25 percent of all fish kills. People use 50,000 products that kill insects, weeds, mammals, and anything that moves; the EPA possesses adequate information on 10 percent of these poisons. In California, which accounts for 10 percent of the world's pesticide use, physicians report 3,000 cases of worker poisonings a year, and many others—perhaps most—go unreported owing to a lack of medical attention and to the illegal status of thousands of Mexican farmworkers who are on the front line of injury.

One of the more tragic pesticide poisonings of a river occurred in 1976 when Allied Chemical Corporation dumped kepone into the James River of Virginia. This nonbiodegradable chemical cousin of DDT will remain in the river and in Chesapeake Bay sediments for—one might as well say—forever. A federal court imposed a $13.3 million fine on the company—the largest penalty imposed to that date for polluting water. Yet that figure pales when compared to the real cost in long-term damage to the ecosystem.

When a train derailed in 1991 and 19,500 gallons of the herbicide metam sodium disgorged from a tanker car into the pristine upper Sacramento River, it poisoned forty-five miles of river at the upper end of a water supply reservoir for 20 million people. The spill forced residents to flee their homes in shock, panic, and haste, but they didn't flee fast enough. Many required extensive medical treatment and suffer long-term symptoms of exposure. All the fish were killed, and tourist businesses along the formerly idyllic river became worthless.

Train wrecks make the news, but the routine application of millions of pounds of pesticides by American farmers polluting tens of thousands of miles of waterways daily goes unnoticed by the public. Though we've known about the health hazards, the birth defects, the poisonings of soil and water, the fish kills, the reproductive problems of birds and wildlife—we've known about it all for decades—agriculture's dependence on the chemical companies grows worse by the year. Sales of pesticides in 1988 were ten times their amount in 1975, and scientists back then were already telling us the problem was severe. In 1989 the U.S. Geological Survey detected pesticides in 90 percent of the streams of the Midwest. Officials suspected that these chemicals caused fish kills in Louisiana in 1991 totaling half a million dead fish.

Atrazine, an ingredient in many weed killers, pollutes the Kansas River for many miles. The water engineer for the city of Lawrence pointed out, "Although restrictions on the amount of atrazine used by farmers on their fields is voluntary, restrictions in the level of atrazine in city drinking water is mandatory." Annual costs to the city specifically for removing this single toxic substance are $280,000.

Many solutions to the pesticide dilemma involve government regulation, research, and agriculture reform. Meanwhile, in buying grocery store produce that is not organic or not screened for pesticides, we cheerfully travel the road of increased use of poisons as we live our daily lives. As consumers, we support the system that delivers the pollution, the worker poisonings, and the accidental spills at factories and train wrecks. One simple and effective solution is to buy organic, pesticide-free produce, though it is not available in many communities and costs more owing in part to lower volumes of sales.

Mine wastes, including acid drainage, have sterilized many rivers, including Appalachian scenic showcases at the upper Sinnemahoning and the Moshannon in Pennsylvania, a state with a better water quality program than most. In the Susquehanna River Basin alone, coal mining rendered 1,350 miles of river to waste; a Pennsylvania Department of Environmental Resources official said, "If it didn't have iron in it, you could bottle it for sulfuric acid." Seventy-five percent of the Susquehanna's problems emanate from old, abandoned mines, but current strip mining continues to degrade entire watersheds and threaten pristine streams that have so far survived. The Cheat River in West Virginia, the Cumberland in Kentucky, and hundreds of smaller streams are likewise polluted with acid. Nationwide, acid drainage affects 11,000 miles of streams, about the same mileage that is protected in the National Wild and Scenic Rivers System.

In the Rockies, toxic metals leach into streams otherwise disguised as sparkling snowmelt, including the San Miguel in the upscale tourist town of Telluride, Colorado. In the San Juan Mountains nearby, open pits, excavated scars, and tailings piles leach wastes in a dozen garish colors to the Uncompahgre River. Colorado's Arkansas River carries lead, cadmium, and zinc from a century of poorly regulated mining—poisons not seen by whitewater rafters on this most popular paddling river in the Rockies. On the Clark Fork River in Montana, copper mining and smelting have transformed one of the northern Rockies' longest rivers into a toxic landmark; this river is the country's largest Superfund hazardous waste area.

The ultimate toxic substance—nuclear waste—has likewise infiltrated the nation's rivers. At the Hanford Nuclear Reservation in Washington, 500,000 gallons of liquid radioactive residue escaped from storage tanks and likely entered the Columbia River. Other radioactive elements sieve toward the Snake River through the porous volcanic aquifers at the Idaho National Engineering Laboratory. Tritium from a nuclear reactor at a weapons facility leaked into the Savannah River of Georgia and South Carolina in 1991. High radioactive levels were found in fish. Oyster beds were closed to harvest, and drinking water supplies were shut down. The worst of the radioactive spills, so far, was into the Rio Puerco, a tributary of the Rio Grande, at Church Rock, New Mexico, on the Navaho Indian Reservation. There, in 1979, a tailings pond of a private corporation failed, releasing 95 million gallons of radioactive waste.

❧ Polluted Groundwater

Underground water deposits account for 96 percent of the nation's fresh water and about half the drinking supplies. Deep in our cultural lore is the image of the unblemished mountain spring—a bubbling source of life itself. As recently as one generation ago, people regarded groundwater as the bastion of untouched quality, as pure as the rain. Now, fossil fuels have acidified the rain, and groundwater holds our worst pollution by toxins. In Nebraska, pesticides tainted 70 percent of surveyed wells. The EPA reported that 20 percent of the aquifers providing drinking water show some degree of contamination.

Nationwide, an estimated 40 percent of all underground pollution leaks from underground storage tanks such as those at the corner gas station. With virtually no new sources of municipal water supply on the horizon in many areas, the imperative of keeping groundwater clean has become more vital than ever to many communities.

Ironically, the pathetic treatment of our groundwater will give rise to new concern for surface water flowing in rivers. Though many cities converted from river water to underground wells so they could sidestep pollution in the past, some are now turning back to rivers as the cleaner alternative. The Merrimack in Massachusetts is a prime example; it was abandoned as a water supply more than a century ago but is now supplying 300,000 people with drinking water. Many New England rivers will experience a similar escalation in the importance of surface water quality as underground sources succumb to toxins. Once polluted, the groundwater stays polluted, without sunlight and oxygen available to break substances down. The hazards of groundwater contamination have only made it more important that our rivers be cleaned up.

While the pollution of groundwater forces renewed dependence on streams for drinking supplies, that change offers only a fugitive's escape from underground poisons. An estimated one-third of all surface water emanates from springs; deteriorating groundwater ultimately means further pollution of rivers.

❧ Polluted Runoff

Dripping, trickling, and seeping from large areas rather than pouring from single points of origin, polluted runoff, or "nonpoint pollution," is the vehicle for a whole stew of contaminants now affecting more miles of rivers than all the point discharges put together. Sixty percent of all water pollution emanates from agriculture, by far the most voluminous source, draining from cultivated fields, feed lots, and pastures laden with silt, phosphates, pesticides, and nitrate fertilizers. In Wisconsin, polluted runoff damages 40 percent of the rivers and 93 percent of the lakes. The situation in other midwestern states is worse.

The problem is not limited to runoff from farmland, but rather to a gamut of runoff that rinses over everything we do to the land. In areas of abusive land use and poor management, polluted runoff is as common as rain. Floating in the overflow of city streets are oil, grease, urban debris, and anything anybody dumps down a grated storm drain. Logging operations, especially clearcuts with bulldozed mazes of roads, cause a slurry of silt that buries the spawning beds of freshwater fish and the habitat of other life in streams and estuaries. According to the EPA, poorly managed logging causes 9 percent of the total pollution of our rivers.

Nitrates from 50 million tons of chemical fertilizer per year eventually accumulate in the streams. In drinking water, the chemicals can cause a shortage of oxygen leading to blue baby syndrome, a condition, sometimes fatal, that affects infants in the Midwest. Twenty-eight percent of the wells in Kansas exceed federal standards for nitrates, carried there by seepage from fertilized fields. Rivers surveyed in the 1980s showed an increase in nitrates at 30 percent of sampled sites—the most striking change in water quality nationwide. Some analysts consider nitrates to be half our total volume of water pollution. An estimated 50 to 70 percent of all nitrates in surface water come from fertilizer or from animal waste. Though often hidden from sight, nitrates are to water quality in the 1990s what raw sewage was in the midcentury years.

Just about the time we had become depressingly aware of the extent of farm waste hazards, an entirely new agricultural predicament came to light. Selenium, a naturally occurring element, is needed by organisms, but beyond minute doses it becomes toxic. It leaches into irrigation runoff water in fatal concentrations and later fills wastewater ponds such as at Kesterson National Wildlife Refuge in California, where ducks and other wildlife have suffered hideous birth defects and died. A 1985 investigation by reporter Tom Harris of the *Sacramento Bee* found selenium poisoning at dozens of sites with irrigation runoff in fifteen western states. Selenium in the Stewart Lake Bird Refuge in Utah drains directly into the Green River, one of the nation's least developed, long waterways outside Alaska. Harris documented the federal administration's selenium cover-up in the 1980s—as appalling as the poison itself. This toxic legacy of big dams and irrigation on unsuitable soils endangers public water supplies, crops, rural residents, and estuaries as large as San Francisco Bay, and contributes to plummeting populations of waterfowl. Mining wastes also cause selenium contamination, including sites at the Weber River in Utah and Jordan Creek in Idaho. Responsible for federal water projects in the West, the Bureau of Reclamation through 1992 continued to ignore rather than solve the problem.

The selenium problem ranks as one of the most notable failures of the Bureau of Reclamation and marked a turning point in public support for that agency's attempts to forever expand and subsidize a huge agribusiness industry. Toxic runoff from water projects that had been so expensively deployed made many people aware of the need for true reclamation—not irrigating undeveloped land but correcting the damage that undiscriminating diversions and irrigation have wrought.

Salinization of water is far more common than selenium pollution and probably more damaging in aggregate. The Colorado River runs up to six times as salty as it did before irrigation systems began diverting water and returning flows laced with minerals leached from cultivated fields. With increased salt that can cause hypertension and health hazards if the water is not treated, the river is piped as drinking water to 12 million people. At the U.S.-Mexican border, the residual Colorado is so saline from irrigation that the U.S. government had to build a $365 million desalinization plant to deliver some semblance of usable water destined by treaty to Mexico. Taxpayers, not irrigators, paid the bills for the pollution emanating from irrigation of the salty lands, many of which were growing surplus crops.

Because many rivers always ran muddy, and because sediment is as common as dirt, people accept it as a benign additive to rivers. Yet 40 percent of the sediment in streams is not natural but washed from cultivated fields (some experts think the percentage is even higher). We allow soil to be eroded into our waterways, in some cases at hundreds of times the natural rates. In Pennsylvania, one square mile of cultivated land loses 7,680 tons of topsoil a year, or 640 dump-truck loads transported to the state's streams, according to the Agricultural Extension Service. Erosion rates on cropland in some other states reach 64,000 tons per square mile. The lower Minnesota River—the color of chocolate milk straight out of the carton—carries the equivalent of one dump-truck load of sediment every five minutes. On the same stream, early explorers had once noted white sand beaches and water so clear that clams could be plucked from the bottom, which is now varnished with shiny brown muck. Nationwide, 2 billion tons of sediment are thought to come from cropland, 1 billion tons from rangeland in the West, half a billion tons from pasture and forest land, and 100 million tons from construction sites, according to a Conservation Foundation study in 1983. Even without toxins, pesticides, nitrates, selenium, or salt, sediment clogs the rivers like piled-up leaves rotting in a rooftop gutter. The Conservation Foundation estimated that nonfarm losses related to sediment total $6 billion a year, including the silting of reservoirs and harbors, foregone recreation, and depleted wildlife habitat.

The most visible economic loss—topsoil erosion—lies at the front end of the sedimentation process. Annual topsoil erosion in the wheat belt of eastern Washington exceeds the weight of the grain harvested there by twenty times. A National Academy of Sciences study revealed that one-third of all valuable U.S. farmland topsoil may already be gone, transported down our rivers where it wreaks damage and results in the "need" for yet more chemical fertilizers to restore "fertility" to the fields. In 1981 the Department of Agriculture reported that the inherent productivity of 34 percent of American cropland was declining because of excessive topsoil loss. An obvious question goes beyond water quality: Where will people farm when there isn't any more topsoil?

The Food Security Act, or "Farm Bill," of 1985 included provisions to deny farm subsidies for crops on previously unplanted, highly erodible soils, and the act funds farmers to convert their erodible lands from cultivation to noncrop uses. Farmers were paid about fifty dollars per acre per year to put 34 million acres of cultivated land in a "conservation reserve." The Department of Agriculture's Economic Research Service reported in 1990 that the program cut "excessive soil erosion" (not total erosion) by one-third. While conversion to wildlife habitat was the goal, many acres simply reverted to weed patches. The program cost taxpayers more than $16 billion in direct payments for a correction that may last only ten years—the term of the farmers' contracts. This act has been called one of the milestones of environmental protection. The fact that a simple revocation of one subsidy and the creation of another is heralded so substantially speaks to the difficulty of dealing with this problem.

Congress largely overlooked the nemesis of polluted runoff in the 1972 Clean Water Act, though it did encourage states to deal with the problem. A Pennsylvania effort in 1979 encouraged local land-use regulations benefiting water quality. But more often, the problem was bypassed through the 1970s because of the more repugnant and unaddressed burden of point sources.

The 1987 amendments to the act established requirements for assessment, planning, and management related to polluted runoff, all the tasks being directed at state governments and reminiscent of the federal Water Pollution Control Act of 1948, which ineffectively called for local action to solve water quality problems. Most state agencies depend on a labor-intensive and diplomatic process to persuade farmers, loggers, ranchers, and others to change the way they've been doing things since their date of settlement. That type of process is clearly in order, but it isn't enough. Thus far, compliance with most guidelines is voluntary. Wisconsin's more aggressive program required cleanup of feed lot operations, where solutions can be as simple as diverting runoff around barnyards and catching the wastewater in ponds. There and elsewhere, progress can be achieved when a dedicated staff from resource agencies works effectively with farmers and others.

At Bear Creek in Alabama, runoff from feed lots was noticeably cut after the Tennessee Valley Authority invested $900,000 and landowners spent $244,000 on solutions. A comparable amount of pollution from a point source would have cost more to correct, yet the nation's needs extend far beyond the reach of programs such as the TVA's Bear Creek demonstration project.

Some clean water advocates maintain that the government shouldn't have to pay farmers to clean up their runoff because they are already being paid by the government. In 1990 farmers received $16 billion in direct subsidy payments—funds that could be tied to water quality improvements so that the taxpayers are not directly funding the demise of their streams when they subsidize agriculture. Conservation plans are now required of farmers in areas of highly erodible soils when price supports are involved, but few requirements exist to implement the plans. Monitoring is inadequate, and many lands are exempt.

For farmers, a critical fact is that water quality improvements not only cost money; they save money as well. Enrolled in a pilot effort to cut polluted runoff, farmers in the Big Springs Basin of Iowa used up to 39 percent less chemical fertilizer or pesticides, saving each farmer up to $4,000 per year, according to the EPA. Most strategies for reducing agricultural waste are aimed at reducing soil erosion—an undisputed long-term benefit to both farmers and streams.

Pine Creek near Cammal, Pennsylvania. This river frontage in the state-owned Miller Run Natural Area is protected, but piecemeal development threatens other reaches along this river and thousands of others nationwide.

Gallatin River above Big Sky, Montana. Like other streams in the West, this one flows through miles of national forest land. Though publicly owned, many of these rivers face threats of logging, mining, and hydropower development.

Potomac River near Paw Paw, West Virginia. This river of the East has partially recovered from pollution of the past and again become a waterway of great value.

Middle Fork of the Salmon River, Idaho. Wild salmon still survive in this river—one of the most pristine in America.

Connecticut River and Holyoke Water Power Dam, Massachusetts. Old hydro-power dams such as this one blocked Atlantic salmon from thousands of miles of spawning habitat.

Kennebec River and Edwards Dam, Augusta, Maine. This antiquated dam may be eliminated, restoring a section of the Kennebec for anadromous fish including salmon.

Grand Coulee Dam, Columbia River, Washington. This dam eliminated 1,000 miles of salmon spawning habitat.

Reservoir drawdown behind Ross Dam, Skagit River, Washington. The stumps of giant trees remain from the old growth forests that existed before the dam was built.

Oldman River in winter, southwest Alberta. An economically unjustified irrigation reservoir may flood this valley and superb fishery of the Rocky Mountain foothills.

Elk Creek Dam, Oregon. This unnecessary dam was halted after one-third of it was built. Oregon Governor Barbara Roberts supported removal of the dam.

Neuse River above Raleigh, North Carolina. This section of river was flooded in the 1980s by a water supply reservoir.

This idyllic valley of the Sierra Nevada was flooded by High Spicer Meadows Dam in the 1980s.

North Fork American River below Iowa Hill Bridge, California. Forty-eight miles of the American River would be flooded by Auburn Dam.

Auburn Dam site, American River, California. Following excavation of the dam's foundation for $250 million, construction was halted owing to earthquake, economic, and environmental problems. New dam proposals continue to threaten the river.

Penobscot River, Basin Mills Dam site, Maine. A hydroelectric dam is planned for this location in spite of efforts to restore Atlantic salmon.

Klamath River below Boyle Powerhouse, Oregon. Hydropower diversions have been proposed here and at hundreds of other rivers.

Snake River above Marsing, Idaho. Polluted agricultural runoff is the major water quality problem in the West and nationwide.

North Branch Potomac River at Westernport, Maryland. Pipes in the middle of the otherwise clear and dark waters of the upper Potomac discharge milky-brown waste from a pulp mill and municipal treatment plant.

Snake River at Star Falls, Idaho. This natural flow of 12,000 cubic feet per second occurs rarely because of irrigation diversions. Most of the time, the riverbed here below Milner Dam is nearly dry.

The dried-up bed of the Snake River below Milner Dam, Idaho. Here, Milner Dam allows irrigation diversions of nearly all the water during most years.

Penobscot River at Old Town, Maine. This dam diverts flows for hydroelectric power, depleting the river and affecting the migration of salmon.

Colorado River in the Grand Canyon, Arizona. Peaking flows for hydroelectric power resulted in 12 vertical feet of fluctuation daily, eroding beaches and wildlife habitat.

Penobscot River near Lincoln, Maine. Riparian zones along rivers constitute the finest wildlife habitat and fulfill other vital functions.

St. John River below Allagash, Maine. Riprap on the banks of the river has destroyed riparian habitat.

Au Sable River near Lake Huron, Michigan. Retaining walls and lawns eliminate habitat for wildlife including mammals, birds, and fish.

Wills Creek, Maryland. Like many other urban rivers, this one is channelized as it flows through the city of Cumberland.

Overgrazing, debris, and a degrading riverbed have ruined riparian frontage here at the Snake River above Idaho Falls and along hundreds of streams.

Flood plain development, West Branch Susquehanna, Pennsylvania. Sited on the flood plain, these mobile homes were pushed by high waters to the edge of the bank.

South Fork Boise River below Featherville, Idaho. This stand of cottonwoods reflects a natural river and a robust riparian community.

Tatshenshini River, northwest British Columbia. This river and the Alsek in Alaska flow through one of the wildest ecosystems remaining on earth. A mining proposal threatened the area until 1993.

North Fork Sauk River, Washington. Rivers flowing through remaining stands of old growth forest have become rare.

Pithlachascotee River, Florida. Blackwater rivers of the South drain some of the least developed lands in the East and ecosystems of extraordinary productivity and diversity.

❧ The Continuing Pursuit

During the past thirty years, our society has eliminated much of the water pollution that we could readily see, but we are left with an insidious legacy of invisible poisons and polluted runoff stemming from the overlooked interface between land and water. Those problems require even greater imagination, money, and commitment.

The EPA estimated that water pollution treatment will require $64 billion a year from public and private sources by the year 2000. Another $10 billion will be needed for toxic waste sites during a twenty-year period beginning in 1989, as reported by author Jeremy Rifkin. Reducing acid rain will cost another $30 billion, and disposing of radioactive waste, $37 billion. This all sounds like a lot of money, and is, but for comparison, the Department of Defense budget was $290 billion for just 1992. That same year, the EPA spent $2.9 billion on the entire clean water program. The cost of the Stealth bomber program alone was estimated at $68 billion. According to the Center for Defense Information, in 1993 the Pentagon spent $38 billion in tax money preparing for nuclear war. And the Department of Energy planned to spend $7.3 billion on nuclear weapons in 1993—41 percent of that Department's budget, which covers all aspects of energy. Even after the Cold War era, the Department of Energy spent $1.5 billion designing *new* nuclear weapons in one year. Many people argue that a change in priorities is in order.

As Jeremy Rifkin has stated in *Entropy: Into the Greenhouse World*, the unpaid bills from illegal dumping, deregulated industries, and shortsighted disposal show that a proverbial Age of Progress was in fact an Age of Illusion that passed the costs to our and future generations. Perhaps in the coming years we will see the conversion of a budget dominated by the production of a war machine to one dedicated to solving the problems that now endanger our nation's well-being more than any imagined enemy abroad. Some of the money intended for missiles can be spent on the poisons infesting our waters and threatening our ecosystems, our drinking supplies, our homes, and our children.

Solutions include continued attention to pollution control programs, a transition to technologies that use materials with greater efficiency and that recover waste materials, and a redesign of human systems for compatibility with nature, such as integrated pest management on farms. Solar aquatic systems can treat wastes from small communities by growing bacteria, algae, snails, and fish as part of the waste treatment process, eliminating the need for chlorine and potentially hazardous chemicals. One community found it could build a solar aquatic system for $4 million when conventional treatment cost $15 million. Other ecologically designed treatment facilities have been developed by the Center for Restoration of Waters, headquartered in Falmouth, Massachusetts, and offer promise in coping with the problems of sludge, chlorine compounds, and high costs in conventional sewage treatment.

Our government has built expensive desalinization plants funded by taxpayers to compensate for irrigation of saline soils where subsidized water grows subsidized crops. Instead, all of that government money could be used to retire the saline lands, stopping the problem at its source, returning habitat to wildlife, and saving a lot of money.

Subsidies that result in waste and pollution, such as tax breaks for mining raw materials but not for recycling, can be eliminated. But the most essential need, as we have seen in other chapters of this book, is for a stable population. While society strived to stop water pollution between 1972 and 1988, the U.S. population increased from 205 million to 245 million, undoing many of the gains.

Citizen action has always helped to solve water quality problems. In the 1980s, Friends of the Earth and other groups filed thirty-eight lawsuits under the Clean Water Act in New York and New Jersey and won fines four times higher than what federal agencies had settled for in similar cases. Pressure from citizen environmental groups led Congress to reauthorize the Clean Water Act and to override President Reagan's veto by a wide margin in 1987. (President Nixon had also vetoed the original Clean Water Act in 1972 but was overridden by Congress.) Hundreds of citizen-sponsored monitoring programs have led to government action to correct otherwise ignored, illegal discharges. These efforts range from ones that are highly organized and government-sponsored to the lone citizen, such as Wayne Dakan, who sampled sawmill waste and delivered the foul evidence to his supervisors in Plumas County, California, with an impatient challenge: "There it is. What are you going to do about it?" Del Wehrspann and Scott Sparlin championed the cause of the Minnesota River in the 1990s, eventually gaining broad community support and a proclamation by the governor that the state's namesake river will be cleaned up.

With the Clean Water Act due for periodic amendments, conservation groups pressed for reforms: provisions to prevent groundwater contamination before it occurs, stricter controls on toxins with an emphasis on eliminating the entire use of certain poisons in the first place, and incentives to help cities keep storm water from overloading their sewage plants when it rains. Also important are water conservation to reduce the amount of water being treated, requirements that states reduce polluted runoff, and regulations on agricultural drains. In California, agricultural districts along the San Joaquin River, for example, dump chemical contaminants far worse than many regulated point sources elsewhere, yet are exempt from regulations.

The 1972 Clean Water Act called not only for the cleanup of polluted water but for the maintenance of still-clean water, yet the government has done little to assure that high-quality streams stay that way. Pristine waters that flow through national parks, wild and scenic rivers, and wild trout fisheries are being polluted under regulations that allow new wastes up to an "acceptable" level. The EPA calls for no degradation of "outstanding resource waters," but most states lack effective programs. Among the states that had nondegradation programs in 1992, only 3 percent of the "outstanding" stream mileage was safeguarded. The National Wildlife Federation called for mandatory federal requirements on outstanding waters and for federal action to prevent pollution of clean streams on federal land.

In spite of all the unmet needs, stopping water pollution remains one of the most popular goals in the environmental field. In 1986 a Harris Poll found that 86 percent of the people surveyed agreed that water pollution standards should not be compromised regardless of financial hardship. A poll by Penn State University researchers found that more state residents were concerned about water quality in 1990 than were concerned ten years before.

As water supply becomes increasingly critical in water-short regions, which at one time or another include all regions, our society can ill afford to contaminate and lose the water sources it already has. Polluted, costly, or unavailable water is bad for ecosystems and bad for business. No matter how expensive, clean water is an economic bargain compared to unalleviated thirst.

New commitments to clean water will be essential if our farms and cities are to survive as we know them, and if natural rivers are to remain or be restored as waterways of life rather than conduits of filth.

Along with halting proposals for large, new dams, the successful abatement of the foulest industrial and urban pollution stands as a success in river conservation. Though much remains to be done, the cleanup already accomplished ranks as the most publicized, supported, and documented of river protection concerns.

In contrast, the least successful effort is immutably related: that of keeping an adequate flow in our streams. Diversions for irrigation or urban development have damaged many rivers nationwide and are the subject of the next chapter.

Chapter Six

The Remains of Rivers

‰ Water and the Dimensions of Loss

People who grow up near streams that run regularly after frequent rains might take for granted that rivers require water. In fact, a river needs an adequate flow as clearly as the human body needs a supply of vitamins, proteins, and fluids; yet diversions and manipulations of flows have ruined thousands of waterways.

At the extreme—which can be seen on too many rivers in the West—the river ceases to exist, a bone-dry relic of an ecosystem remaining after the flow is shunted away in canals and ditches for irrigation. But long before that termination, the dimensions of loss owing to instream flow problems are apparent in many ways.

When diverters systematically take more and more water, shallows and sloughs are the first areas to dry out, yet they often comprise the most productive spawning beds and rearing areas for fish. If the volume of a river drops too low, its temperature rises too high. Above seventy degrees Fahrenheit, oxygen supplies dwindle. Species by species, fish and invertebrate life die as water temperatures climb. Trout are the first fish to go; carp are among the last. Depleted flows in winter cause temperatures to drop lower than they otherwise would and result in anchor ice on the bottom of streams, glazing shut important gravel beds and shelter.

Beyond these direct effects, diversions and altered flows below dams establish a chain of events affecting the entire form and structure of the riverbed. In the spring, two or three months account for 40 to 70 percent of the stream flow in most American rivers; 70 percent of the runoff in the West comes with snowmelt in April through June. The disparity throughout the year has long been the rationale for water agencies to store runoff in times of high flow and release it later, yet streams and ecosystems have evolved under the natural regime for millions of years and in many ways depend on it. Biologists liken the natural hydrograph of rivers—ranging from high to low flows on an annual basis—to that of an electrocardiogram. Its vacillations, which some people regard as annoying, are as important to the river as the heartbeat is to the patient.

With effective flood control, high waters no longer scour and reform the channel. As a result, pools gradually fill with silt, and riffles become eroded and lowered. Eventually, the pool-and-riffle sequence on which aquatic life depends is replaced with a constant glide that denies both the shelter of deep water and the aeration of riffles needed by invertebrate life and spawning fish. In 1984 the U.S. Fish and Wildlife Service estimated that 67 percent of the nation's stream segments with water resource degradation suffered because of flow alteration (chemical pollution was the problem in 56 percent of degraded streams; habitat loss affected 49 percent).

The issue of healthy flows in rivers extends beyond the problem of diversions. For peaking power a few hours a day, hydroelectric dams release flushes of water that pose far more difficulties than those expressed in signs warning wading anglers of dangerously changing river levels. Normally stabilized by the perpetual give-and-take of erosion and deposition, beaches subject to such frequent flushing erode at rates that cause their disappearance in a matter of decades, years, or even days.

Silt, once flowing naturally in rivers, is trapped behind dams, and the clean water that is released erodes shorelines but deposits nothing. This pattern of all-take and no-give causes a degrading riverbed. Because islands—refuges for wildlife—owe their existence to deposits of silt, sand, and gravel, the elimination of bedload movement leaves nothing for reconstruction while erosive forces go unchecked or are aggravated by the clear waters below the reservoirs.

In a depleted river, the hyporheic zone, or the biologically enhanced ground that is permeated by river water, becomes drained, causing the loss of an important source of invertebrates and nutrients. Even worse, groundwater is sucked out of the banks when a degrading riverbed is lowered, robbing the flood plain of its vital underground water supply and leading to biological deserts where riparian gardens had flourished. Little of this linkage of loss may be evident for some time. It often occurs gradually, the ever-diminishing cycle spanning several generations, leading people to say mistakenly, "It's always been this way."

A healthy aquatic community depends on the functioning of all its members. Alder trees—a riverfront mainstay needing high groundwater levels along streams—accumulate beneficial forms of nitrate in their leaves at highly enriching levels, not lost on the riparian way of life. The leaves fall into the river. Fungi and bacteria digest the alder greens, and the combined detritus creates food for larvae of caddis flies, mayflies, black flies, stoneflies, salmon flies, and hundreds of species of insects that feed dozens of species of invertebrates and fish. Biologists Mark Sosin and John Clark reported that a ten-pound northern pike requires 100 pounds of minnows that ate 1,000 pounds of invertebrates that ate 10,000 pounds of aquatic plants. The good pike stream must be a good insect stream, and before that, a good algae stream, and before that, a good *water* stream with adequate flows and an adequate variation of flows based on the patterns of the millennia.

The rivers are not just long rights-of-way for moving water that one might compare to traffic on a highway. Each waterway is intricately varied and diverse. Once lost, subtle but important features of the ecosystem may not be remembered by the casual observer. Our eyes for beauty do not penetrate the surface of the water to see if the stream is functioning properly or naturally. Working on instream flow problems of the Northwest, American Rivers' Lorraine Bodi said, "People look at a river, and if it's pretty, they think it's healthy."

The rivers' world is under attack, and the losses range from the desiccated beds of thousands of western streams to garden greenways of the East whose water is being tapped for cities. Problems that plague the stonefly, which requires fine flecks of properly rinsed gravel, plague the outermost ripples of the riparian community, including the multibillion-dollar commercial fishing industry offshore and the recreational industry of sport fishing, which forms the economic backbone of many rural communities.

❧ A Wide Scope of Difficulties

Diversions for irrigation make possible pastures and crops in all western regions where rivers flow, but if one were to set a map of the irrigated land of the West on top of a map of decimated fisheries, the overlap would be almost total.

While irrigation seems all-important in the areas where it is practiced, it accounts for only 10 percent of the nation's farm acreage. Except for parts of California, little of the irrigated acreage is dedicated to crops that cannot be grown economically elsewhere, and well over half the amount of water that is used, even in California, is for pasture and forage for livestock. In many regions, all of the irrigation is for cattle, though most of the nation's beef is raised in the temperate South and Midwest.

The "miracle of irrigation" formed the basis of settlement for much of the West, but instead of miracles, aquatic and riparian communities face disasters in stagnant pools and chalk-dry riverbeds more appropriate to Death Valley than the Rocky Mountain foothills and other regions.

Irrigation accounts for 85 percent of the withdrawals from all rivers in the United States, and 90 percent in some arid states such as New Mexico. In Montana, 96 percent of the consumed water (water taken from rivers and not returned later on) is used by agriculture. In that picturesque state, where recreation ranks as the second-largest industry, the Beaverhead River's fishery contributes $2.3 million to the economy annually, but it lay nearly dry in 1989. Fish died by the thousands, and biologists estimated that recovery would take five to eight years, assuming normal rain and snow. Fishing outfitters on the world-renowned Big Hole River lost their jobs by June because of diversions for ranchland. In a perverse reversal of normal fluvial logic, the Big Hole and many other western rivers *decrease* in volume as they flow downhill; one diversion after another taps the river and reduces it when it should be getting larger.

Low flows mean that pollution grows worse without the counteragent of dilution. Arsenic in the Missouri River, for example, reached alarming concentrations in low-water years of the 1980s.

In California, it is no coincidence that 40 percent of the natural flows are diverted and 90 percent of the riparian habitat is gone. On the Trinity River, flow reductions of 90 percent caused salmon reductions of 90 percent when water was tunneled out of the basin and ditched south by the Bureau of Reclamation to Central Valley farms growing cotton—a surplus crop.

In New Mexico, the bed of the Rio Grande lies as dry as ancient adobe for many miles below Elephant Butte Dam. The river doesn't necessarily benefit when that reservoir fills; in fact, it can get worse, because an interstate compact allows upstream irrigators in Colorado to divert more than their usual amount, leaving a parched riverbed far upstream from Elephant Butte. In Arizona, the nation's oldest federal irrigation project set a pattern by drying up the Salt River.

With an appetite for water that borders on the extravagant, Idaho irrigators divert nearly all of the Snake River from Milner Dam, where an upstream basin dumps a ponderous volume of 12,000 cubic feet per second into the reservoir and almost none comes out except by way of canals. The Snake has the dubious distinction of being the largest river in America that is dried up at a single dam.

Unlike Milner Dam, which was constructed by private canal companies back in 1906 when it might be argued that we didn't know any better, McPhee Dam on the Dolores River in Colorado was built by the federal government in 1979, but it, too, cuts flows from one of America's great desert canyons. The Bureau of Reclamation releases a stream of 60 cubic feet per second where more than 1,000 cubic feet per second used to run in the springtime.

In 1990 the Arkansas—one of the six great rivers draining the Rockies—ran dry by the time it crossed the Colorado line into Kansas, though a compact gave the latter state 40 percent of the flow. Following the river's course downhill, the flow became less and less, then it was gone, and then the cottonwood trees for fifty miles died. Considering our treatment of rivers, *High Country News* publisher Ed Marston wrote, "In their rhetoric, the West's leaders always speak of water as the region's most precious resource. But in action, the West treats water as if it were in infinite supply and without intrinsic worth."

Problematic as they might be, diversions causing low flows and dry streams present only one of the difficulties regarding healthy river flows. A second major source consists of the unplanned effects that dams have on stream morphology—the shaping, maintenance, and form of the riverbed and its shorelines.

Once-legendary flocks of ducks no longer congregate in the Chesapeake Bay at the mouth of the Susquehanna River. The suspected cause is the lack of scouring action brought by ice, once delivered by the river in springtime but now detained in a chain of four hydroelectric dams. On many streams, flood flows are needed to wash previously deposited silt out of the interstices in gravel beds, restoring spawning habitat for fish.

On the Milk River in Montana, cottonwoods die and will likely go extinct because of a lack of flood flows and silt below dams—a scenario of ecological impoverishment that is under way but undocumented on many rivers of the Plains and throughout the West, according to biologist Cheryl Bradley and other researchers.

Flow manipulation by dams on a reach of the Missouri River reduced flood plain wetlands by 67 percent. With silt and organic detritus settling in Missouri River reservoirs instead of going downriver, fish populations have declined by 80 percent since 1940. In 1992 the Nebraska Game and Parks Commission proposed that residents dump organic debris such as leaves and trimmed branches into the river to replace some of the lost nutrients.

The silt detained in reservoirs even causes problems at the ocean. Rivers in southern California no longer deposit millions of cubic yards of beach-making sand at the coast as they once did after heavy rains, and erosion by waves and ocean currents whisks the existing sand away with no replacement in sight. As the National Research Council reported in 1991, "Restoration of the flow regime is one of the most neglected aspects of stream and river restoration."

Not only dams, but levees cause indelible effects on the structure and therefore the health of a riverway. Along the Mississippi, levees on both sides of the river force floods higher and higher in a constrained channel. Although floods in 1973 moved only 60 percent of the volume measured in 1844, the constriction caused by the levees forced the crest to be 2 feet higher. A medium flood level of 600,000 cubic feet per second at St. Louis reached 29.2 feet on the gauge in 1880, but the same discharge topped 35 feet in 1980—6 feet higher for the same volume of water.

Constrained by levees, flood waters from twenty-four states flow improbably above the level of the flatlands and even above the elevation of rooftops on either side of the Mississippi River. These levees have decimated the ecosystem by barricading wetlands and creating current where none used to be. The pent-up river now poses dangers of catastrophic floods by overtopping the levees or eroding through them. During an unprecedented siege of rainstorms in June, July, and August of 1993, the Mississippi River system flooded beyond historic levels, nearly topping even the fifty-one-foot-high St. Louis flood wall.

To the very end of the Mississippi, levees channelize the flow, carrying sediment to the deep waters of the ocean instead of depositing it on the swampland of the river's alluvial fan. Consisting of sediment up to 40,000 feet deep, the Louisiana coast is naturally subsiding as the silt compacts, and without a new accretion of silt, the land has sunk below sea level, creating many problems. The levees sluice the sediment straight to the sea, where the river's load of phosphorus upsets the balance of life in the Gulf of Mexico.

Going from sea level back up to the continental divide, both a dam and levees manipulate flows amid a Rocky Mountain paradise of scenery at Jackson Hole, Wyoming. Below Jackson Dam in Grand Teton National Park, an excellent trout fishery faded to mediocre, in part owing to dam-induced flow reductions in winter, wiping out invertebrate life that the trout need. Below the park, levees crowd this scenic gem into a straitjacket, blocking water from wetland sloughs and carrying constant current where there would have been riffles mixed with pools.

In both the Mississippi River Valley and Jackson Hole, the alternative exists to move levees back in rural areas, giving the river room to flood, and to construct ring levees to protect the more urban or developed centers. Ring levees would keep floods out of the towns but would not extend up and down the river for miles on either shore. Dr. Raphael Kazmann, professor emeritus from Louisiana State University and author of the text *Modern Hydrology*, states that ring levees could protect most developed real estate and still leave the river free to overflow in perhaps 90 percent of its flood plain. He stated, "If we hadn't built levees and encouraged people to invest in the flood plain, this disaster of 1993 wouldn't have happened." When asked about the difficulty of making the change after the great Mississippi flood, he responded, "Would we rather have *this* kind of flood reoccurring? We've spent billions of dollars of public money on flood control in this country, and now we have a $10 billion disaster relief bill and even greater damage from a single flood. A one-time expense to redesign the system would be better than this kind of reoccurring loss."

To carry out such reform, Dr. Kazmann recommended that flood control responsibilities be turned back over to local government—a theme in keeping with other current political movements. If each area is paying for its own flood control, large levees will not be built around low-value agricultural land. The hydrologist pointed out areas that had historically been flooded regularly, where people "expected" the high water. "People can manage their land for that. It's the unexpected disaster that hurts, such as what we've seen in 1993." Other experts also suggest that a new Mississippi levee should be designed to allow inundation of lower-value land and believe that the owners should be compensated when the government gives up on its futile attempts to keep flood waters out of everywhere.

Seeing the futility of living with the hazards of the flood plain in the aftermath of the 1993 Mississippi flood, unprecedented numbers of people in 200 different towns along the river and its tributaries wanted to move to higher ground if given an opportunity. This led water policy analyst Gilbert White to say that in sixty years of work he has never seen such interest in relocation. New legislation increased the money available for relocation from $39 million to $105 million in late 1993—still a small portion of total disaster aid.

Water policy changes have followed in the wake of all our largest floods, such as the massive dam-building program after the high waters of 1936 and the flood insurance improvements after 1972. The difference, in 1993, was that relocation, flood plain management, and wetlands protection were at the center of the arguments, offering some possibility that reforms to save money, avoid human suffering, and restore riparian habitat might gain ground.

Few politicians have been interested in facing the ultimate failure of levee systems, concluding—if they think about it at all—that the price will be paid after they have left office. But Dr. Kazmann argued that it may be different following the 1993 floods because now we lack the money to re-build and maintain both the levees and the infrastructure that led to so much damage. Any efforts at reform will encounter intense political pressure to do simply more of the same—to rebuild flood walls higher, larger, stronger, and more expensively, causing ever-worsening floods.

The history of river development has shown that after much political anguish and compromising, fifty interstate compacts or international treaties govern how rivers are divided for consumption among U.S. states and the three nations of North America, and thousands of state and local decisions have also divided the waters for a century. The needs of the rivers were ignored. For the time being, the purveyors of water have taken whatever they could and escaped the consequences of hydrologic chaos and bankrupt ecosystems.

ᵉ Extinction on the Agenda

One of the more complex and consequential problems of river flows occurs on Nebraska's Platte. With its South Fork wending 450 miles from the Front Range of Colorado and the 665-mile-long North Fork crossing Wyoming, the main stem continues another 310 miles to the Missouri River. The upper two-thirds of that length harbors habitat of continental significance. Like an hourglass, the flyways of migratory birds constrict at this centerpoint, with birds arriving in autumn from as far as Siberia, and in spring from the Gulf of Mexico and beyond.

The endangered whooping crane depends on the river, and 540,000 sandhill cranes comprising 80 percent of the world population must stop to feed here, as 97 percent of their optimum habitat nationwide has been lost. The endangered least tern uses the Platte as one of three prime stopover areas. The threatened piping plover and 2 percent of the bald eagles in the forty-eight contiguous states congregate here. Among midcontinental waterfowl, 40 percent of the mallard ducks, most of the white-fronted geese, and up to 30 percent of the pintails touch down to rest and feed along this reach of the Platte.

The river is vitally important, but because of flow reductions, it supports just a shadow of the ecosystem it once did. Habitat losses dangerously constrain the endangered and other species to a small slice of the land and river they once used, and proposed new developments spell doom. Sixteen upstream dams and many diversions cut the river's flow to 30 percent of the natural level and altogether eliminate the scouring of regular floods, a critical process in maintaining the riparian environment that was characteristic of the Platte of old.

While upstream impoundments on other rivers such as the Milk in Montana cause the elimination of cottonwoods and thereby trigger a collapse of riparian ecosystems, here on the Platte the dams curiously spawn a new abundance of willows and cottonwoods because high water no longer scours the flood plain. Ironically, however, similar ecological collapse results.

Rather than needing brush and trees, the cranes need open areas on sandbars and in shallow water to assure their safety from predators such as coyotes, which could otherwise hide in the vegetation. Even in the relatively open areas that remain, 67 percent of the shorelines are overgrown. Aggravating this fundamental shift in balance, the upstream dams trap silt, causing the river to erode faster in a downward motion, thus carving deeper and narrower channels and allowing yet more plant growth to take hold on the bars. The Platte, where the term "a mile wide and an inch deep" was coined, now flows through narrower, braided channels separated by brush-covered islands.

One might think that if bird species needing willows and cottonwoods could migrate to the Platte from rivers now depleted of those plants, and if the cranes could migrate to rivers where cottonwoods fade toward extinction, things might work out. But nature doesn't work that way. Other features make the Platte just right for the cranes and make other rivers essential for the other species.

Attempts to reinstate some of the Platte River flows and habitat proved to be a jurisdictional and political imbroglio. The states hold the authority to appropriate water, and each maximized irrigation. Even if Wyoming or Colorado allowed healthy instream flows for wildlife—and they don't—Nebraska could simply divert the water when it reached the first Cornhusker headgate. Nebraska sued Wyoming for excessive diversions, arguing on behalf of endangered species. Meanwhile, Nebraska pushed for more in-state agricultural development and opposed conservation groups fighting to retain water for wildlife. Several new dams and diversions could further reduce flows and augment habitat problems. Confusing concessions have been suggested for building the projects while mitigating losses; none of them offer much in the way of confidence that habitat quality won't continue to get worse instead of better.

The Platte is an excellent example of regional irrigation interests refusing to give up modest amounts of growth to prevent species from becoming rare and, instead, allowing species to become endangered, thus forcing society to spend extravagant amounts of money attempting to prevent extinction.

A Platte River Management Joint Study pursued compromises, private wildlife groups bought land, the U.S. Fish and Wildlife Service proposed a refuge, and efforts at basinwide water planning addressed both water transfers and modified operation of dams. The Fish and Wildlife Service reviews along with lawsuits by the National Wildlife Federation and the Environmental Defense Fund halted new dams, including the Narrows Unit proposed by the Bureau of Reclamation. Two Forks Dam on the South Platte was stopped. A local referendum halted the Nebraska Mid-State Project, which would have diverted more than half the Platte's existing flow. But fourteen projects remain at some active level of consideration; the combined effects would cut river flows to 15 percent of their historic level.

Beyond all the political and administrative intransigence, the opportunity exists to correct some of the damage. Licenses issued by the Federal Energy Regulatory Commission for two Nebraska projects, including Kingsley Dam, expired in 1987. While FERC granted annual renewals, river protection groups intervened, attempting to improve flow conditions through the relicensing process.

For now, the main progress has been to block the new dam and diversion proposals, which really isn't progress at all but simply a reprieve from further losses of species that would otherwise accelerate the downward spiral from the rare, to the endangered, to the extinct. Yet it is many people's hope that through continued negotiation, a greater willingness to compromise, and persistence from wildlife groups and agencies, the coming years will see an improved flow regime for the critical species of the Platte.

❧ Defying Logic and Gravity

It may seem that in an age when the federal government slashes funds for basic human services, when environmental concerns have taken firm root, when the electorate decries the national deficit along with welfare and subsidies, one would expect that public policy about water would change to reflect all those realities. But at the Animas River in New Mexico and Colorado, the expectation of government largess lives on, and water developers hope to defy both gravity and the logic of the times by diverting enormous flows out of the river.

While truly severe social, economic, and environmental problems demand attention and solutions, the federal government in southwestern Colorado proposes to build the Animas–La Plata Project, diverting up to 460 cubic feet per second, or one-third of the water from the Animas River in the postcard-perfect tourist town of Durango. The government would then pump the water 900 feet uphill to irrigate alfalfa at a project cost of more than $640 million. Considering typical Bureau of Reclamation cost overruns, the final price may be closer to $1 billion.

This hay-growing scheme ranks as the most expensive water project in Colorado history. To pump water from the Animas to the neighboring La Plata River Basin would require energy sufficient to fuel a city of 62,000 people if the full project is ever built—energy that will be decreasing in supply and increasing in expense during the coming decades. Land for one of the project's reservoirs was condemned from the Colorado Nature Conservancy, eliminating critical elk range, impossible to replace. Instead, feed for cattle will be grown. Irrigation will leach through lands laced with dreaded selenium; dozens of Indian family wells are already tainted with the toxic element, sometimes causing sickness. What's left in the way of runoff will be returned to the San Juan and Colorado rivers for downstream use at cities and farms in Arizona, California, and Mexico. Junior water-rights owners on the Animas River downstream in New Mexico will see reductions in their water supplies, while the new lands at

7,000 feet above sea level—with a decidedly shorter growing season—will get the water. The lower Animas, where cottonwood forests shelter bald eagles, offers the finest riparian habitat in New Mexico, but would be impoverished by the reduction in flow. A $3 million rafting industry in Durango, forming a substantial component of the region's economy, will be forced out of business because the diversion will exhaust the river halfway through the whitewater run. As American Rivers director Kevin Coyle said, "Once we do all of that, then they'll be able to grow surplus crops."

The Bureau of Reclamation calculated project costs with a 3.25 percent interest rate. At a reasonable 8.5 percent rate, however, the benefit-cost ratio would return only sixty cents on the dollar. Even this ratio overstates the benefits, as it accepts the Bureau's plethora of boldly optimistic assumptions underpinning this classic case of pork barrel.

In a 1987 political advertisement to ratify a repayment contract for the project, supporters asked, "Why support the Animas–La Plata project?" and then answered, "Because somebody else is paying most of the tab. We get the water. We get the reservoir. They pay the bill."

Taking the opposite view, local archaeologist and educator Lew Mattis said, "It just doesn't make sense to divert all that water from a river and then spend valuable money and scarce energy pumping it uphill to irrigate surplus crops." Mattis has fought the project for years.

Among a group of New Mexico landowners and farmers opposing Animas–La Plata, farmer Tommy Bolack said, "They're planning to spend a lot of money pumping water up to irrigate fields underlain by selenium. That's just one of the concerns the Bureau of Reclamation didn't address, and the reason they didn't is that people would be concerned."

The only feature that sold Animas–La Plata to a skeptical Congress was its provision for Indian water rights. Indian Congressman (later Senator) Ben Campbell of Colorado pitched Animas–La Plata to his colleagues as a service to families who still carry their drinking water in buckets. But the neighboring Dolores River project provides for those families' needs.

According to reporter Steve Hinchman of *High Country News*, only 4 percent of the water in Phase 1 of the project, to be funded by the federal government, would be delivered to the Indians. This is because facilities are not available to get the water to the reservation, where it can be used. Delivery of the rest of the Indian water is dependent on Phase 2, which is unlikely ever to be built. Not only is it the most marginal part of the project, but it would also have to be funded by nonfederal money, such as state funds. Dividing Animas–La Plata in two is thus an economic sleight of hand whereby sponsors have evaded federal cost-sharing requirements for Phase 1, which will serve white farmers.

If the Indians ever do get their water, their tribal government will likely try to sell it for the construction of coal-fired power plants. The cost of development of that water tops $5,000 per year per tribal member. If history provides any clues—and there are plenty—that kind of expense for native people is not likely to be borne by the state of Colorado, though that was ostensibly the plan as Phase 1 was being sold to the Indians and the rest of the public. And, if history is any guide, coal-fired power will not be allowed in this San Juan Mountain air basin—one of the cleanest remaining in America.

Topping the charts of irony, the pumping of water presumably to serve coal-fired electricity would consume vast amounts of electricity produced at other Bureau of Reclamation projects, which cause their own long list of problems. In testimony to the Office of Management and Budget, the Bureau of Reclamation stated that the 160 million kilowatt-hours of electricity a year needed to run the pumps could make the Animas–La Plata Project so expensive that the federal government would have to subsidize its operation or shut it down.

More to the point of real support for Animas–La Plata: it would provide water to non-Indian irrigators for $4 per acre when it costs the federal government $673 per acre to do the job. Dissent within the Indian community grew with the election of Ray Frost to the Southern Ute tribal council in 1993. Frost asked, "Why is it called an Indian project if it does not help the Southern Utes?"

For more than a decade, a campaign against Animas–La Plata was led by local resident Jean McCullough of Taxpayers for the Animas River, which successfully fought variations of the plan that were even worse than the current one. Assuming volunteer duties after McCullough's death,

Michael Black said, "It's a foolish plan that will cripple tourism in Durango." Black and others argue that the project—originally planned for the upper Animas River but reduced and redesigned six times—should be scrapped completely and the Indians given adequate water rights and the ability to use them in alternative ways. This could require some creative water law, but the Animas River defenders believe that new legal formulas allowing the Indians to sell water for downstream use at power plants and at existing water projects would be better than Animas–La Plata and, in fact, that real water needs could be met in that way while benefiting the Indians. Additional options considered by the Sierra Club Legal Defense Fund include providing the Utes with more water from the nearby Dolores River project and building a smaller dam on the Mancos or La Plata rivers.

Unswerving state support for the project is based on the nearly religious notion that Colorado should use the water—no matter how badly it bankrupts state coffers, federal taxpayers, and the environment of New Mexico and Colorado—rather than let the water "escape" to the lower Colorado River Basin, where Arizona or California could put it to use in their tightening urban crunch. This kind of provincialism has a seventy-year history going back to the original efforts to divide the waters of the Colorado River Basin among seven U.S. states and Mexico.

One Animas–La Plata delay in 1991 stemmed from a U.S. Fish and Wildlife Service ruling that the diversion would adversely affect the endangered Colorado squawfish and razorback sucker that survive in the San Juan River, downstream. To meet fishery needs, the Bureau of Reclamation proposed to release extra water from Navaho Dam—an entirely separate facility on the San Juan River. This was approved by all relevant parties except the most important one—the Navaho Indians, whose water and reservation are at stake. The Bureau's next proposal was to scale back the project temporarily, eliminating the diversion to the La Plata River Basin but leaving many of the other problems intact.

The little-known Animas is one of the largest rivers in Colorado surviving without a dam, and its riparian community is among the finest in the entire Southwest. While river advocates and federal agencies, including even the Bureau of Reclamation, seek to restore adequate flows to rivers elsewhere, the unspoiled Animas still faces the threat of destruction by a new project of profoundly low value with the nation's taxpayers footing the bill.

An environmental impact statement, updated after a 1992 lawsuit by the Sierra Club Legal Defense Fund and others, will presumably consider overlooked factors, though the Bureau of Reclamation's 1993 draft was so incomplete that the U.S. Environmental Protection Agency flunked the report and did not give approval. Meanwhile, the project cost goes up by $40 million each year. Rising costs of electricity needed to pump the water, along with water quality permits that will be required, cause Michael Black to believe that Animas–La Plata will never be built. But the project doesn't die. As with the Auburn Dam site in California, public money continues to be spent on more studies, more plans, and more compromises. Black said, "If you come back here in ten years, I suspect that we'll still be working on this."

↬ Fighting the Dominant Culture

Outside the Colorado River Basin, many Indian tribes have taken a different approach to water and the way it flows in rivers. Different, that is, from the approach of the white irrigation society, and similar to cultures that sustained life on the continent for 10,000 years without squandering economic or ecological capital and without causing species to go extinct and food sources to disappear. In 1990, for example, the Shoshone and Bannock tribes in Idaho secured water rights to the Snake River, much of which they intended to use as instream flows to repair low-flow damage caused by white irrigators and to supplement supplies for migrating salmon.

Directly east of the Snake, on the Wind River Reservation in Wyoming, the Shoshone and Arapaho gained rights to a substantial 500,000 acre-feet of water—one-third of the water flowing past the reservation. The Indians planned to use 80,000 acre-feet of their water to restore a blue-ribbon trout fishery designed to attract anglers from all over the country. But in 1992 a Wyoming Supreme Court ruling took back the water, once again giving the state control of it.

Responding to the Indians' right to a portion of the river and to repair the streams that had been dried up by irrigators with no recognition of instream needs whatsoever, Justice Richard Macy ruled in favor of the irrigators and against the Indians with the following logic: "Water is simply too precious to the well-being of society to permit water-right holders unfettered control over its use."

For the Indians, dissenting Justice Michael Golden wrote that the "expropriation of Indian lands" in the last century is being paralleled now with the "same fate for their water resources. I cannot be a party to deliberate and transparent efforts to eliminate the political and economic base of Indian peoples under the distorted guise of state water-law superiority."

Giving the state authority means giving the irrigators authority. Wyoming and most other states in the West act in perfect concert with white irrigators. During the dry summer of 1992, Wyoming state engineer Jeff Fassett bluntly stated, "Fishery rights don't exist."

Though the Winters Doctrine, named for a 1908 court case, gives Indians water rights based on the treaty establishing their reservation, the Wind River Shoshone Indians are barred from using their water for fisheries and instream flows that would generously repair some small part of the damage done by irrigators. The court rather required that natives use their water just as the white society has used it—for irrigation. Otherwise, the Indians forfeit their rights. If forced to irrigate, the tribes warned that they will divert the water for their own farms and that other farmers will be in worse shape than if the flows were assigned for instream enhancement. Their opponents apparently relied on the Indians' unwillingness to farm. Facing the prospect of an unfriendly U.S. Supreme Court reflecting the views of conservative members appointed in the 1980s, the Indians decided to accept the state decision without appeal.

Unfortunately for rivers as well as for Indians, the Wyoming court ruling sustains the diversions and the dried-up riverbeds and encourages the Indians to do as their preemptors have done: divert more water for irrigation, build more dams for water supply, and destroy rivers that have been the basis of so much life.

❧ No Immunity for Rain-fed Rivers

While many of the dramatic causes of flow problems in rivers occur in the arid or semiarid West, the East enjoys no immunity, and with a growing population, diversions imperil more and more streams. Some have been affected for a long time, such as New York's Croton River, whose rich aquatic life was lost long ago to diversions to New York City.

Many depleted flows are caused by hydroelectric generation; the Hawks Nest project on the New River of West Virginia cuts flows in a five-mile reach from an average of 9,000 cubic feet per second to 25. Reviewing the project for relicensing, the U.S. Fish and Wildlife Service recommended a minimum of 2,000 to 4,000 cubic feet per second; the Federal Energy Regulatory Commission "compromised" with a minimum of 100 cubic feet per second. Conservationists appealed the ruling.

A plan to tap the Farmington River in Connecticut and pipe it to the city of Hartford provided the stimulus for a wild and scenic river study in 1990. Inclusion in the National Wild and Scenic Rivers System would limit the severity of the diversion or perhaps ban it.

Statewide interests in neighboring Massachusetts enacted one of the nation's stronger instream flow laws aimed at avoiding depleted riverbeds. The law prohibits any transfer of water from one basin to another without an act of the legislature.

Upper Darby Creek in central Ohio may be the best example of an eastern river recently threatened by diversions. The Nature Conservancy considers this small river one of the biological gems of the Midwest. Cutting through dolomite and limestone, the creek runs high in carbonate content, providing the chemistry and raw materials needed by mussels to produce their shells. The clean water and healthy volume of runoff in Big and Little Darby creeks support an astounding eighty species of fish and forty species of mussels, with thirty-one species of reptiles and amphibians in the watershed. The Scioto madtom—a secretive member of the catfish family—lives in lower reaches. Fourteen local species of fauna in Darby Creek appear on Ohio's list of endangered, threatened, or potentially threatened species.

Darby Creek dam proposals were defeated in the 1960s and 1970s, but a plan by the city of Columbus to divert flows from the headwaters persisted. Proposing to skim only high runoff, city spokespeople suggested that the effect on stream life would be minimal. Yet species breeding in the spring, including many darters, require the high flows for health and maintenance of gravel spawning beds. Ohio Rivers Unlimited and the Darby Creek Association fought the proposal, finally securing agreement from Columbus in 1992 that the river should be protected.

Diversions for urban uses have affected hundreds of rivers. During the 1989 drought in the upper Mississippi River Basin, the combined effects of many communities extracting water left rivers nearly dry, including the Mackinaw in Illinois.

While diversions threaten eastern streams, advocates there find solutions more often than they do in the West, where aridity, population growth, and the irrigation and cattle industries continue to dominate the political scene. But most important, a long history of legal advantages has favored development over protection in the West.

ᴥ A Stacked Deck

Western water law is notoriously complex and arcane, guarded by its lawyers and purveyors and mystifying to nonirrigation interests that would like to have some influence over this entirely public resource. The subject, however, need not be so intimidating. The basic principles are not really that difficult to understand.

During early development of the West, the only thing anyone had to do to secure a supply of water was to take it. If the diverter put the water to "beneficial" use, meaning irrigation, mining, domestic, or industrial supplies, the user automatically enjoyed a legal right to continue the diversion, forever. Later, the filing of paperwork established "rights" for the water, but the rubric remained about the same.

While some states require a "reasonable" use of the water, the breadth of definition allows just about any withdrawals for irrigation. When crops consume two acre-feet of water per year (one acre-foot would cover an acre one foot deep), farmers on the Egin Bench in southern Idaho apply twenty acre-feet, effectively raising groundwater to the root zone of the plants. State water agencies have considered this a "beneficial" and "reasonable" use. Irrigation canals sometimes leak 30 percent or more of the water they carry. That, too, is "reasonable." A large percentage of the federally supplied water that feeds the leaky canals, flooded fields, and over-watered acreage grows surplus crops, considered "beneficial" though the government pays some farmers not to grow them. Rice, cotton, wheat, and barley routinely qualify.

There is no doubt that the public owns the water. The law is clear on this point. Diverters secure only a right to use the vital fluid and are entitled to retain that right only if the use is beneficial and only if the water is in fact used and not hoarded.

To leave water in a river to maintain some semblance of aquatic life has not been considered a beneficial use until recent years. Indeed, anyone who left his or her share of a water supply in the riverbed stood to lose those rights, which were quickly claimed by the next "junior" water-rights holder. This remains the case in most of the West. While safeguards exist on paper to prevent unauthorized expansion of the acreage to be irrigated with a given supply of water and to avoid unreasonable diversions, their effect is about nil. Beyond the legal safeguards for irrigators, the water masters or ditch riders—the officials responsible for policing the system—don't bother to monitor many areas.

Preference for water supply is given to those who got there first (except for the Indians, who were really there first but who hadn't done the paperwork and usually didn't divert their water from streams). A claim before 1910 usually assures the irrigator along a large stream of a plentiful supply. Little or no attention need be directed to water conservation, which can often make it possible to grow crops profitably with far less water—often with one-third the amount that was necessary only fifteen years ago. After senior water-rights owners take their share, whatever water is left goes to the junior water-rights holder, a process that is repeated until either the water or farmland is exhausted, and it's often the water that gives out first.

The settlers structured the legal system to expedite development of the West, and that's what it did. Irrigators have appropriated virtually all supplies in farming regions. Some of the water is claimed several times, and dry streams are the result.

Since the mid-1960s, some irrigators have reduced their application of water considerably. In many areas, sprinklers replaced surface irrigation, which had cyclically flooded the entire field. The sprinklers require less water—only one-third the amount that surface irrigation of crops requires. They also reduce labor costs and soil erosion, which is extreme with surface irrigation, accounting for a 25 percent loss of fertility on the Snake River plain in Idaho, for example.

Unfortunately, the conversion rarely results in more water being left in the rivers. The irrigators either use the saved water to expand acreage (sometimes illegally) or pass it on to junior water-rights owners (sometimes selling it in an illegal practice called "spreading"), or the canal companies continue to divert the full amount and simply run it through the canal system, from which it leaks into the groundwater or spills back into the river much farther down. Though the water may eventually come back to the river, a dried-up streambed is left in the interim.

Beyond the water saved by sprinklers, vast additional potential exists to reduce the amount of irrigation supplies that are needed, and doing so often *increases* crop yields. Laser leveling of fields saves great amounts of water. Curtailment of sprinkling on windy days can cut demands by 40 percent. Drip irrigation, whereby water is percolated to the root zone of plants from hoses with holes in them, can cut application to a fraction of the amount that even sprinklers use and can also sharply reduce herbicide use because only the crops—and not the weeds—are being watered.

Before the 1970s, efforts to protect streams from excessive irrigation withdrawals would have brought about dumbfounded amazement followed by political lynchings. Withdrawals of 100 percent of the flow in even large streams still goes unquestioned at many outposts in the West, from the Gila River in Arizona to the Powder in Oregon.

But in the 1990s, where strong, determined interest exists, the most common approach to the problem of dried-up streambeds is for states to claim water rights for instream flows. This constitutes a public right to a certain amount of water that will be left in the stream. In 1955 Oregon became the first state to adopt a program for the reservation of instream flows. In 1969 Montana allowed this; all western states but New Mexico have now adopted similar programs. However, a new state right for instream flow assumes the date of the right's establishment, and herein lies the problem: a water right dated anytime after 1980 is essentially worthless because it applies only to the water remaining after all the preexisting rights are satisfied. In low-water years—when it counts—the stream may already run dry before the recently declared public right is satisfied. But at least the instream right prevents yet more diversions that could dry up the stream even in wet years.

Not only are the instream rights largely ineffectual in times of drought, but they are established only through an elaborate process, consuming time and political capital. The entire water industry usually resists instream flow designations. They are accomplished stream by stream and mile by mile in states that contain up to 90,000 miles of waterways. After fifteen years of effort, Idaho, for example, had only 300 miles with instream flow rights. Furthermore, the decisions made by state water boards can be subject to veto by commodity-dominated state legislatures.

Federal reserved water rights are a separate method of reserving water for instream flows. This doctrine maintains that the federal government has the right to adequate flows to sustain federal lands such as national parks, wilderness areas, wild and scenic rivers, and national forests for specified purposes. Upheld by courts, these federal rights are based on the date of the designation of the land—not the date of any recent claim for water—and thus often predate the rights of irrigators. To put it mildly, this fact has caused intense controversy in the West, and the actual exercise of the federal reserved water rights has been limited. Fear of the federal rights has caused a stalemate on the designation of many new wilderness areas, such as in Colorado, with western politicians stonewalling new proposals that do not explicitly forego reserved water rights for the wilderness land.

Diversions for hydroelectric proposals are handled differently from other water rights. The Federal Energy Regulatory Commission, state water departments, and sometimes public utility commissions require approvals for new hydro projects. Agencies can require that certain minimum flows remain in the rivers when producers divert water to power plants. The need for minimum flows used to be ignored in the permitting process, but most agencies now give this at least minimal consideration. Some states mainly seek to protect irrigators' flows rather than those needed for stream life, and FERC often rules for flows far less than those recommended by fish and wildlife agencies. Though the agencies never require the optimum conditions for stream life and frequently fail to reserve adequate minimum flows, the instream requirements have nonetheless become a way to reduce the impacts of hydro dams and occasionally to stop them altogether.

A few states have acted to protect flows in larger streams that were not yet fully appropriated, the Yellowstone River being the model case. In the late 1970s, Montana established flow requirements aimed at protection of fish, wildlife, and hydrologic processes, all of which were threatened at the time by diversions for coal processing. For many large rivers, however, it is too late to secure meaningful flows because all the water has been given away. The question for river conservationists becomes one of sustaining stream life in its crippled condition and of reinstating the needed water.

One approach to putting water back into the streams is to buy or lease it from the irrigators who hold the rights. In 1989 Montana passed a law allowing the state to lease water from irrigators to meet emergency demands of trout streams that had been reduced to trickles by the combined effects of drought and diversions. Though the plan was voluntary and gave irrigators an opportunity to make money without even farming in a dry year, the water lobby yielded only after facing the threat of a statewide initiative addressing the instream flow issue. Montana accomplished little in actual amounts of leasing, but water use reformers heralded the case as a modest step away from the traditional grip of irrigation on water supply.

On the Henrys Fork of the Snake River in Idaho, The Nature Conservancy leased stored irrigation water on an emergency basis to keep rare swans alive in the winter of 1989. On the main stem of the Snake River, Idaho Power Company has leased great amounts of water from irrigators, incidentally alleviating some instream flow problems because the needs for power and for instream flows just happened to occur at the same time. Colorado cities are acquiring irrigators' rights and transferring water to urban development, but fish and wildlife agencies in Colorado and elsewhere don't have the needed money to purchase such rights. Critics of these marketing programs argue that the public should not have to buy what it already owns—the right to healthy streams. They maintain that any waters not genuinely being used for other beneficial purposes should revert to the streams as a matter of simple enforcement of the appropriation doctrine, without the government having to compensate anybody.

Reform-minded people have sought to change the basic incentives of existing water law, all of which move water from streams to ditches as rapidly as is humanly possible. Now, irrigators who save water run the risk of losing rights to it under a "use it or lose it" doctrine. Other rules make it difficult for irrigators to sell water—a complicated and risky process but one that could effectively retire salty soils from cultivation and avoid urban water crises that otherwise promise another round of new dam proposals. Yet, for all the talk, the changes toward marketing have been slow or nonexistent in most areas. Because irrigators may lose the rights to unused water, and because the water is nearly free, and because regulations make it difficult to sell water, there are no economic incentives to use less. To change the incentives, laws must be changed. But a rewriting of water law literally means amending the constitution in some states, and reformers may as well talk about revising the Bible in the irrigation belt of America.

In Oregon, a law seeking effective use of water enables irrigators to sell 75 percent of saved amounts while 25 percent goes to restore instream flows, but the measure has been sparingly used owing to legal complications and a persistent reluctance by irrigators to give up water rights no matter what.

Some authorities on the subject, such as lawyer Jeff Fereday in Boise, Idaho, say that existing law contains an elegance that can allow it to serve new needs and to bring greater efficiency to long-standing uses. Perhaps the reinterpretation of "reasonable" and "beneficial" use could go far toward solving problems by denying the right to divert water wastefully. If new methods are meanwhile established to safeguard the flows that are returned to the streams, the general health of rivers will improve. These half-steps toward reform have normally been frustrated by water users. Ironically, the irrigation industry's reluctance to compromise has led to more extreme proposals, and to greater success in cracking the shell of laws protecting diverters.

Frustrated by the full deck stacked against them, conservationists in

California sued Los Angeles for diversions that were ruining the ecologically vital Mono Lake. Invoking the "public trust doctrine," the National Audubon Society drew upon a strain of venerable American case law that is traceable to the Roman codes and the law of England. Audubon maintained that the water and the lake constituted public resources that could not legally be decimated even by a city that "owned" the water rights. In a milestone case, the court agreed that the water rights did not entitle Los Angeles to ruin public property—in this case, the lake. Other cases in Idaho and elsewhere confirmed the legitimacy of the public trust approach in questions of water allocation. This may be widely invoked if more moderate approaches to returning water to dried-up streambeds are not successful. Unsatisfied by years of effort to establish new instream flow reservations that aren't very effective, Phil Wallin of River Network said, "The public trust doctrine may be the only answer."

People have been tinkering with the legal system, trying to get irrigators to conserve water, trying to get authorization for individuals to donate their rights for instream flows, trying to change the pricing structure, trying to buy and lease water, trying to invoke the Endangered Species Act and fisheries laws, but none of this has amounted to much in comparison to the wide scope of the dried-up riverbeds. Many water law reformers now go further and argue that the existing laws of prior appropriation are unjust in giving all the water to select groups of users simply because they got there first, especially when one considers that, in fact, the life of the stream existed first. Professor Charles Wilkinson, one of the authorities on western water law, believes that our society has to recognize the fatally flawed reality of the doctrine of prior appropriation. As applied, it fails to recognize that water has multiple uses, that streams should be able to exist as streams, and that water is essential to fish, wildlife, recreational users, and ecosystems that are cornerstones of our society.

Nationwide, the water development system has failed in that it has taken away too much. Forty percent of some urban water supplies go for the life of lawns, but the life that was lost at Mono Lake or in the salmon redds of the Yuba River in northern California offered more life than that of Kentucky bluegrass in the desert, more life than that of surplus cotton. And beyond this theme, we can have adequate lawns and thriving farms by consuming far less water under a new ethic of resource use that is reasonable, efficient, and economic.

❧ With Intent to Reform

Diversions under water rights administered by the states are one aspect of the problem of adequate flows in rivers, and the management of federal dams is another, quite different from the first, though the water industry doesn't want people to realize that fact. The water diverters would like everyone to believe that the diverters "own" the water, whether it comes from natural stream flow or from federal dams.

With federal water projects, the water users' rights are subsumed and new ones created under varying formulas, differing by state and by project. Many of the formulas are negotiable, temporary, or changeable by federal agencies or by Congress, unlike the right to take water from rivers under state laws. In addition to matters of water rights or contracts, federal agencies must be concerned about a whole body of law, frequently at odds with water diversions, including the National Environmental Policy Act, the Clean Water Act, and the Endangered Species Act, which are applicable to management of the dams.

Importantly, federal dams are mostly paid for by taxpayers and hydroelectric users—which is to say, everybody. Federal projects are thereby more vulnerable to democratic processes that reflect changing times, while state water law remains more insulated, rigid, and protective of the status quo. It is in the federal arena where reformers thus far have had the most success in restoring health to streams.

Recognizing the need for change in 1993, House Interior Committee Chair George Miller said, "You can't let people who placed a claim on a resource forty years ago continue as they did when their claim today is so politically weak. It is not the dead hand from the grave that should dictate water policy today."

With the Central Valley Project of California, the federal Bureau of Reclamation operates sixteen dams, including an enormous one on the major river of the state—the Sacramento—and on the American, Stanislaus, and Trinity rivers. The dam building is over, and the losses of wild rivers under flatwater is permanent; but even worse than that, changes in the flows below the dams have left hundreds of miles as only the crippled remains of rivers. Irrigation canals totally dry up a ten-mile section of the San Joaquin below the Bureau's Friant Dam, and sixty-nine unregulated agricultural discharges pollute that river. The diversions have annihilated salmon runs, decimated resident fish and riparian life, and created health hazards. Shasta Dam on the Sacramento results in reduced flows, altered temperatures, and barriers to migrating salmon and other species, driving them toward extinction.

At the Sacramento–San Joaquin delta, where dozens of streams issuing from the Sierra Nevada merge, some of the largest pumping plants in the world lift the accumulated waters into two giant canals bound for the San Joaquin Valley and southern California. Diversions and habitat loss in the basin have caused a 99 percent loss of winter salmon; populations of those fish and of delta smelt hover just above extinction. The pumps, sucking water uphill to corporate farms, kill 80 million striped bass a year. The Central Valley Project has also contributed greatly to the loss of wetlands, reduced from 4 million to 0.3 million acres in the Central Valley. An original 15 million waterfowl have decreased to 3 million. Stemming from the project, water quality problems, including selenium, pesticides, and intrusion of salt water, threaten both the delta, from which 20 million people drink, and San Francisco Bay, the greatest estuary on the West Coast.

A huge state water project, along with dams and diversions by dozens of irrigation districts and cities, all contribute greatly to this ecological house of horrors, but the federally sponsored Central Valley Project is the cornerstone of ruin to waterways spanning 400 miles of geography from north to south.

The project was built with federal money, and now it is operated with federal money. Interest is not charged to irrigators, deadlines for paying back the cost of irrigation facilities to the federal government were postponed, fish and wildlife mitigation was overlooked or token amounts undertaken provided they were funded by taxpayers, and any semblance of payback was erased with exceptions to irrigators who officially lack the "ability to pay" and can thereby get the water for $3.50 or less per acre-foot, the closest thing in the world to a free lunch.

Controversy has arisen elsewhere over the antiquated Mining Law of

1872 because miners make $3.9 billion from public lands each year and return nothing to the public. But the hard-rock giveaway pales in comparison to the big-water giveaway. The National Wildlife Federation claimed in 1993 that the Bureau of Reclamation's failure to enforce repayment provisions on irrigation projects may cost taxpayers $2 billion. With the Central Valley Project and other dam-and-canal networks throughout the West, the taxpayer not only allows the water to be taken and the streams to be destroyed, the taxpayer pays for it. The public coughs up a subsidy for the Central Valley Project amounting to many millions per year; former California Resources Secretary Huey Johnson estimated the subsidy at $200 per acre-foot.

The situation is typical throughout the West. The federal government spends more than half a billion dollars a year to provide cheap irrigation water, which may seem bad enough when the national deficit and cuts in programs such as Medicare are considered. But even more largess stems from the fact that 38 percent of the acres served with the subsidized water are planted with crops in chronic surplus, for which price supports and other subsidies are paid to curtail production. Succinctly put, the government pays to send water to irrigators and then pays the irrigators not to grow crops with it. The U.S. Department of Agriculture reported in 1986 that $730 million was paid in crop supports on lands also receiving federally subsidized water. In California, 43 percent of the acreage served by the Bureau of Reclamation grew surplus crops. If that's what's being grown, why is it so important for so much tax money to be used to destroy so many rivers?

On average, western farmers received $54 an acre in water subsidies in 1986, according to Department of Interior figures. The federal government received a total of $58 million from irrigators but had to pay another $534 million to cover their program, and $203 million of this water subsidy went to surplus crops.

Irrigators of the Bonneville Project in Utah pay $17.84 an acre for water costing the taxpayer $306 an acre to deliver. The Garrison Diversion Project in North Dakota will charge $39.78 for water costing $759 an acre to deliver. New Melones Dam on the Stanislaus River will benefit 400 farmers to the tune of $1 million each over a fifty-year period, if they ever choose to buy the water. According to Congressman George Miller in 1987, the Columbia Basin Project in Washington will yield a subsidy of $4.4 million per farm; the Central Valley Project will provide a subsidy of $1.8 million to each 960-acre spread.

In Colorado, irrigators pay fourteen cents for every dollar's worth of taxpayer-subsidized water from the Bureau of Reclamation. Meanwhile, $209 million was paid to Colorado farmers in crop subsidies; one-fourth of this acreage also received subsidized federal water, according to a *Denver Post* exposé on the subject in 1992. The same crops thrive on nonirrigated acreage in the Midwest and in other regions where farmers are put out of business by competitors basking in the federal endowment to the West. If the subsidy were going to family farmers on 160-acre parcels, as intended in the legislation making the irrigation program a reality, there would be less objection, but much of the giveaway—especially in California—goes to corporate giants with tens of thousands of acres.

Daniel Beard, staff director for the House Interior Committee in 1991, summed it all up: "We're taking money out of taxes, handing it to a very small number of people, and destroying rivers when we do it." (Beard later became commissioner of the Bureau of Reclamation in the Clinton administration.)

Seeking to force some integrity into this bankrupt system, the Natural Resources Defense Council (NRDC) sued the Bureau of Reclamation when it prepared to renew water delivery contracts from Friant Dam on the San Joaquin River in California. At giveaway prices, the diversion of 2.2 million acre-feet of water a year has spelled ruin for that once-vital artery of the San Joaquin Valley. The habitat of an estimated 100,000 adult salmon was destroyed, capable of supporting a $150 million industry. Fisheries consultant Bill Kier said, "We have overseas people banging on California's door for salmon. So why is water wasted on surplus crops like cotton?" The NRDC argued that the Bureau should at least write an environmental impact statement as required by the National Environmental Policy Act. The agency responded that it could not alter the status quo—the irrigators presumably had the right to cheap, subsidized water without environmental controls or oversight, all this to last forever because they struck up a good deal forty years ago. During the Bush administration, Interior Secretary Manuel Lujan agreed to do the impact statement but rendered it moot by renewing the contracts in the meantime.

Purveyors of the status quo were scrambling and spending a lot of money to keep ahead of the brilliant lawyers at the NRDC, but when Representative George Miller of California and Senator Bill Bradley of New Jersey also sought reform, the old-boy water industry knew it was in big trouble.

Miller and Bradley, as chairs of their respective Interior committees, introduced legislation to reauthorize the Central Valley Project. Their bill provided 800,000 acre-feet for fish and wildlife, 200,000 acre-feet to correct damage done to the salmon and steelhead fishery of the Trinity River, and 230,000 acre-feet for wildlife refuges—all of it totaling a modest 15 percent of the project's supply. New emphasis was given to urban water deliveries, and irrigators' fees would gradually increase to cover the government's full cost, but only when irrigators use more than 80 percent of their contracted amount. As a reform bill, this one was arguably conservative, yet it marked the most significant effort ever to redirect a reclamation project toward fixing the problems that the project had created.

Governor Pete Wilson opposed the bill; he reportedly had received $400,000 in just one night at a campaign fundraiser in the Westlands Water District—the hotbed of corporate recipients of the Central Valley Project subsidies. Blowing a familiar smoke screen, California Senator John Seymour argued, "My priorities have always been people and jobs first and animals and plants second." Among other things, Seymour ignored a major source of jobs existing without the subsidies but being lost because of the water projects—the once-great California salmon industry.

The Miller-Bradley bill, called the Reclamation Project Authorization and Adjustments Act of 1992, passed, and a complaining George Bush signed it, largely because it offered water development approvals in Utah and elsewhere in the West. (Though the act authorized completion of the Central Utah Project, it also required water conservation and protection of wetlands and instream flows.) President Bush vowed to work to undo the California reforms when reelected. He and Seymour were then both voted out of office. In 1993 George Miller announced to a conference of river conservationists that "we now have the opportunity to save—and 'save' is the operative word—the Sacramento River delta."

George Miller and Bill Bradley's visionary step could be a turning point against the subsidized destruction of waterways. The NRDC's Karen Garrison said, "The passage of the 1992 act is a resounding endorsement for a whole new direction for western water management." It is possible and quite likely that some of the best river conservation in the 1990s will result from the Bureau of Reclamation reprogramming other projects. The reforms that the Reclamation Act of 1992 so sensibly mandates for the Central Valley can be applied elsewhere, though the interests that have stymied reform for decades will be hard at work. Governor Wilson predicted legal challenges to the new law and pushed a plan for state takeover of the project, seeming to ignore the fact that it was a big money-loser while California was already saddled with budget deficits of up to $14 billion a year. In a *San Francisco Chronicle* interview on October 31, 1992, Jason Peltier of the Central Valley Project Water Association said of the new law: "We'll do anything and everything to keep from being harmed. If that means obstructing implementation, so be it."

While some of the water users dug in with a siege mentality, the politics in 1993 did appear to have changed with the start of the Clinton administration. Assuming new duties as the commissioner of the Bureau of Reclamation, Daniel Beard recognized the irony that his agency has had "a lot of bad successes." He identified the need "to change not only the way we do business, but the approach to the way we solve problems—the need to change the culture of the agency."

⚓ To Spare the Grandest of Canyons

After Glen Canyon Dam was built on the Colorado River just upstream from the Grand Canyon, conservationists considered the resulting flooding by Lake Powell in the early 1960s to be the greatest loss on any desert river. It spurred David Brower of the Sierra Club and others to defeat two additional dams proposed within the Grand Canyon. Yet the damage was far more insidious than just the flooding of Glen Canyon. Downstream from the dam, the greatest of all American canyons faced growing problems from the manipulation of the Colorado's flows.

Glen Canyon Dam was considered a silt trap that avoided the hasty obsolescence of Hoover Dam, downstream. And, in a fashion, it works. The prodigious runoff of silt for which the Spanish named the Colorado now settles nonstop on the bottom of Glen Canyon Reservoir, which itself will be full of silt within a few hundred years or perhaps much less. Meanwhile, cold, clean water is jettisoned from the bottom of the dam. Though dazzling to behold, the clean water unnaturally scours beaches and banks in the Grand Canyon, washing them away as a degrading riverbed without depositing any new silt. The cold water also destroys the endemic warmwater fishery, including the endangered Colorado squawfish and humpback chub.

The Bureau of Reclamation aggravated a bad situation when it rewound turbines at Glen Canyon Dam for higher output in the mid-1980s. Then the Western Area Power Administration—the federal power brokerage with authority to schedule hydroelectric releases—adjusted management for all-out peaking power. By releasing huge amounts of water a few hours in the afternoons, the dam generated electricity when Southwest utilities were willing to pay the most so that people could keep their air conditioners turned up high.

The beneficiaries, who were residents in several western states, including purchasers of large wattages for irrigation pumping, paid some of the lowest rates in America—some paying one-fourth the average cost of electricity nationwide. They paid as little as one-third the cost of other rate-payers even in their own market area. Adding further insult to the rivers of the Southwest, some of the income generated by wreaking havoc on the Grand Canyon was seen as justification for new, energy-consuming developments such as Animas–La Plata and the Central Utah Project.

The effect on the Grand Canyon was akin to running a nonstop parade of bulldozers down the river. The old reservoir releases had eroded seriously enough, but the new peaking surges fluctuated twelve vertical feet every day. Each time the water went up, it flushed sand and silt in a flood downstream to Lake Mead, behind Hoover Dam. Every time the water went down, the saturated banks, without time to drain slowly, slumped into the river. This mass wasting caused truckload-size chunks of shoreline to avalanche into the Colorado. Idyllic beaches where river runners camped were there one year and gone the next, and in the short turning of the calendar, riparian habitat was becoming a thing of the past. Shoreline erosion threatened to destroy Anasazi ruins dating back many hundreds of years. Extensive studies for the National Park Service, U.S. Fish and Wildlife Service, and Bureau of Reclamation documented the problems.

The plight faced by the Grand Canyon exists to some degree below dozens if not hundreds of dams. Extreme effects were felt below Glen Canyon Dam owing to the nature of the peaking schedule, and the losses attracted media attention because, after all, this is the Grand Canyon in one of America's most beloved national parks. But Hells Canyon of the Snake River is no less affected; power releases there since the 1960s caused most beaches to disappear, and with them, the riverfront ecosystem of America's second-deepest canyon, along with riparian habitat far richer than that of the Grand Canyon. In flagrant form, the problem exists below Oahe Dam on the Missouri River and affects vast cottonwood forests there. In subtler form but perhaps no less deadly in the long term, riverbeds are in the process of degrading below dams in many regions. Except for the extraordinary cases, little research has illuminated these problems.

Though a grassroots campaign to stop the Western Area Power Administration from instituting the radical peaking releases at Glen Canyon Dam had failed in the mid-1980s, river conservationists grappled with the problem anew when the devastation was seen firsthand. Boaters, for example, were left with their craft stranded on rocks high above the water whenever the dam tenders shut off the flow, every day. A concerted campaign by the Grand Canyon Trust, American Rivers, the National Wildlife Federation, and rafting groups pressed the federal government for reform and sued the Bureau of Reclamation, asking the agency to write an environmental impact statement.

Arguing the familiar old line that the Reagan and Bush administrations had employed for everything from acid rain to sockeye salmon, the Bureau of Reclamation said that more study was needed. The agency agreed to do environmntal investigations for five years. But at that point, opponents argued, there wouldn't be anything left to study. Interior Secretary Lujan reluctantly called for an interim schedule for less destructive releases, but immediately added a rider allowing exceptions for economic reasons, as if the entire issue were not an economic one.

Because of the artificial flow regime and the losses it caused, American Rivers named the Colorado the "most endangred river" of 1991. A bill to limit the extreme hydroelectric releases progressed through Congress, but then advocates had to fight a scheme by western senators to force tax-payers to reimburse the Western Area Power Administration for foregone profits—a subsidy that would have amounted to $93 million according to the National Wildlife Federation. Taxpayers nationwide already subsi-dized the Western Area Power Administration by picking up the tab for interest on loans—a federal subsidy of $400 million a year that utility rate-payers in the rest of the country would have loved to enjoy themselves.

David Marcus, an economist hired by American Rivers, reported that reducing the peaking flows would add only four cents a month to the av-erage utility bill of Glen Canyon Dam beneficiaries. The utilities' own worst-case scenario added only three dollars a year to consumers' bills, still keeping them far below rates that nearly everyone else pays for elec-tricity.

Reflecting on the arguments for and against protection of the Grand Canyon, journalist Jim Bishop wrote in *High Country News*, "It is no small irony that, had the federal government managed its dams more prudently in the past, taxpayers and ratepayers might never have discovered a per-vasive, socialized empire in the West, held together for the most part by conservative politicians fond of making speeches about the free market and rugged individualism."

Following a lobbying blitz with nationwide grassroots support in 1992, Congress mandated releases more amenable to the canyon environ-ment but included subsidies requiring taxpayers to fund related environ-mental studies. The new flow regime does not solve the problems created by Glen Canyon Dam, but it corrects some of the worst aspects of hydro-electric domination. The Grand Canyon act does nothing to reinstate the vital flow of silt from the upper basin. The Bureau of Reclamation curso-rily considered a pipeline to transport the silt from the inlet of the reser-voir to the dam, a costly alternative. Perhaps, someday, solutions of that type will be the only workable response to keep reservoirs from filling with silt. Many of these pools will inevitably mimic the fate of Austin Lake in Texas, 96 percent filled with silt in only thirteen years, and Little Pine

Creek Reservoir in Pennsylvania, filled with mud in thirty years. Some dams on the Missouri River lose one-quarter to one-half percent of their capacity every year.

Like the Central Valley Project reform, the Grand Canyon case is not a complete solution—not even close—but it represents a turning point when the managers of dams and reservoirs were forced to recognize the needs of rivers. House Interior Committee Chair George Miller said that the Grand Canyon act "sets a precedent for going back and re-thinking a dam project." Perhaps the protection of the Grand Canyon will signal the beginning of greater reform. With modest concessions by highly subsidized electricity rate-payers, other projects can be brought into a line of compromise to retain at least a semblance of the natural rivers that once existed. Beyond federal dams, hundreds of private projects will be relicensed by the Federal Energy Regulatory Commission, presenting an opportunity for reform on a large scale.

With growing attention to the problems and intricacies of the flow of water in rivers, both the dried-up streambeds below irrigation canals and the disabled streambeds below dams and behind levees can be improved. Many of the rivers can flow with health and vigor once again, affirming life, as they always used to do.

Chapter Seven
The Riparian Edge

❧ Lifeways of the Continent

Lewis and Clark wrote of a continent "lush and beautiful beyond compare." Following rivers, their route offered a tour of riparian America—the riverfront zone of fruitful, wetted life. The vegetation along the water's edge might be thought of as a landward extension of the river, revealing itself in textured green instead of the blue or brown of the river's liquid center.

In 1803, Meriwether Lewis and ten recruits began their 981-mile-long journey down the verdant Ohio River by keelboat. The next year, the full "Corps of Discovery" began the ascent of the cottonwood-fringed Missouri—our second-longest river at 2,315 miles—into the heart of the West. Then they descended the Clearwater, Snake, and Columbia to the Pacific.

More than purple mountains or fruited plains, what they saw were waterfront sycamores, black willows, and silver maples in their passage through the East and Midwest, followed by plains cottonwoods shading riverbanks of the prairie. The narrowleaf cottonwood thrived at high western elevations, and red cedars darkened streamfronts of the Pacific Northwest. Today, many riverbanks remain lush and beautiful beyond compare. And many don't.

The river's edge is not as simple and discernible as one might expect. Along the Withlacoochee River in Florida, for example, the boundary seems to come and go—is it land or is it water? A primordial landscape of wetlands harbors life in jungles of complexity. Broadleaf trees stretch skyward across that southern flatness. Cypress "knees" protrude from the water with rounded heads on thin, muscular pillars that may "breathe" for the flooded entanglement of cypress roots. Curtains of moss hang from every living surface. Turtles and alligators hunt at the watery edge; opossums, raccoons, and armadillos scavenge the banks. Startlingly red heads of pileated woodpeckers and a body-length whiteness of egrets dazzle the eyes. This is the riparian zone in the Deep South.

Along the James River, an elegant landscape begins at the shore and reaches outward from the banks, supporting life enriched by plentiful Virginia rainfall. While more succinctly defined than at the swamp-blessed Withlacoochee, the edge of the James hosts a mixing zone with land frequently nourished by floods and with soil wetted by the capillary action of water drawn from the river. Underfoot lie the gritty gravel bars from ancient floods that softened the Appalachian Mountains, but more commonly, one steps into the dank sogginess of sedges, leaves, and roots in rapid rot—a greenhouse and nursery of life. A child of this abundance, the wood duck leaps to a sudden, whistling-wingbeat flight from the hardwood bottom of the James River.

The prairie wanderings of the Smoky Hill and Republican rivers join into the sluggish midwestern artery that the Indians called the Kaw but road maps call the Kansas. Along its shores, the riparian buffer of plant life snakes across the plains like a river itself, perched only slightly above the muddy flow, upon which the trees are utterly dependent. Here, the eclectic hardwood forests of the East intermingle with the simplified forests of the West, variety being the outcome. The region's vast, dry grasslands, splendid in their monotony, lie streaked with threads of riparian life, green in spring and summer, golden yellow in fall, gray in winter, but sheltering throughout.

Winding from its headwaters in the Flattops Wilderness, the Yampa River arcs across northwestern Colorado to its confluence with the Green River more than 200 miles below, much of the corridor hosting a refuge for narrowleaf cottonwood, Fremont cottonwood, box elder, red-osier dogwood, and many species of willows. Though constricted in canyons, the riparian community broadens in valleys and "parks"—riparian openings in an arid land. Like swaths of a painter, tiers of cottonwoods across the flood plain succeed one another in groves whose ages date the flood cycle of that great river, undammed until 1989 and now dammed only once. The Yampa offers one of the finest riparian communities remaining in the West.

≈ A Rich Interface

All rivers possess important riparian zones, roughly equivalent to flood plains, which account for about 7 percent of the landscape nationwide. The riparian zone, however, extends somewhat beyond the flood-prone acres, incorporating adjacent land that is heavily influenced by the river and its companion groundwater.

Each riverfront practices life support at its finest. When left intact, riparian landscapes absorb flood waters and diminish their effects—no small consideration, as floods account for 70 percent of the "natural" disasters in the United States. These lowlands store groundwater by detaining it in porous soils and then rationing it out slowly in drier months.

The species of plants in riparian zones vary by region, but all hold the earth together by stabilizing streambanks with a gripping and tenacious latticework of roots. They filter sediment and protect rivers from polluted runoff originating behind the riparian zone; one mature tree might filter out as much as 200 pounds of nitrate from overfertilized runoff in a year. Researchers D. C. Wilkin and S. J. Hebel reported in 1982 that sediment accumulated in forest flood plains of the Midwest at ten to twenty tons per acre per year. In contrast, flood plains cleared for crops resulted in no accumulation at all, but rather in erosion at the rate of fifteen to sixty tons per year.

As vegetation takes root along the wet edges, streams typically respond by "aggrading," meaning that sediment is beneficially trapped to become lodged as sandbars and silt deposits. Riparian plant life thus helps to shape the earth around it. Cottonwoods benefit from this process; they can germinate in a small amount of silt on gravel bars, but then they need further silt built up to create a terrace that slowly amasses itself above the river level. And the entire riverfront community benefits: with the aggrading action of silt deposits, downcutting of streams is halted. Water then returns to previously dried-up shorelines that had signified abused riverbanks.

People have been fooled by an apparent paradox: vegetation along rivers results not in lower flows, as one might expect from trees transpiring water, but in higher flows of a year-round nature owing to self-maintenance of streambeds and water tables. The Bureau of Land Management (BLM) at one time clearcut cottonwoods from southwestern streams, falsely believing that doing so would free up more water for ranchers and irrigators. Instead, without a vegetated shoreline, the streams eroded their banks, drained groundwater, and dried up sooner.

A healthy riparian zone is populated by natural wonders. The mainstay of riparian environments, 65 to 100 species of willows hybridize from species to species, and as many as 10,000 seedlings can blanket a half-acre mudflat. Towering over the willows are sycamores—giants of the bottomland community—with camouflage-patterned bark. These trees can live for 400 years, and they rank as the largest tree in eastern North America. Sharing sandy soils with silver maples, sycamores don't mind prolonged flooding and can withstand silt deposited to depths of several feet around their trunks—a suffocating burden to most other trees. Becoming hollow with age, these guardians of the riverfont mature into apartment complexes for raccoons, gray squirrels, yellow-throated warblers, swallows, swifts, the rare prothonotary warbler, and on and on.

Wildlife, which has been lost so profoundly in other cultures and on other continents, even including so much of Africa, remains a symbol of North America. Among all possible natural emblems, ours is the fish-eating bald eagle, dining at riparian gravel bars and nesting in trees along the water. No animal quite epitomizes the riverfront zone as well as the beaver, at home in water and along its edge. On small streams, this superbly adapted fur bearer establishes ponds that raise water tables and cause the riparian acreage to expand, benefiting a host of creatures from the microscopic to the moose—a riparian wader and grazer that ranks as the largest member of the deer family ever to have lived. Otters are likewise emblematic of the riverine way of life. Our most primitive land-dwelling carnivores, these sleek, whiskered members of the weasel tribe date back 30 million years. They once ranged throughout the United States, but farming has eradicated them from the heartland and, owing to riparian destruction, few remain elsewhere.

According to the U.S. Environmental Protection Agency's *Livestock*

Grazing on Western Riparian Areas, more than 75 percent of all western wildlife species depend on riparian habitat. Among neotropical migrants—an especially threatened group of songbirds—80 percent depend on riparian zones for nesting or migration, and in the Southwest, researchers found that removing 70 percent of the trees in riparian areas cut the number of birds by at least half. Even considering all the losses, the wildlife of America continues to define the character and lore of this land, and among all wildlife zones, the waterfront is the most important, yet the most affected by change.

Bears, moose, muskrats, wood ducks, egrets, alligators—yet another *Peaceable Kingdom* could be painted of the riparian lifeway, no less critical to people than it is to these other creatures. The riverfront is central to community identity as it flows through pastoral landscapes, towns, and cities. The local chamber of commerce advertises Boise, Idaho, with a poster of its riverfront and only a backdrop of the city. Farmington, New Mexico—otherwise a bleak new metropolis founded on irrigation, mining, and oil drilling—shows its best face at a spacious new park along the Animas River. The riparian corridor can at once be a place to walk on a summer night, a home for an endangered amphibian, and the fundament of a whole neighborhood's real estate value. From farms along the Cumberland to Indian villages along the Yukon, how many images of homelands are remembered with the green curves of river life running by?

❧ Under Siege

The riparian greenways we know today represent a fraction of those seen by Lewis and Clark. The U.S. Fish and Wildlife Service estimated that 70 percent of the riparian habitat nationwide has been lost or altered. Other estimates reach 90 percent. Among 121 million acres in the 100-year flood plain (the area likely to flood once every 100 years), only 23 million acres remain in a relatively natural condition, according to one Fish and Wildlife Service report in 1981. Within those areas, only 5 perent of the natural vegetation still exists. At least 6 percent of the land nationwide once supported riparian vegetation; only 2 percent still does. Along the lower Mississippi, only 5 million of 21 million acres of forest wetlands remain. In California, a state with 12 percent of its land in parks or preserves of some kind, only 10 percent of the riparian habitat remains intact and only 1 percent is protected. By the 1890s, settlers had transformed the banks of the Gila River in Arizona from a cottonwood and willow bosque to an arid, quarter-mile-wide strip of dust-blown waste. In Colorado, where 90 percent of the native riparian habitat has been turned into something else, small remaining riparian zones provide habitat for 60 percent of the state's wildlife species. The wildlife of the riparian zone is not doing well.

Losses nationwide are the result of public policies supporting the flow of tax dollars for new roads and sewer lines that encourage development along rivers, of dams and levees ostensibly providing flood control and thereby enticing development on flood plains, of public permitting of grazing and gravel mining on bottomlands, and of subsidies for agriculture and logging. Additional riparian losses accumulate in a socially passive arena in which developers can build where they choose without concern for essential flood plain functions or for the usefulness of what will be lost.

While laws regulate how many ducks a hunter may shoot, the greater effects of habitat disruption on waterfowl and other riparian species are too often ignored, calling to mind a medieval English quatrain:

> The law locks up both man and woman
> Who steals the goose off the common,
> But lets the greater felon loose
> Who steals the common from the goose.

Unexpected losses also occur from invading plant species introduced or benefiting by our tinkering with land and water. Tamarisk—a shrub that chokes out other species and offers a drab wasteland of unpalatable foliage for wildlife—now monopolizes shorelines of the Southwest. The invader accounts for 40 percent of all vegetation along the lower Colorado River; on another 43 percent of the waterfront, tamarisk is mixed with other plants. Native cottonwoods and willows have declined to 0.8 percent of the riparian landscape, as reported in *Down by the River* by Constance Hunt. Meager efforts to restore native vegetation are foiled by saline irrigation return flows that cause a salt buildup in the river and along the shores. Thus, the tamarisk, an alien shrub from Mediterranean areas, thrives along the dam-controlled rivers and has rendered once idyllic shorelines of native plant life to a distant memory with little prospect of recall. Worse, the thorny, gray-green Russian olive tree grows taller and spreads farther from the water line than even tamarisk and has displaced the willows and Fremont cottonwoods in riparian belts as vital as the San Juan in New Mexico.

Many riparian areas fit the definition of wetlands, with standing water part of the year, hydric or water-influenced soils, and plant life adapted to undrained flats. Nationwide, an estimated one-half of all wetlands have been lost; on the alluvial plain of the Mississippi, 78 percent are gone. Yet wetlands sustain an estimated one-third of endangered and threatened species. Agriculture accounts for 87 percent of the nation's reduction in wetlands; urban development, 8 percent.

While much riparian acreage has been lost as a result of dams, hydro-electric projects, and diversions, as discussed in earlier chapters of this book, even greater areas have been sacrificed to channelization, including levees and riprap, to land development, and to cattle grazing.

₰ Draining Rivers Faster

Channelization—the process of excavating a waterway or hardening its banks with levees or rock armor called riprap—not only ruins streambeds but also riparian communities by sucking out groundwater, eliminating flood flows and sloughs, and bulldozing vegetation. Tens of thousands of miles of stream frontage have been sacrificed with the objective of keeping water away from property. Riprap and levees disconnect a river from its flood plain, at great loss to the riparian ecosystem.

When wetlands are drained, riverbanks reinforced to retard erosion, and channels deepened, some local flood or drainage problems may be temporarily solved. However, the secondary effects are formidable, and the long-term success of the manipulations are fraught with hidden costs and frequent failure.

Channelization, meant to whisk away floods from upstream reaches, causes worse flooding downstream because the water has to go *someplace*, and after channelization, it goes there faster. Downstream communities respond by digging extensions of channels or by mounding up extensions of levees, pushing the accumulating problem to yet another luckless area—such as the other side of the river. This self-defeating cycle of human intervention feeds on itself until the system fails, with massive losses realized in both human and natural communities along the river.

Streams, of course, meander and overflow their banks for a reason, and that is to gradually dissipate the energy of the flowing water. In the process, erosion damage is decreased, flooding elsewhere is lowered, groundwater is replenished, and fertile soil is deposited. Recognizing these benefits, farmers of the British Isles in the 1800s diked their fields, not to keep flood waters out, but to funnel them *in*, reaping the harvest of fertile silt that settled on the flooded land in a process called warping.

Too often, our treatment of streams fails to recognize their intrinsic qualities. Waterways are channelized by farmers and ranchers for drainage, flood control, and shoreline reinforcement; by local governments for flood control; by the Army Corps of Engineers for navigation projects; and by highway departments that relocate portions of thousands of streams for roads. An Arthur D. Little study in 1973 estimated that more than 200,000 miles of stream channels had been modified. For barges alone, 26,000 miles were channelized at a 100 percent subsidy to the barging industry. Half the prodigious length of the Illinois River is constrained by levees, and 3,123 miles of smaller streams in Illinois were channelized. A 155-mile-long section of the Rio Grande between El Paso and Fort Quitman, Texas, was reduced to 88 miles by channelization that cut off broad meanders.

In northwestern Ohio, Mike Fremont of Ohio Rivers Unlimited estimated that 80 percent of the streams have been turned into drains, with devastating effects on the whole riparian community. Simply by driving across the Midwest on interstate highways, one can see hundreds of streams and riparian draws that have been excavated into straight-line ditches to get water off the land and to make bottomlands easier to farm. The U.S. Soil Conservation Service, established to protect soils, was responsible for 21,401 miles of channelization as of 1979, much of it in the South and Midwest.

Most channelization has been stopped, not only because of wetlands, stream devastation, and conflicts with downriver communities, but also because channelization works poorly in the long term, going against the grain of natural processes and working against efficient principles of hydrology and physics. A doubling of velocity in channelized rivers quadruples the water's erosive force and increases by sixty-four times its capacity to push stones along the riverbed. These dynamics deliver a cyclone of new problems, not the least of which is the stream's destructive force magnified upon the manipulated banks of the channelization "improvement," naively intended to tame the high flows. Streams tend to reestablish meandering patterns, requiring constant drag-line and bulldozer maintenance if the dug-out profile is to last.

Yet some threats of new channelization remain. In 1970 Congress authorized the Army Corps of Engineers to spend $32 million to channelize 17.4 miles of Mill Creek in Ohio. In 1992 the project, still unfinished, was estimated to cost $341 million. Confident that the times have changed, Mike Fremont said, "Once we stop this plan we'll begin to restore the damage already done to Mill Creek."

On the Ouachita River in Arkansas and Louisiana, the Corps still plans to finish the Ouachita–Black River Navigation Project, cutting off meandering bends and heaping 162,000 cubic yards of mud from each bend into hardwood riparian forests and wetlands.

In California, levees and riprapped shorelines gird the banks of the Sacramento River for much of the waterway's 370-mile length—not exactly channelized but lined with levees and revetments that change a meandering river of riparian wealth into an outsized sluiceway of sterile design. A riparian forest of 800,000 acres in 1848 was reduced to 12,000 acres by 1988. One section between Redding and Red Bluff remained intact, though threatened by a Corps proposal. Local farmers, owning 80 percent of the frontage, wanted completion of the riprap as a barrier to the migrating river.

Wildlife interests, determined to stop the plan, organized the Sacramento River Preservation Trust. The group found that twenty-five of forty-one riprap sites failed to prevent erosion. Believing that any "benefits" are thus short term, the Trust questioned the Corps' use of a fifty-year life span applied to the benefit-cost ratio. Each acre of river bottom "saved" from an undercutting current cost the taxpayers $29,900. Alternatives were outlined for public acquisition of the erosion-prone land—far cheaper than riprapping it—thereby compensating the farmers and protecting both the riparian forest and the hydrologic process. Some farmers responded by clearcutting their cottonwoods so there wouldn't *be* any forest to protect. With a low-key approach, The Nature Conservancy launched a program to buy the woodlands where farmers wanted to sell, and to negotiate management agreements for many tracts. State voters meanwhile authorized $4 million for riparian purchases in an initiative sponsored by the Planning and Conservation League in 1988. The U.S. Fish and Wildlife Service bought 2,000 acres by 1992 and hoped to acquire another 16,000 acres of contiguous habitat from willing sellers. For all the initial hostility, 62 percent of the owners said they would sell if the price were fair.

Here and elsewhere, scrutiny has shown that reserving riparian habitat as a natural system is not only essential to the health of the river, but also cheaper than channelization and riprapping.

‌ To Pave and to Mow

The greatest threat to undamaged riparian habitat and the streamfronts of America is from new land development—homes, vacation cottages, and suburban sprawl along shorelines. Population growth, watershed development, and the resulting loss of riparian habitat ranked among the leading concerns of river conservationists surveyed by the River Network in 1993.

No reliable documentation of land development along riverbanks is available, but few riparian areas in heavily populated regions of the country have escaped. All that one must do to grasp the widespread nature of the conflict is to drive or canoe along private-land rivers in the East, Midwest, or on the West Coast. Riverbanks are used for industry and commercial development, or roads, railroads, and farms, or houses and second homes, or mowed lawns that look pretty and keep the bugs down but cut wildlife and bird habitat to the nubs.

In the 1978 Nationwide Outdoor Recreation Plan, the Department of Interior reported that 81 percent of the river miles in the Mideast region had moderate to heavy shoreline development. Urban development on all types of land in the United States increased by 88 percent from 1960 to 1990, and the rate of growth along riverfronts—often preferred real estate—may have been higher.

In the north-central highlands of Pennsylvania, Pine Creek and Loyalsock Creek have carved deep folds into the Appalachian Plateau, leaving terraces and flood plains of green and forested beauty. The riffling waters are good for fishing and cool summer swims, making the valleys attractive for home sites and weekend retreats. Fields of open space—once the centerpieces of mountain farms—have been whittled away piecemeal by development that includes ten-room homes as well as trailers on cinder blocks. While Pennsylvania has bought some critical parcels as state forest, and a local conservancy was formed to acquire additional tracts, much remains vulnerable to subdivision. The Beaverkill and Willowemoc river systems in the Catskill region of New York—deep in the lore of trout fishing in America—are similarly threatened, as are thousands of other streams nationwide. Peter Lavigne of the River Network reported in 1992 that land development posed the primary threat to rivers in New England, where people fleeing the crowded megalopolis have resettled along idyllic riversides even in times of economic recession.

Ironically, water quality improvements have led to a new development boom along waterways that for a century smelled too foul to live with. This phenomenon appeared as early as the 1970s along streams of the Appalachians, where government reclamation cut acid mine drainage along some scenic waters, such as the Clarion River of Pennsylvania. At a river-planning symposium in 1980, Bart Hague of the Environmental Protection Agency proposed a synchronized program of pollution control and shoreline protection, but action on the latter issue remained spotty and piecemeal, if not entirely ignored. Regarding urban pressures that arose in the wake of pollution cleanup along the Connecticut River, journalist Richard Conniff wrote, "If they could fix 'the sewer,' isn't it reasonable to think that, with care and a little sacrifice, we can figure out how to save the landscape too?"

Local land-use regulation is the most common, reasonable, and promising means of keeping riverfronts from being lined with parking lots, homes, and groomed lawns. Local ordinances protecting open space and agriculture can help to sustain natural riverbanks, but flood plain zoning is the key approach. Based on frequency of flooding, local governments can ban conflicting land uses from lowland areas because of the hazards affecting neighboring property, the public costs incurred with flooding, the environmental effects of earth moving, sewage disposal in gravelly soils or in wetlands, and habitat loss. Flood plain regulations have been supported by the courts for more than thirty years.

In 1960, seeing the wisdom of flood plain zoning, Congress created the Flood Plain Management Service to assist local governments in regulating their riverfronts. For years the program had negligible effect. In 1973 the National Water Commission reported that $56 billion had been spent through dam construction and other structural means to protect property from floods, yet the damage increased each year. After finding that flood losses rose higher than ever, even after forty years of increased spending for flood control, the Army Corps of Engineers in 1974 advocated flood plain management, writing, "Floods are 'acts of God.' But acts of man cause flood damage."

In spite of these arguments, and in spite of decades of labor by land use planners, who were led eminently by Ian McHarg of the University of Pennsylvania with his appeal for "design with nature," local governments scarcely regulated flood plains at all.

Facing deficit-fueling expenditures for disaster relief in the wake of floods, the federal government had finally, in 1968, instituted a flood insurance program that provided subsidized insurance to people already owning buildings on flood plains, but only if local governments controlled future development to limit additional damage. The response to this sensible carrot-and-stick program was nil. When the most damaging flood in American history up until that time occurred with Hurricane Agnes in 1972, only a few communities that were inundated from New York through Virginia had qualified for the insurance program.

With teeth this time, Congress substantially strengthened the effort by barring federal insurance of mortgages—required by every bank—from properties in communities not participating in the insurance program. A sensitive nerve had been struck; many governments rushed to comply with the needs of constituent bankers, realtors, developers, and homeowners.

The program could have been a model of combined regulatory and economic incentives for land use reform. Unfortunately, the Federal Emergency Management Agency (FEMA) was lobbied heavily by builders' associations and chambers of commerce and set guidelines that do not ban harmful development from 100-year flood plains, but only from flood "hazard" zones, allowing giant loopholes for "flood-proofing" in much of the riparian area. Development may proceed if it will not increase the level of a 100-year-frequency flood by more than one foot. While the most damage-prone building was stopped on the lowest land, development that was somewhat safer and more expensive proceeded on acreage still vulnerable to floods. Environmental damage was intensified when people simply dumped earthen fill onto the flood plain to raise floor levels above the high-water mark. On a case-by-case basis—as the regulations are administered—it is difficult to prove that one house will change the flood levels, though the cumulative effect of development and urbanization certainly does aggravate flooding. Further illustrating that an inadequate amount of land is zoned, 31 percent of the claims for damage are outside the 100-year flood zone altogether, according to an analysis by Jon Kusler and Larry Larson, who in 1993 represented associations of state wetlands and flood plain managers.

FEMA also granted dubious exemptions for flood plains behind levees, such as in Jackson Hole, Wyoming, and for flood control dams, no matter that these solutions have often proved unreliable. Breached levees at Wilkes-Barre, Pennsylvania, in 1972; Linda, California, in 1986; and the Mississippi River Valley in 1993 are just three examples of disastrous flooding where people had been lulled into a false sense of security. Rapid City, South Dakota, flooded in 1972 when a skyful of black clouds dropped its load between the city and Pactola Dam, which was thought to provide more than enough upstream flood control.

Even with adequate regulations, existing development on flood plains promises costly damage for generations to come. Floods accounted for $3 billion to $4 billion in annual losses nationwide in the 1980s. In spite of flood insurance restrictions, damage in 1992 was the worst to that date, and all previous records were eclipsed by the great flood of the Mississippi in 1993, when losses exceeded $10 billion.

Made flaccid by compromise and delay, the flood insurance program actually subsidizes bad decisions by insuring people who build on the flood plain and by paying people to rebuild in the same place after floods occur. Among 22,000 flood-prone municipalities nationwide, all but 4,000 had some kind of flood plain regulations in 1993, yet few of these truly protect flood-prone land from all development. The number of dwellings on flood-prone land has increased 40 percent since 1968, when the insurance program was started.

In the 1980s, $438 million was paid by the government for losses on 18,000 buildings that incurred damage of 50 percent or more of their total value. Unfortunately, the funds are used for rebuilding and not for relocating, even when damage is so great. The federal program has chronically run in the red, and even with very low premiums, only 15 percent of flood-prone homeowners insure themselves. In August 1993, with thousands of payments yet to be made for the great flood of the Mississippi, the program was essentially bankrupt with a $50 million deficit and no end in sight. On top of this heavily subsidized effort, disaster relief funds in huge amounts are still appropriated by Congress, including about $10 billion for the 1993 Mississippi flood that caused an estimated $20 billion in property damages.

The 1993 flood, with a reported crop loss of $6.5 billion, made apparent a clutch of paradoxes regarding federal policy for agriculture as well as for land development. In past years the government has paid for farmers to drain their fields and channelize wetlands, which aggravates flooding by speeding up runoff. The government pays the same farmers not to grow surplus crops on the "improved" land, and then it pays other farmers for flood damage when their property growing surplus crops is flooded. Though the farmers' losses generate a lot of sympathy, many of these tracts may more appropriately be regarded as "farmed flood land" than "flooded farmland." Some of this acreage never should have been cultivated in the first place.

Rather than help farmers pay to restore farmlands damaged by the 1993 flood, the federal government could buy the land, return it to wetland habitat, and encourage the farmers to cultivate elsewhere. This may be a very economical approach. According to the Soil Conservation Service, the cost of reclaiming one acre of land covered by one foot of sand is about $3,200. Sand deposits over much of the farmland on the Missouri River flood plain range from six inches to ten feet deep. Removal costs thus range from $1,600 to $32,000 per acre where preflood land values were only $600 to $1,100 per acre.

For all its shortcomings, the flood insurance program still helps to curtail rampant development along many riverfronts and produces at least minimal zoning where otherwise there would be none. In addition, the program incidentally offers the most widespread approach for saving riparian habitat.

Reform of federal policy could keep more development off flood plains and provide incentives for relocation rather than rebuilding after flood waters recede. To establish an effective federal flood insurance program, in fact, may be the most important public action needed to protect riparian land. Introducing a bill to reform flood insurance in 1993, Representative Joseph Kennedy of Massachusetts said that the existing program is "like a poorly built ship . . . riddled with leaks that threaten to sink it and soak the taxpayer." He added that the subsidized insurance "encourages people to build where the undeniable logic of nature says they shouldn't." Kennedy's bill, also sponsored by John Kerry of Massachusetts in the Senate, would prohibit flood insurance policies in swiftly eroding areas. The bill would phase out much of the development that is the most costly; buildings resulting in two or more insurance payments of more than $1,000 since 1978 represent only 2 percent of the program's policies but account for 47 percent of the dollars paid out of the fund. Opposing reform, and apparently oblivious to the billions of dollars in disaster relief that taxpayers spend, the spokeswoman for an organization called Defenders of Property Rights argued, "If it's a risk an individual is willing to assume, then let them take it."

Meanwhile, any municipality may exercise the option to regulate its flood plain with greater effectiveness than FEMA demands. Lycoming County, Pennsylvania, for example, requires that all development under its jurisdiction be set back fifty feet from waterways, a distance that is increased when slopes are steep. Unfortunately, Pennsylvania, like many other states, allows local land-use ordinances to supersede county ones. Most local officials are unwilling to exceed federal flood plain requirements, depending instead on the "hammer" of the federal agency as a scapegoat for action that is unpopular with local developers. Wisconsin and a few other states require flood plain management by local communities, and a few states, including Maine, mandate setbacks from waterways, adding greatly to the likelihood of open space protection in riparian zones.

Taking a different approach by targeting an individual river, New Hampshire in 1987 and Vermont in 1988 established commissions to protect the Connecticut River Valley landscape by properly guiding development. And in Minnesota, the state legislature created a consortium of eight counties, called the Mississippi Headwaters Board, with a mandate to protect riverfront values, including flood plains. Counties must meet minimum standards involving open space, with restrictions on tree cutting and sewage systems. Along "wild" stretches of the river, ordinances require 200-foot setbacks and 10-acre lots for subdivision or development. In other reaches, 150-foot setbacks and 5-acre lots apply. The upper Mississippi is the longest corridor in America protected by local governments, helping to sustain a vastness of riparian marshes and forests at the headwaters of our largest river.

?? The Imprint of the Cow

In 1980 the Department of Agriculture estimated that more than half of all western rangelands had deteriorated to less than 40 percent of potential productivity. At the leading edge of this national disgrace, riparian areas were hit the hardest. If that much value has been lost to cows, imagine the effects on native plant life and wild animals. These are the first to go when the range suffers, succumbing far sooner than cattle, which are cared for in winter, guarded from predators, fed hay, watered, vaccinated, and husbanded for market.

The data indicated that riparian habitat was in its worst condition in history. Federal policies and neglect from 1980 through 1992 made things worse. And a lot of land is at stake. Cows are permitted on 70 to 91 percent of all public property in the West (the estimates vary), which together constitutes 48 percent of the total land area in those eleven large states. Vegetation is chomped to the roots even along the riparian zones in Grand Teton, Capitol Reef, and Great Basin national parks in Wyoming, Utah, and Nevada. Much of the privately owned land in the West is also grazed.

Problems are not limited to the West and Midwest but also extend to the East, where cows have unrestrained access to rivers. Though the Pennsylvania Game Commission provided free fencing to farmers so that cows could be limited to necessary access to streams, few farmers took advantage of the offer.

In the well-watered East, the problems can be solved more easily because vegetation recovers more readily. Indeed, a cow in the East can live on half an acre. In the West, ranchers need a minimum of eight to ten acres per cow on productive private land, twenty-five acres on much of the public land, and much more land in the less productive areas. And in the West the effects of grazing are more lasting, owing to erosion and invasions by noxious plants. Riparian overgrazing ruins entire ecosystems in the West, and the opportunity to reform beckons because of public ownership of land.

On an acreage and mileage basis, overgrazing by cattle may exceed the impact of all land development on river frontage. But unlike the hundreds of billions of dollars worth of infrastructure in houses and highways already constructed on flood plains nationwide, much of the overgrazed range in the West is theoretically easy to fix. Doing so would infringe on relatively few people and impact an economy that is negligible to the nation overall. Protecting riparian areas, in fact, would improve that economy.

Overgrazing now strips native vegetation bare; aspens, willows, forbs, and bunchgrasses are replaced by sagebrush, thistles, and cheatgrass. Trampling by cattle and the eradication of deep-rooted, native grasses allows soil to be compacted, with less capability of retaining water. With their vegetative line of defense gone, streams are gutted into ravines that expand when flash floods chew away the once-willow-brushed flats and turn the land into a Gobi Desert of erosion. Where it had historically been contained like juice in an uncut orange, groundwater bleeds away through the sliced face of deepening ravines. Heavily grazed, Strawberry Creek in northwestern Colorado knifed gullies thirty feet deep, sucking ground-water from the surrounding landscape. In Montana, researchers found that soils along an ungrazed stream retained 772 percent more water than soils along a grazed reach.

Virtually hundreds of streams make case studies of abuse by cattle: Tonto Creek in Arizona, Bear Creek in Oregon, Big Creek in Utah, and so on. Large rivers assume even more of the burden: the San Juan in Utah, Smoky Hill in Kansas, the Missouri in Montana, Owyhee in Oregon, and Humboldt in Nevada.

If untended by cowboys—as nearly all cattle are—range cattle gravi-tate to riparian areas and stay there, denuding the greenery even when for-age is available in upland tracts. Until recent years, some livestock grazing manuals blithely referred to riparian habitat as "sacrifice areas."

The American Fisheries Society stated that overgrazing reduced sport fish numbers by 50 percent on an estimated 60 to 90 percent of 68,600 miles of streams in western national forests. Bureau of Land Management acreage is affected even more.

Under the rule of the cow, 10 percent of the American West has fallen into a state of desertification—our own human-made Sahara, larger than the thirteen original colonies. This land represents the worst of the over-grazing, and here, reversal from the devegetated, dried-out, wind-blown, erosive fate will be difficult if not impossible.

At Marsh Creek—the otherwise pristine headwaters of the Middle Fork of the Salmon River in Idaho—endangered salmon in teeming num-bers have spawned in the past. The stream looks pretty and the grass sprouts green, but 200 cows crowd in thick groups by the water in sum-mertime. They tramp and eat vegetation, causing banks to erode, spawn-ing beds to clog with silt, and the salmon to slip further toward extinction. Nearby, in marked constrast, Cape Horn Creek has seen no grazing for many years; its spawning habitat is excellent. Not blind to the difference, Forest Service range managers, after decades of neglect, called for a two-thirds cutback in grazing along Marsh Creek. Ranchers complained, and the Forest Service managers were overruled by desk-bound Bush admin-istration officials, who ordered that the plan be halted and that all copies of the revealing government report be held from public distribution, according to an exposé by *High Country News* writer Florence Williams. The Idaho Conservation League negotiated an agreement with the Forest Service and the ranchers in 1992 and then found that the ranchers and the government violated nearly every aspect of the agreement. The League then sued the agency; its public lands director, Michael Medberry, said, "Legal action is the only antidote for the high-handed political meddling that has kept the Forest Service from issuing a grazing plan which protects salmon habitat."

In *Moment in the Sun*, Robert and Leona Train Rienow wrote about the unexpected severity of grazing problems. "We have exchanged an eternal wonder for a beefsteak." And it's not many beefsteaks at that. The notion that the West feeds the nation its meat is a myth. All public land in the West accounts for 3 percent of America's beef—less than the annual fluctuation in the amount of beef Americans eat. For this, enormous subsidies are required. While grazers paid $1.86 in 1993 for one Animal Unit Month (the forage needed to graze a cow and calf for one month), the program cost the government $3.21 per AUM, and grazing fees on comparable private land cost more than $10 per AUM. According to the General Accounting Office in 1988, the BLM recovered only 37 percent of its costs for the program; the Forest Service recovered 30 percent. The government was losing $75 million a year by allowing public lands to be ruined by grazing.

The subsidy to all permittees averaged $40,000 each per year in the mid-1980s. A bill to gradually raise grazing fees on public land passed the House in 1990, 1991, and 1992, but western senators blocked each effort. A 1993 bill would have raised the fee to $5.25 per AUM, and Interior Secretary Bruce Babbitt planned to raise the fees on BLM land. Western senators again blocked reform, perhaps only temporarily. Meanwhile, soil science professor Harold Dregne at Texas Tech University estimated that the loss of the cows' own forage value beneath the hooves of overgrazing in the West was $200 million a year.

While sympathy endures for small operators in the West, the ranching industry has been isolated by scientific studies and an awakening to real-world economics. The General Accounting Office found that public land was being overgrazed (1988), effective land-management planning was not occurring (1990), grazing of too many cattle was common (1990), and cattle were favored over wildlife (1991). Incongruous with federal law, all this occurs while Congress mandated the BLM to provide "harmonious and coordinated management of the various resources of the public lands without permanent impairment of the productivity of the land and the quality of the environment." Explaining some of this discrepancy, BLM management in local areas is heavily influenced by advisory committees loaded with ranchers. While the cattle industry gets a lot of public relations mileage out of the image of the lone cowboy at work on the range, half the public grazing allotments are controlled by only 1,000 permittees—many of them large corporations. In all, only 35,000 ranchers graze on 270 million acres of public domain. Thus, the equivalent population of one small city the size of Missoula, Montana, accounts for a dominant use of 11 percent of the United States. On BLM acreage alone, 21,000 ranchers graze their cattle while 196 million people visited for recreation as early as 1978. The figures support what *High Country News* publisher Ed Marston wrote: "A rancher's political influence is roughly one hundred times greater than that of a non-rancher in the West."

Leaning on the image of the cowboy and on the rest of the nation's ignorance or apathy regarding subsidies and ruined water and habitat, the cattle industry, with western senators in heel, continued to block meaningful reform. Hope grew in 1993 that the Clinton administration would bring about change. The new BLM director, Jim Baca, came to the job with an impressive record of government reform in New Mexico. In a July 1993 *Sierra* magazine article he said that he wanted the agency "to move away from the consumptive era. . . . We're just borrowing this land from our kids. We shouldn't be rushing to cut the last tree and graze the last blade of grass." Baca, however, was out of office the next year.

The greatest irony is that change need not be so painful. Solutions do not require the removal of all cattle—slight as that effect might be on the cost of hamburger. Under contract for the U.S. Environmental Protection Agency, Ed Chaney, Wayne Elmore, and William S. Platts outlined solutions in *Livestock Grazing on Western Riparian Areas*. Reviewing case studies throughout the West, these highly qualified authors illustrated the success of the rest-rotation approach, whereby cattle were moved into and out of riparian areas rather than just into them. Cottonwoods, previously eaten or trampled at the seedling stage, increased from 20 per 100 acres to 2,000 per 100 acres. The cattle simply needed to be channeled by fences to adequate water sources but excluded from the rest of streams. With noneroding banks, the previously degraded Mahogany Creek in Nevada saw summer flows increase by 400 percent and water depth increase by 50 percent. Management of cattle along West Rocky Creek in Texas resulted in a stream flow rising from zero under degraded conditions to 4,000 gallons per minute. Fencing at Huff Creek, Wyoming, led to an 80 percent reduction in streambank erosion, a doubling of riparian area, a narrowing of the creek channel, and a 1,100 percent increase in Bonneville cutthroat trout. With better range in all these areas, more calves survived, and they gained weight faster. The streams improved and the ranching improved.

Reductions in cattle numbers were not always required, but even with decreases, riparian rebirth was not assured until somebody fenced all cattle from critical streamfronts. Ranchers vehemently oppose fencing requirements, such as those introduced in a bill in the Kansas legislature in 1992. The fences can cost up to $4,000 a mile. Alternatively, cowboys can do the job; where employed, they can move cattle through riparian areas quickly. This may make good sense in public land areas, while fencing along major bottomlands and where cattle spend winters will still be needed.

Impressive restoration projects are carried out by government agencies in pilot projects, by ranchers seeking to mend their own lands, and by consortiums, such as the Northwest Colorado Riparian Task Force, composed of grazing, government, and wildlife organizations. The Toiyabe National Forest, with an unexpected 1,200 miles of streams in the most arid state of Nevada, set a goal of restoring 95 percent of its degraded range to "satisfactory" condition—a big step, though "satisfactory" might be considered a modest expectation for land belonging to the American public. New standards limited grazing to a harvest of 45 percent of the vegetation in riparian areas. That represents a lot of grass but significantly reduces the routine of cows eating everything. Forest Service officials weathered a storm of protest from entrenched ranchers complaining that the federal government had no right to regulate federal land. In the early 1990s, aiming to retain control of the public property, ranchers launched a new "sagebrush rebellion," including county ordinances intended to ban federal managers from making reforms. The ordinances were widely believed to be unconstitutional, but nonetheless served to intimidate federal officials who had to live in the same communities.

Success can be found in southern Idaho, where restoration consultant Bruce Lium restored native vegetation to large tracts of overgrazed land near Silver Creek, planting 18,000 willows and shrubs on one 500-acre tract after cattle were totally removed following a new owner's purchase of the ranch. Lium said, "It has been truly remarkable to observe how quickly mismanaged land will respond when given a chance." Acquisition of overgrazed land by The Nature Conservancy has resulted in improved habitat along the Snake River in southeastern Idaho and the South Fork of the Kern in California.

Along the Yampa River in Colorado, a Nature Conservancy program strives for teamwork with ranchers, aiming for better management through voluntary agreements and only occasionally through easements or acquisition. "We could never buy enough land to protect the cottonwood corridor," explained project manager Jamie Williams in Steamboat Springs. "Instead, we're working with ranchers to accomplish habitat goals within the economic and traditional dictates of this valley. We may be able to buy a few of the most important tracts but will seek ranchers' initiative for management of other riparian land. A number of the larger ranch owners are receptive to this approach."

Aware of the significance of the riparian landscape, of the effects posed by grazing, and of the potential for his program on that cottonwood-lined riverway, Williams added, "The Yampa provides us with a real opportunity to establish a model of cooperation between ranching and conservation, a collaboration that seems so basic at its heart, yet grand enough to have implications reaching far beyond the river basin itself."

⮚ Beyond Regulation

Though land acquired for preservation will never amount to much as a percentage of the American riverfront, public acquisition of riparian acreage is the most complete means of protection. A number of our finest riverscapes have been safeguarded this way, and many more can be saved.

Sizable blocks of land may be needed for state or national parks, but riverfronts come in thin strips where modest acreage can go a long way. A whole mile of frontage 100 feet deep totals only twelve acres. Yet even with streams in the National Wild and Scenic Rivers System, few parcels are bought by government agencies.

More common in the 1990s are innovative programs of private land trusts. Early efforts such as those of the Western Pennsylvania Conservancy, which bought exquisite frontage along the Youghiogheny River and Slippery Rock Creek in the early 1960s, increased dramatically. Eastern Pennsylvanians incorporated the Brandywine Conservancy in 1967 as a forerunner of many river-based associations. At first motivated to stop an industrial park in Chadds Ford—a landscape made famous in the paintings of Andrew Wyeth and deep in the heritage of the American arts—the Brandywine group expanded its efforts to secure easements and donations covering several thousand acres, halting the suburban gridiron in riparian valleys between Philadelphia and Wilmington. In a neighboring watershed, residents organized the Schuylkill River Greenway Association in 1983, launching a program to protect and restore a river heavily degraded by coal mining, suburban development, and inner-city encroachments, including the Schuylkill River Expressway with its rush-hour traffic bound for the heart of Philadelphia.

With a heritage of concern for public spaces, New England became a beehive of land trust activity. The Nashua River Watershed Association protected 6,000 acres in Massachusetts through acquisition and other means. Nonprofit conservancies seek greenway protection through a combination of acquisition, easements, and flood plain regulations for parts of the 130-mile-long Housatonic River in Connecticut and for the Hudson River in its 150-mile reach of tidal water from Manhattan to Albany.

Even the Blackstone River in Massachusetts and Rhode Island, earlier blocked by one dam per mile and garishly dyed with toxins, is recovering. A bi-state park, dedicated in 1992, commemorated success in establishing a greenway of public land along the river. A greenway is likewise proposed by the Cahaba River Society for that stream in Alabama—one of the more ecologically diverse and valuable southern waterways. The Passaic River Coalition in New Jersey advocated flood plain acquisition as an alternative to a proposed flood control diversion that would cost $1.2 billion to construct and $2.1 million a year to maintain. The coalition's message was "use the money to buy the land," thereby solving problems more completely. The Army Corps of Engineers had already enacted a successful program of open space protection rather than floodway channelization along the Charles River in Massachusetts. Wetlands along the eighty-mile-long river held 50,000 acre-feet of flood runoff—the volume of the average flood control reservoir in New England. The Corps found it cost-effective to protect the wetlands rather than damming or channelizing the river. The Corps likewise established a greenbelt rather than concrete channels along Indian Wash in Scottsdale, Arizona.

Along with many other riparian projects nationwide, The Nature Conservancy in 1987 set up a Connecticut River Protection Project to save 7,000 acres along New England's largest river and especially at the rich tidal wetlands near its mouth. Dennis Wolkoff of the Conservancy called the Connecticut "the ecological thread that ties New England together."

In Oregon in the late 1960s, Governor Tom McCall led passage of a law to establish a Willamette greenway for 255 miles. Before the program stalled out in the 1980s, the state had bought 12,000 acres of shoreline along 70 miles of Oregon's heartland river where pollution had been curbed and salmon populations restored. Elsewhere in the West, $7 million was spent by public agencies on a greenway along the South Platte in Denver, and conservancies have bought or obtained donated easements to protect river frontage along the Niobrara in Nebraska, the South Fork of the San Miguel in Colorado, the McCloud in California, and Icicle Creek in Washington. The Conservation Fund, a national organization headquartered in Arlington, Virginia, has acquired important riverfronts along the North Branch of the Potomac in West Virginia and Maryland, the Hudson and Salmon rivers in New York, the Deschutes in Oregon, and in other areas of the country. Dozens of other associations, from the Yakima River Greenway Foundation in Washington to the Saco River Corridor Commission in Maine, labor to establish public open space by dealing constructively with landowners and local governments.

In an age of limited government involvement and shrinking horizons of public agencies, more attention falls on what Glenn Eugster called "cooperative regional approaches"—a complex mix of private and public solutions that can be centered around riparian habitat. Eugster pioneered innovative programs at the National Park Service's Philadelphia office by providing technical assistance to local government and river groups, and in the 1990s sought to do the same for wetlands through his job with the Environmental Protection Agency. Based on widespread support, the cooperative brand of conservation emphasizes that riverway protection does not threaten existing landowners and economic enterprises but enhances them by championing the fundamental ingredient of wealth—a healthy environment.

After serving as director of American Rivers in the mid-1980s and becoming one of the foremost professionals in the field, Christopher Brown now leads the National Park Service's Technical Assistance Program for River Conservation. Embracing the cooperative approach and having nothing to do with national parks or any ambitions of setting up new ones, experienced staff help state and local groups and governments to craft conservation plans that suit their needs and political possibilities along scores of rivers nationwide.

⊷ A Reactionary Response

While efforts to safeguard riparian habitat always faced opposition from people who profit by riverfront development and also by people fearing change and distrusting the government, opponents of protection organized themselves in the 1980s and 1990s as if mobilized for war. With names such as Alliance for America, People for the West, National Wetlands Coalition, and Multiple Use Land Alliance, the opponents of river and land protection launched on attack, frequently bankrolled by private and corporate interests in mining, logging, grazing, and real estate. This self-proclaimed "Wise Use Movement" was called the "resource abuse movement" by others. Claims founded on distrust of government proved difficult for conservationists to counteract. Strategies underpinned by fear became impossible to overcome in some of the rural forums where new dramas over the fate of the American landscape were acted out. Fighting a wild and scenic river proposal, the spokesman for a landowners' group along the West Branch of the Farmington River in Massachusetts referred to an Army Corps of Engineers reservoir that had displaced nearby residents many years before and said, "Anything that smacks of that sort of control, I'm against." He had overlooked the fact that the wild and scenic river program was set up to ban new dams, not build them, and to sustain the status quo, not change it.

With mailings titled "Your land has been stolen!!" a Farmington group calling itself "Friends of the Rivers" led people to believe that their land would be condemned with wild and scenic river designation, though the proposal called for no acquisition of any kind and expressly banned condemnation or eminent domain. No federal involvement in management was proposed, but landowners resisting 100-foot streamside setbacks for new construction convinced their neighbors that a national park "takeover" was under way. As reported in the *Litchfield County Times* on February 28, 1992, a "Friends of the River" leader referred to other national wild and scenic rivers and proclaimed with remarkable imagination, "Whole towns have disappeared." Under the program, towns have not been threatened, but rather safeguarded from destructive dams and hydroelectric projects. Homes and farms have likewise been safeguarded.

Nonetheless, the rhetoric of fear found fertile soil among a segment of the rural populace in Massachusetts that had shunned three years' worth of local public meetings on the subject but now came out angrily to vote after receiving the mailings of "Friends of the River." The townspeople in all three of the communities bordering the river in Massachusetts voted against designation, reversing the votes of support that they had passed only eight months earlier. Phil Huffman, the National Park Service planner who had patiently and skillfully aided the municipalities in developing local protection plans for the Farmington, responded, "Through their fear of change, they lost the best chance they had to keep things the way they are." Resisting the paranoid approach, towns along a lower reach of the Farmington in Connecticut held firm in support.

Encountering "wise use" antagonists in the state of Washington, lawyer and conservationist Douglass North advised river protectors to inform people before alarm and lies are spread about what will happen if riverfronts are saved, and to disassociate themselves from government by reiterating that protection programs limit what bureaucrats at the Army Corps of Engineers, Federal Energy Regulatory Commission, and other agencies can do to damage the river. Regarding the "takings" issue whereby governments at all levels are challenged on their legal authority to regulate land use or pollution, North advised people to clearly identify public values that are threatened by unfettered motives of private profit.

Chuck Hoffman, a consultant to local governments, private groups, and river management agencies, has been dragged through more than one riverfront war and emerged with both landowners' confidence and protected streams. In his populist style, he advises conservationists to take landowners' concerns seriously with strong information programs and effective public involvement every step of the way.

❧ Restoration

Across much of the continent, the opportunity for saving unspoiled land has gone the way of coal-stripped mountainsides in West Virginia and housing tracts in Arizona, but unaccepting of the loss, people have launched efforts to restore damaged places, lending a helping hand to reinvigorate the works of nature. Riparian habitat enjoys benefits from this movement, with big possibilities on the Kissimmee River in Florida.

In the 1960s the Army Corps of Engineers straightened this penultimate nourisher of wetlands, ninety-eight miles long, into a ditch of fifty-two miles to better serve ranchers and housing developers. Everglades National Park began to dry up, Kissimmee waterfowl declined by 90 percent, bald eagles declined by 74 percent, and three out of every four fish disappeared. Lake Okeechobee—the second-largest freshwater body wholly within the United States—was markedly affected by the manipulation of its Kissimmee source, renamed ditch "C-38."

In the 1980s public outrage at these losses led to the nation's most ambitious blueprint to restore a channelized river. This time, the Corps would recreate a stream, undoing with costs of compounded interest the damages it had caused twenty years before. The dug-out channel would be backfilled, meanders reinstated to forty miles of the Kissimmee, and 30,000 acres of flood plain and wetlands recreated. As of 1993, plans had been drawn up but the work had not begun. To reclaim half the original river, agencies proposed a $280 million appropriation.

Like the gentrification of some urban neighborhoods, restoration in many regions gained momentum where the time and place were right. At Grays Run, Pennsylvania, Trout Unlimited members and Boy Scouts stabilized damaged banks. At New Mexico's Blue Water River, volunteers replanted riparian species on the flood plain. At Lagunitas Creek north of San Francisco, hundreds of people converged for a weekend of stream restoration labor, building check dams in eroding gullies. The Nooksack Salmon Enhancement Association in Washington fenced cattle from streams and placed gravel, logs, and root wads to recreate fish habitat.

David Rosgen—a protégé of the great hydrologist Luna Leopold—carried out a remarkable reinstatement of the Blanco River in Colorado. As a result of abuse, the stream had fanned out over a 400-foot width of barren gravel bars. Rosgen transformed the Blanco back into a deep channel of pools and riffles. His hydrologic formulas replicated nature's way, and now the stream continues the healing process in its riparian landscape.

In California, some 300 projects were under way at riparian areas of urban streams. In 1986 the state unfurled an Urban Streams Restoration Program that achieved great success by 1993, with $1.4 million made available to cities, counties, and community groups for streambank stabilization and natural flood control projects. In the San Francisco Bay Area twenty years previously, people had bodily blocked chainsaws from clearing riparian forests along Tamalpais Creek but ultimately failed to halt a channelization project. In contrast, citizens in the early 1990s not only stopped plans to bury Wildcat Creek in nearby Richmond but launched a program of benign channel improvements instead, such as removing troublesome obstructions while still leaving a natural channel. The approach is typical of many sought by the Coalition to Restore Urban Waters, headquartered in Portland, Oregon, and promoting better use of city streams nationwide.

In the 1970s George Palmiter, without formal training, devised means of using fallen logs and resident rocks to redirect the flow of small streams that had eroded banks and been troublesome to riparian landowners. This Ohioan with a native sense for the force of flowing water capitalized on the principle of letting the stream do the work of maintaining adequate flows. With efforts carried on by his son, his techniques—known as the "Palmiter method"—are used as an alternative to channelization on hundreds of miles of midwestern streams and require one-tenth to one-third the cost of conventional channelization.

Perhaps the most challenging riparian restoration project fell on the shoulders of Lewis MacAdams. In 1991 he advocated restoring the fifty-mile-long Los Angeles River from a concrete trough so wide, so flat, and so paved that city bus drivers practiced parking there. This ultimate extension of the American riparian nightmare shows only two miles of banks that support life. MacAdams determinedly noted, "It took 40 or 50 years to mess up the river, so it will probably take that long to fix it."

Taking a sweeping view of riparian restoration in 1991, the National Research Council reported that "because a river and its floodplains are intimately linked, they should be managed and restored as integral parts of an ecosystem." The Council recommended at least fifty large rivers for lengths of 120 miles or greater to be designated as "reference reaches" for protection in all regions of the country. The Council also recommended a stream restoration target of 400,000 miles within twenty years—about 11 percent of the nation's total stream mileage.

Part of a larger movement for environmental restoration across the nation, riparian habitat restoration is already the object of dozens of efforts to remove cattle, debris, and development; to reinstate vital floods and natural flows; and to replant the riverfront kingdom with native grasses, sedges, willows, cottonwoods, and sycamores. Directing a model program that successfully doctored dozens of abused landscapes in the redwood country of northern California, Nancy Reichard noted, "We now see more interest in restoration than in preservation of unspoiled places. People would rather go out and plant trees than get involved politically."

Appealing to both the nurturing and the fix-it mind-set, restoration efforts avoid irksome showdowns with hostile forces. While arguments can be made that a full-force battle must be waged to save the remaining streams that are not yet spoiled, riparian restoration can also go far toward reanimating the lost qualities of rivers.

⮞ A Riparian Initiative

Much as Jamie Williams seeks protection and restoration of the cottonwood corridor along the Yampa River in Colorado, David Pashley seeks a new brand of preservation in the humid forests of the lower Mississippi. Bottomland hardwoods once extended from the confluence with the Ohio River to the Gulf of Mexico in an emerald swath 600 miles long greening two-thirds of Arkansas and Louisiana. Only patchworks of old trees now survive in one of the more economically impoverished valleys of the nation.

Before tropical rain forests made the news, the hardwood forests of the Mississippi were being cleared and burned to grow soybeans in the 1970s. Lower crop prices stalled farmland expansion in the 1980s, providing the opportunity to save or restore some of this heartland ecosystem. Pashley's Nature Conservancy program seeks to preserve forest cores and to establish buffers from civilization, but also to address economic recovery of a sustainable type. The group seeks a regional management plan to connect protected lands with greenway linkages. The riparian protection efforts along the Mississippi and the Yampa are just two examples among many that are capturing people's imagination.

Through the combined nationwide efforts to stop destruction of the remaining riverfront legacy and to restore at least enclaves that have been lost, riparian protection can go far toward creating a better future for the rivers of America. Much as the term *wetlands*, coined in the 1950s, led to a widely recognized movement that may mature in the 1990s, a riparian initiative is needed to fully recognize the value of our riverfronts.

This idea might be brought into perspective with a historical view of conservation, which shows successive movements to protect various types of landscapes in the nation. Though all of these efforts continue unfinished, their inception offers a chronology of awakening opinion to the value of nature. In the late 1800s and early 1900s, national forests were set aside for watershed protection and sustained timber yields. In the same era, some of our scenic treasures were safeguarded with the creation of national parks. Then wildlife refuges were designated as the needs of migratory birds and popular wildlife species came to light. Later, wilderness was preserved, initially with an emphasis on the high country of the West. In the 1970s, reaches of undeveloped coastline were safeguarded as national seashores and in a few state coastal zoning programs. During the same decade, "parks for people" became a goal, achieving varied success near urban centers. In the 1980s and 1990s, movements gained force for retaining old-growth forests, wetlands, and a few of our finest deserts.

Now, there is growing recognition that riverfronts constitute a vital part of critical hydrologic systems, that wildlife and plant life need these areas, and that the water's edge shines as a recreational and community centerpiece. Perhaps a riparian initiative will be the next great movement on behalf of the landscape of America.

Chapter Eight

The Heart of the Ecosystem

❧ One Organism

Earlier chapters address the issues of dams, water pollution, stream flows, diversions, and riparian habitat, but the larger ecosystem also determines the health of a river. Likewise, the qualities of a river provide the foundation for the well-being of the greater ecosystem—the community formed by the interaction of all plants and animals within their environment—a complex, flourishing tapestry of life that in many ways functions as one organism, so dependent are its members on one another.

From the wanderings of the moose to those of the invisible protozoan, the fitness of rivers depends on the intricate matrices of all life, seen in every stream but dramatically evident in an unspoiled watershed of the north.

❧ An Ecosystem of Primeval Splendor

Flowing through three of the wildest political subdivisions on earth—the Yukon Territory, British Columbia, and Alaska—the Alsek and Tatshenshini rivers bisect the St. Elias Mountains, traverse the largest parklands complex in the world, and form a riverscape of primeval splendor.

Mount Fairweather, visible from the Alsek, rises 15,300 feet from its starting point at the ocean—the greatest vertical relief veering from any coastline on earth. The glaciers feeding these rivers constitute the largest nonpolar ice fields in the world. The basin houses one of the densest concentrations of brown (grizzly) bears, which depend on salmon, still ascending the Tatshenshini in age-old abundance as they once did the Columbia. Besides being the bears' storehouse of food, the river valley provides a corridor vital for wildlife travel and genetic exchange. Visitors here can see bald eagles, wolves, and the rare glacier bear—a silver-blue variety of *Ursus americanus*. A whole cast of other species populates this northern Eden spanning six biogeographic zones.

Accessible by road at a remote gold rush site in the Yukon called Dalton Post, the Tatshenshini flows into British Columbia and through a forested landscape of increasingly grand scale. As tributaries pour in, mountains climb higher to snowfields and craggy summits. Recently glaciated flanks now blanketed with wildflowers lead hikers up to the perches of Dall sheep—a snow-white variety of bighorn. With exciting whitewater and a breadth of view growing ever wider, ever higher, ever overpowering, the Tatshenshini converges with the massive flows of the Alsek River just above the Canadian-U.S. boundary.

The Alsek River also begins in Yukon Territory, flows from Kluane National Park and then through the northwest corner of British Columbia, and finally into Alaska, transporting glacial meltwater through a raw-boned wilderness of ice age wonder. At the appropriately named Turnback Canyon, the Tweedsmuir Glacier pushes against the fat, churning river, squeezing it into a constricted maelstrom between ice field and canyon wall. After the Tatshenshini joins at a spacious confluence backed by Teton-like peaks, the Alsek tears on down through the heart of the St. Elias Range. At one place, the river sprawls two miles in width, with breaking waves scattered throughout as in a rough day at sea. Glaciers abutting the river disgorge house-size icebergs into the water, and then the current lofts them away, floating their broken remains past a coastal rain forest, which from a distant view resembles the vine-clad, tropical mountains of Kauai in the Hawaiian Islands. The Alsek then completes its route to sea on the western side of Glacier Bay National Park and Preserve, the quintessential ice-bound landscape with an untouched wilderness of coastal mountains, glaciers, and estuaries. In all the world, there is no other place like the Alsek River Basin.

The first modern-day descent of the Tatshenshini and Alsek was likely made by Richard Norgaard and three other people in 1972, but few followed until the late 1980s, when the rivers became known as two of the most spectacular anywhere. Global river explorer Richard Bangs called the Alsek "probably the most visually spectacular river in the world." No other runnable river travels so far through such ice-bound country; twenty-four glaciers can be seen from one spot. To float the lower Alsek is to enter a time machine and float a river of the ice age, complete with everything but mammoths and mastodons.

Rising 6,000 feet above the confluence of the rivers, roughly two-thirds of the way through the 160-mile wilderness river reach from Dalton Post to the Gulf of Alaska, Windy Craggy Mountain stands as a landmark. Encircled by this park complex of two nations but in a donut hole of un-protected land belonging to the province of British Columbia, the moun-tain was proposed as the site for an open-pit copper mine by Geddes Re-sources in the mid-1980s. The corporation would level much of the mountain and crush it to extract its ore, which would be shipped to Japan.

Geddes would mill the sulfide-bearing rock on the site, exposing it to air and an abundant seventy-five inches of precipitation a year, resulting in acid mine drainage fifteen miles upstream from Glacier Bay National Park. Waste materials would accumulate in hazardous tailings, most to be dumped onto a glacier. The most toxic 224 million tons would be dumped into the bottom of a mountainside reservoir, impounded by an earth-fill dam 360 feet high, located squarely in the most seismically active zone of North America. The continent's largest earthquake occurred here in 1899, throwing mountains up forty-seven feet. The dam's failure to contain the wastewater, virtually assured in the long term, could result in acid drain-age to the entire lower Alsek River, where even minute quantities of heavy metals and acid are toxic to salmon and other life.

The mine would employ 600 people for its life of twenty years. The Geddes plan assumed that an acid-drainage catastrophe could be averted at least until the company abandoned the site, though tailings would re-main hazardous for thousands of years, if not geologic time.

Conservationist Ric Careless of Tatshenshini International led the fight against the mine in British Columbia: "This river has cast a spell that has invoked a deep sense of caring and commitment in people I've talked to all over the continent. And it's no wonder. It's North America's greatest wilderness, threatened by one of North America's biggest mines."

Geddes president Gerald Harper took a somewhat different view: "The Tatshenshini isn't pristine wilderness, it's barren ground." Encouraging approval for the mine, he argued in these terms: "We can't enjoy this planet unless we have the cash to do it with."

Beyond the scenario of milling Windy Craggy Mountain to its root and rendering this river system to an acid-drained sewer of mine waste, there are problems with the proposal. A 700-foot-long bridge would cross the Tatshenshini at the O'Connor River. Then twelve miles of road would be blasted and bulldozed along the Tatshenshini to the center of this great wilderness, to become a mine-truck thoroughfare with one load of ore rolling out every ten minutes, night and day. Roads being roads, traffic would include hunters, off-road-vehicle drivers, and everything that can be packed into a pickup truck.

The ore would be trucked across the mountains and down along the Chilkat River, a narrow corridor that constitutes the Chilkat Bald Eagle Preserve, where 3,500 of the big birds feast on chum salmon in the largest eagle congregation on earth. If anyplace can claim to be the valley of America's national emblem, this is it. The road would be widened to accommodate the ore trucks. Admittedly, there would be problems with trucking, and to avoid them, Geddes proposed as an alternative a slurry pipeline to cross 200 salmon spawning streams and dump 360,000 gallons of wastewater per day into the heart of the southeastern Alaskan fishing grounds, among the finest in America. Under either plan, the small Alaskan town of Haines, dependent on a $41 million annual commerical fishery and on tourism, would become an industrial port for oversized ore ships after the harbor is dredged and enlarged.

As for Geddes' side of the argument, the corporation claimed that $8 billion worth of copper can be extracted, though copper is not a scarce commodity in the world market.

The fight to save the Tatshenshini and Alsek became the leading environmental battle in western Canada and perhaps the finest example of a conservation effort cooperatively waged by river and parklands supporters in these two countries that share the most spectacular wild riverscapes on earth.

Before he was elected vice-president, Senator Al Gore introduced legislation to proclaim the area a World Heritage Site and to request review by the International Joint Commission, which mediates disputes between the countries. Glacier Bay National Park superintendent Marvin Jensen—with a career full of river experience—supported protection, but James Ridenour, Director of the National Park Service in the Bush administration, opposed Gore's measure with an opinion that overrode all other concerns: Congress should not dictate international agreements to a Republican administration. The United Nations enacted the World Heritage designation for Glacier Bay National Park anyway, the designation specifying that nations are not to take any deliberate measures that might damage directly or indirectly the cultural and natural heritage of the designated site.

Tatshenshini International pushed harder for national park status on the British Columbia lands. Peter Enticknap of Haines led the Alaskan fight to safeguard the entire Alsek watershed; Tom Cassidy of American Rivers accomplished what needed doing in Washington, D.C.; and Ethan Askey, John Mikes, and many other British Columbians continued to press for decisive action in their province.

In 1991, provincial voters ousted an administration dominated by the resources extraction industries. With the New Democratic Party taking charge, hope grew for the survival of this wild place. Support from Vice-president Al Gore pushed the issue into the international spotlight, and in 1993 the province approved a 2.5-million-acre Tatshenshini-Alsek Wilderness Park, to be joined with other protected lands for a 21-million-acre international preserve—the largest in the world. The Alsek became the first major watershed in North America to be protected from its headwaters to the sea. British Columbia Premier Michael Harcourt acknowledged that the mine would be incompatible with the new designation. "This is one of the most spectacular wilderness areas in the world, and today B.C. is living up to its global responsibility to keep it that way," Harcourt said. The preservation of these rivers and their watersheds marked one of the great conservation victories of all time; Tom Cassidy commented, "This ranks with stopping dams in the Grand Canyon."

Vice-president Gore and Premier Harcourt joined in a historic handshake regarding the Alsek and Tatshenshini in November 1993 at a conference sponsored by American Rivers. Honoring the two statesmen, the concluding banquet was attended by 1,100 people celebrating the twenty-fifth anniversary of the National Wild and Scenic Rivers System and also the Alsek-Tatshenshini victory. Referring to this and other environmental initiatives of his administration, Premier Harcourt said, "Someday our dream will be the dream of everyone, where rivers run free and we never hear the phrase *endangered species*. Quite simply, we owe it to our children to leave this planet a better place."

Significant in this story of river protection, the Alsek-Tatshenshini was probably the most publicized fight to save a river from threats to its surrounding landscape. Over the years, many mine proposals have been battled by conservationists, for example, at streams threatened by coal stripping in the Appalachians, at the White Cloud Mountains of Idaho in the late 1960s, and at Crested Butte in Colorado in the 1970s. But few of those fights were conducted explicitly to save a river.

Here at the Alsek and Tatshenshini, the waterway is seen as the highlight, the living entity representing the entire landscape. The salmon—so dependent on the water—are recognized as the building block of a vast community of life. Traveling by river, in fact, is the finest way to see the area. The Alsek-Tatshenshini case is perhaps the best illustration of the importance of surrounding landscapes to rivers, and also of the vital role that rivers play within their greater ecosystems.

ᴥ Beyond the Waterfront

As the heart of ecosystems, rivers are not just important in the remaining wilds of the north, but everywhere. Working for the River Network, Peter Lavigne wrote of streams a continent away from the Alsek: "The rivers of New England are the ecological infrastructure of the region . . . the veins and arteries of the watershed body."

Unfortunately, much of the nation has been parceled out and now requires complex restructuring to even imagine what originally existed. Of 232 types of ecosystems in America, few have been protected even as token samples, and even fewer contain significant rivers protected within them.

Rather than integrating the concerns of watersheds, we have historically separated them, because in breaking the wholeness of the world into parts, we can effectively isolate and commodify those parts. When we see a mountain as only a disconnected hillside bearing copper above the Alsek, coal along the Cumberland River in Kentucky, or gold at the Feather River in the Sierra Nevada, the mountain appears less consequential. Even our more progressive environmental measures often fail to relate an understanding of the entire system of life.

There have been attempts. In the 1950s and 1960s, conservationists and farmers formed "watershed associations" that the federal Soil Conservation Service promoted to deal with the larger picture of stream basins. The associations preached the gospel of the land-and-water interface—what is done up above affects the stream down below. Their efforts, however, usually stopped at voluntary measures for soil erosion control and local improvements and failed to halt the larger wave of destruction across the country.

In the 1950s, thinking more of efficiency than ecosystems, the President's Water Resources Policy Commission recommended a shift in federal emphasis from the study of individual water courses to whole river basins, and in 1965 the Water Resources Policy Act authorized the formation of river basin planning commissions with state and federal participation. Water development was still the main focus. However, from the Sacramento to the Susquehanna, the new efforts failed to justify big new projects, which had been the lingering hope of political supporters who felt they only needed to jump through the hoops of basinwide planning in order to sustain the status quo in development. But neither did the commissions make the leap for effective protection of biological assets of rivers and ecosystems, which were being lost so rapidly with so little apparent concern for the consequences. Failing to deliver old-style development, raising the disturbing specter of concern for larger life systems, and lacking a reliable power base, many of the river basin commissions were disbanded in cost-cutting measures.

The late 1960s saw new and genuine interest in the broader spectrum of environmental issues, maturing in 1970 with the National Environmental Policy Act, which required that environmental effects of federal projects be evaluated. In 1973 the federal Water Resources Council expanded responsibilities in water project planning, though still failing to identify ecosystems as a central concern.

A movement toward whole systems had been growing, but a 1980s interlude, beginning with the Reagan administration's total disbanding of the Water Resources Council, saw stern resistance to federal measures for protection. This occurred even while some of the old concepts of watershed associations were being bolstered with naturalist philosophy and recycled as "bioregionalism," and as the concern for ecosystems grew among biologists, resource agency personnel, and the public.

❧ Struggling to Sustain Diversity

In spite of the Endangered Species Act of 1973, government administrators and the public only gradually became aware of a crisis of extinction, and even more gradually realized the importance of ecosystems to the survival of whole threatened communities of life. For years, endangered species were considered something of a bird watchers' topic, a back-seat environmental issue when air and water pollution occupied the headlines.

Breaking through the news barrier in the late 1970s, the snail darter—a three-inch-long perch—was thought to live only in one reach of the Little Tennessee River, and for a while became the most publicized fish in America. Lawsuits to spare this endangered species sought to halt Tellico Dam, an admittedly indefensible project even to its sponsor, the Tennessee Valley Authority. In spite of ample evidence of the dam's absurdly high cost relative to benefits, and ignoring a decisive administrative halt to the dam, Congress ultimately approved it in a travesty of legislative proceedings. During a late-night subterfuge, an amendment that was neither read, debated, nor seen by any but a few congressional members called for completion of the dam "notwithstanding the Endangered Species Act or any other law." The TVA obediently flooded the Little Tennessee. (The fish, fortunately, was later found in several other streams.)

The snail darter controversy was followed no less painfully by that of the northern spotted owl of Oregon and Washington and the sockeye salmon in the Snake River, and in the process, the public began to realize what biologists had known for a long time. Without protection of habitat and ecosystems, one species after another succumbs to threatened, endangered, and eradicated status in spite of expensive efforts to salvage individuals from the abyss of extinction. As House Interior Committee Chair George Miller said in 1993, "The case in the Northwest is not about the owl. It's about the absolute existence of the forests of the Pacific Northwest."

Nowhere are the problems of biological diversity more severe than in rivers and streams. More than 700 species of fish live in North American fresh waters, a relatively unnoticed cornerstone of the earth's community of creatures. In a natural stream, an abundance of diverse life accompanies these fish. For example, one waterway of three-foot width was found to host 1,044 invertebrate species. That study happened to be made in Germany, but could as well have been in many regions of North America. Biologists identified 388 algal species in just one stream in Ontario. The cast of freshwater creatures has been a rich one, but its future is precarious.

An alarming biological survey by The Nature Conservancy found that about one-third of all freshwater fish species in the United States are threatened or endangered. Dr. Larry Master, The Nature Conservancy's chief zoologist, found 103 species to be endangered, 114 threatened, and 147 deserving special concern. Other biologists reported for the American Fisheries Society that 214 separate runs of Pacific salmon, steelhead, and cutthroat trout stocks are threatened, 101 of them near extinction. Biologist James Karr of the University of Washington reported that populations of 40 to 70 percent of all fish species have experienced major declines in the last century. Since 1900, 40 species of American fish have gone extinct, 19 of them since 1964 and 10 of them in the 1980s.

Two-thirds of all crayfish species are rare. Most waterfowl populations are losing numbers perilously. Ducks on the Pacific Flyway declined by 20 percent between 1984 and 1985 alone, while Central Flyway ducks declined by 30 percent. Other birds are likewise affected. For example, piping plovers and interior least terns, added to the federal threatened and endangered species list in 1985, depend heavily on sandbars and islands of the upper Missouri River, where habitat loss and selenium poisoning from irrigation systems threaten the sparse remaining populations. In California—an exceptionally rich state for diversity of species owing to variations of geography and climate—a Nature Conservancy study found 40 percent of the aquatic communities to be rare or threatened.

The disquieting national study by Dr. Master at The Nature Conservancy found that 20 percent of all aquatic species are threatened and concluded that riparian development and habitat loss were the key reasons for decline in 93 percent of the cases. The zoologist noted that "the health of aquatic habitats in North America continues to decay" and that the trend is likely to get worse until we see "a major commitment to conservation of entire ecosystems."

In *Saving the Planet*, the World Watch Institute reported that scientists estimate one-fifth of all plant and animal species will disappear during the next twenty years if business continues as usual. Recognizing the epidemic of extinction, percipient author Thomas Berry used the term "supreme pathology" in describing the effects of modern civilization on the environment. In *Dream of the Earth* he wrote, "The change that is taking place in the present is not simply another historical transition or another cultural transformation. Its order of magnitude is immensely more significant in its nature and in its consequences. We are indeed closing down the major life systems of the planet." Professor E. O. Wilson, the eminent Harvard biologist, likewise raised the concern and asked about the ultimate ramifications: Is humankind suicidal?

Freshwater ecosystems are far more endangered than terrestrial ones. Like fish species, one-third of frog and toad species are either endangered, threatened, or of special concern, compared to 13 percent of terrestrial mammals, 11 percent of birds, and 14 percent of land reptiles.

Molly Beattie, director of the U.S. Fish and Wildlife Service in 1993, reported that 45 percent of all endangered species are in fresh water and that aquatic ecosystems will be one of the highest priorities for protection by her agency in the 1990s.

Ironically, aquatic ecosystems have probably received the least attention, according to J. David Allan, a professor of conservation biology at the University of Michigan. Fish have had few advocates, and invertebrates even fewer. The aquatic species, of course, live underwater, where, unlike the American bald eagle or the African elephant, they are not seen.

Few people keep life lists of fish the way bird watchers do for birds, though the number of species for each group in the United States may be about equal. If the aquatic species could be seen, many would not look appealing to the average viewer the way kit foxes or pandas do. But the endangered forms of aquatic life have their own inherent right to exist and, in fact, compose building blocks for other lives, the footing on which the pyramid sits—one whose top is occupied by bears, eagles, and people. Furthermore, aquatic ecosystems may be the best indicators of total ecological health, because they reflect the conditions of the entire watershed.

Among the uncharismatic aquatic creatures are freshwater mussels, which have even fewer supporters than cold, scaly fish but are vital to the quality of rivers. Mussels cleanse the water daily, removing bacteria and suspended organic particles by means of their own filtering system. Seventy-five percent of freshwater mussel populations face critical or declining levels. In the Ohio River Basin, where half the nation's 330 species of mussels live, 20 species have already gone extinct. Mussel larvae attach themselves to fish gills, which breathe for them until the larvae mature. Some fish, such as sturgeon, in turn depend on the mussels as food. Likewise, mammals and birds depend on these and other invertebrates. The diet of the Everglades kite, for example, depends on a single species of freshwater snail.

Near the Bruneau River in the middle Snake River Basin, five species of snails have been listed as endangered. This raised concern and sometimes ridicule in the local ranching community, which fears that the few numbers of snails may gain some kind of administrative preference over the plentiful cows. Tirsh Klahr of the Idaho Conservation League perceptively countered, "The Bruneau snail and the Bruneau rancher are both threatened by the same plight—mismanagement of the groundwater aquifer. Over-pumping of the aquifer is not only drying up the snails' habitat, but it is also impacting ranchers in terms of increased pumping cost and the cost of drilling deeper wells to replace those that dried up."

The fascinating case of the Colorado River's endangered fish illustrates the connections among native species, dams, water quality, flow regime, and riparian habitat. The Colorado squawfish and razorback sucker evolved more than 3 million years ago and are found nowhere else in the world. The bonytail chub and humpback chub are also endangered. All face multiple hazards of mismanagement. The basin's reservoirs have flooded some of the best habitat, and while the fish used to migrate hundreds of miles up and down the river system, dams have blocked the migration routes. Cold and clear releases from the reservoirs have eliminated the warm water and silt that had been present for millennia and are needed by the native fish. Irrigation wastewater has polluted spawning areas with fatal levels of selenium. Diversions, development, and riprap have blocked access to the flooded bottomlands needed for feeding during the spawning period.

Assaulted on all fronts, the fish are limited to only 25 percent of their historic habitat—a situation worse than that faced by Columbia River salmon. Furthermore, the fourteen native Colorado River species must compete with forty nonnative species as voracious as the northern pike of the Yampa River. Old-style management by some state fish and wildlife agencies favors introduced game fish that are not native to the area; these agencies still stock the more sporting exotics where they sometimes threaten native fish. Though no less deserving of life, the squawfish, chubs, and suckers unfortunately lack the charisma of trout and pike, and suffer as a result.

The U.S. Fish and Wildlife Service and Bureau of Reclamation have worked to alter release schedules from federal dams such as Flaming Gorge on the Green River in order to accommodate the endangered fish. The Colorado Nature Conservancy has acquired riparian frontage, hoping to sustain bottomland flooding in a few important areas. Much more needs doing to tip the balance back toward the native fish.

Elucidating a great deal about the endangered species problem, Robert and Leona Train Rienow wrote, back in 1967, in their prescient masterpiece *Moment in the Sun*, "In crowding and exploiting a species into extermination we not only tear asunder the interdependent web of life of which we are a part, but we obliterate some of the wonder of creation and rob ourselves of a joy of coexistence that is priceless."

In 1993 the Wilderness Society proposed an American Lifelands Conservation Act with the goal of preserving enough of the American landscape to assure the existence of healthy populations of every species in every type of ecosystem. Speaking for that organization, T. H. Watkins wrote in the spring 1993 issue of *Wilderness*, "The preservation of species habitat, we are convinced, is the single most important conservation goal that now faces us, just as the preservation of pristine wilderness areas was thirty years ago."

With a total of about 1,000 species declared as federally endangered and another 3,700 on the waiting list for consideration in 1993, the job of protecting one species at a time appears hopeless. The more plentiful the threats to extinction grow, the more obvious it becomes that trying to save one species at a time works poorly, if at all. The ecosystems that sustain the species are first of all endangered, and efforts to sustain those systems are what is necessary to avert whole groups of extinctions and a collapse of the natural world as we know it.

⮞ A Pervasive Problem

The plight of extinction surfaces in the altered ecosystems of rivers nationwide. The Tennessee River Basin, for example, has been incomparably rich through the ages of evolution, with more kinds of mussels than any other river system in the United States and with 224 species of fish. In comparison, 95 fish species live in the St. Croix of Wisconsin, 88 in the Savannah of Georgia, 70 in the Hudson, 43 in the Columbia, and 31 in the Colorado. The Mississippi, with its great length, holds even more species, with 300. Yet the Tennessee system has suffered systematic destruction by dams, canals, and channelization, and its richness has been multiply diminished. Twenty percent of the basin's mollusks are extinct, and 45 percent of the remaining species are endangered or seriously depleted. Dredging of the Tennessee-Tombigbee Waterway caused at least 15 species of fish to be eliminated from the rivers, and at least 99 species of snails became extinct, threatened, or endangered, as reported in *Water Quality in North American River Systems*. Invasion of habitat by the exotic zebra mussel has escalated the threats to native species.

Nearby, the fertile Cahaba River in Alabama ranks as one of the nation's richest rivers in numbers of species per mile. One of the longest free-flowing rivers in the South, it extends 200 miles from the Appalachian foothills of northern Alabama and across the coastal plain to Selma, passing broad sandbars and hardwood bottomland forests with abundant wildlife. The river provides habitat for the threatened Cahaba shiner and more than 130 species of fish in all. Already stressed by urban development, rural subdivisions, sewage, siltation, and water supply withdrawals, dismaying new threats occur at methane wells where gas is extracted from coal seams. A half-million pounds of caustic salts per day could be discharged into the Cahaba. Repeated efforts to designate portions of the river as part of the National Wild and Scenic Rivers System failed under intense lobbying pressure from land developers.

Aquatic species of the Midwest may be even more affected by ecosystem changes than those of the South. According to Dr. James Karr, the number of fish species in midwestern rivers has declined by 45 to 70 percent since 1850.

Introduced species pose yet another threat to river life nationwide. In Montana's Flathead Lake, the mysis shrimp, an exotic species, was introduced as a food source for salmon, which had been doing just fine on their own. In twenty years' time, the shrimp had outcompeted the salmon for the lake's supply of plankton, which had been the fish's main food source. The salmon population disappeared, as did the great congregations of bald eagles that had come to feed on the salmon after they spawned upstream at McDonald Creek in Glacier National Park. This problem of alien species is common. One study found that in 77 percent of the cases of introduced fish species—many of them deliberately stocked—native fish declined.

In the Sacramento River system, the listing of the winter run chinook salmon as endangered, along with lawsuits by conservation groups and a failure of the state to act, finally prompted the National Marine Fisheries Service to take action in 1993, requiring sixty-four water agencies that have been damming and diverting water in the basin to relinquish emergency flows for the fish. Other Sacramento River Basin species on the verge of extinction include the delta smelt, western yellow-billed cuckoo, bank swallow, giant garter snake, and Swainson's hawk—all taxed by the loss of aquatic and riparian ecosystems.

Even the Willamette River in Oregon, considered a success for pollution abatement and open space protection, suffers from a lack of holistic effort. Species other than game fish and anadromous runs have largely been ignored, and biologists call the aquatic ecosystem a "basket case."

In *Restoration of Aquatic Ecosystems*, the National Research Council reported, "Just as clear-cutting a diverse, complex forest ecosystem and replacing it with a stand of Douglas fir produces a tree farm rather than a restored forest, so, too, does taking a highly disrupted and polluted river system and merely abating the pollution fail to suffice to 'restore' the river." Recognizing the limits of common riverfront protection approaches, the authors wrote, "Greenways along waterways in cities usually serve as parks rather than as a means of restoring the natural functions of rivers." The view of the Council's authors—greenways are fine, but they do not constitute ecosystems—challenges river conservationists to reach even further to protect what is left of the original legacy of America.

ᴥ Dismantled Watersheds

The importance of ecosystems to river health is nowhere more apparent than in our treatment of forests. To them, the health of rivers is inextricably linked.

Forests hold soil and prevent siltation; they cast shade to guarantee cool waters; and they contribute essential nutrients to streams. With a thick sponge of humus, forests store water, releasing it slowly to rivers. One study found that undisturbed forests contained 137,000 pounds of humus per acre, each pound capable of absorbing two pounds of rainwater. But after forests were cut, only 20,000 to 70,000 pounds of humus per acre were found, and sometimes none at all.

Runoff after heavy logging produces violent flushes of high water choked with battering rams of dead-wood debris. Because the runoff occurs so quickly, the streams then become reduced and pathetic spectacles of missing water—water that went to the sea or the muddy bottom of the next reservoir long before its time. Even during the extraordinary floods of 1964 in northern California, observers in airplanes reported clear water flowing from streams draining a Nature Conservancy preserve on Elder Creek while other streams ran high, thick, and brown with silt from logged-over mountainsides.

The silt is not just a roily brown mess that can be forgotten after the

Lifelines: The Case for River Conservation

high water recedes. It settles on gravel beds used for spawning and traps newly hatched fish inside the encased mud, or prevents water from flowing through the gravel and thereby denies oxygen to the fish eggs. The silt frequently seals off the gravel beds from spawning altogether, as if a lead-weighted trap were thrown over the riverbed, and the effect on invertebrates is even worse. Much as riprap and levees disconnect a river from its flood plain, silt actually separates a river from its *bed*.

The forests of the East and South—once magnificent beyond compare in their diversity and extent—were virtually all cut. Portions of those regions have rebounded with second- or third-growth forests of respectable integrity. Much reclamation work is possible in these areas if land development and the biological pauperization of tree farms can be avoided. But in the meantime, the timber industry has been cutting the last and finest old growth in America at a breakneck pace in the lush forests of the Northwest, Alaska, and the northern Rockies.

Controversies have intensified to a kind of civil war in recent years over the fate of the old growth that remains—12 percent or less of its original extent in Oregon and Washington, and almost nothing in most of the rest of the country.

Fisheries biologists attribute many extinctions of salmon and steelhead runs in the Coastal Range and Cascade Mountains to logging and related road building. Surveys in 1991 by researchers Sedell and Everest of the Pacific Northwest Research Station of the U.S. Forest Service documented declining fish habitat since the 1930s, with an average loss of 60 percent, mostly associated with logging, road building, and grazing.

Federal and state scientists surprised nobody in 1990 when they surveyed Jim Creek in the Swan River Basin of northern Montana and found increases in sediment and small gravel after heavy logging. "Based on predicted embryo survival, bull trout, a species of special concern in Montana, will experience 100 percent mortality," the biologists calmly reported. Sidestepping both dissent within its ranks and criticism from the outside, the U.S. Forest Service in the late 1980s planned to log 1.2 million acres of roadless forest in Montana.

Most timber sales lose money for the government—a typical situation throughout the Rockies. In Idaho, 172 timber sales were planned in roadless areas for the five-year period beginning in 1993, many of them money-losers. Using government data, the Wilderness Society reported in 1993 that taxpayer losses to uneconomical national forest timber sales averaged $238 million a year since 1989. Hundred-year-old lodgepole pine trees were sold to timber companies for about a dollar each. Sales on three-quarters of national forests nationwide lost money.

Overt political pressure by western senators and congressmen on Forest Service officials is a primary reason for this breach of economics, logic, ethics, and good forestry. Senator Larry Craig of Idaho, for example, wrote to Forest Service Chief Dale Robertson to express discontent that industrial cutting was not proceeding fast enough in his home state. Craig called the cutting rate a "drastic under-accomplishment" and admonished Robertson as follows: "Dale, I am very disappointed with the Forest Service's accomplishment and accountability for timber output in Idaho and the Nation as a whole." Craig's May 23, 1991, letter, leaked mysteriously from the bureaucracy and published in the Idaho Conservation League's October 1991 newsletter, demanded in the tone of a humiliating parent that Robertson submit monthy personal progress reports to Craig's office itemizing efforts to speed up the liquidation of Idaho's forests. It is individuals such as Senator Craig, enjoying campaign contributions from forest industries, who thus dictate the management of these enormous, irreplaceable ecosystems owned by the American public.

Seeking to remedy the situation, the Clinton administration initially proposed a reduction in the deficit timber sales that would have saved taxpayers $274 million during a five-year period. Instead, obstinate pressure from western senators resulted in Clinton dropping the reform in order to pass his deficit reduction budget in 1993. Spokespeople for the administration said that other attempts would be made to bring economic sense to the federal timber program.

Studies such as those of the unfortunate bull trout in the Swan River Basin are increasingly common, but not as common as they might be. Al Isaacson worked as a hydrologist for the Forest Service at the Panhandle National Forest in northern Idaho. In a September 1992 *Sierra* magazine interview he stated, "When we told the Forest Service they shouldn't have a [logging] project because it was going to harm the water resource, they told us that they wouldn't believe us without monitoring data. So, we went out and began monitoring. Their next step was to cut off the money for monitoring so we wouldn't have the data." Extensive logging ensued along the once-pristine Coeur d'Alene River.

At the Siuslaw National Forest in the coastal range of Oregon, trees grow better than in any other national forest anywhere—and so do fish. On this stage of conflict, up to 10 percent of the salmon and steelhead in the United States outside Alaska return to spawn in a forest that was being cut at a rapid rate. Heavy rains in 1975 resulted in 245 landslides causing gross siltation, 89 percent of them due to logging and related road building. A study indicated that half the fish habitat in the forest was lost owing to soil erosion that occurred between the beginning of logging in the 1940s and 1976. The cutting continued anyway. A lawsuit in 1984 by the National Wildlife Federation temporarily halted the chainsaws on the unstable Suislaw hills. After six years of litigation, timber sales resumed in 1990 with restrictions designed to retard the loss of habitat.

Throughout the Northwest, biologists report that the amount of spawning habitat declines every year. At the southern Oregon coast, coho salmon runs are nearly extinct. Once abundant, the bull trout survive in only 11 percent of their former northwestern range—the roadless 11 percent.

At the South Fork of the Trinity in northern California, fisheries interests won a four-year court battle to stop timber salvage sales because of sedimentation damage to anadromous runs. At the time of the decision, only seven chinook salmon and thirty-five steelhead returned to the once-teeming tributary.

Not only the northern spotted owl, but old-growth species of many kinds are threatened, as are public water supplies. Residents at Belitz Creek on the Oregon coast protested logging on Forest Service land critical to their domestic water supply. The Mount Hood National Forest alone yields drinking water to fifty-four communities, including Portland, and a soil suitability study found that 30 percent of the land designated for logging in that forest was too steep to avoid erosion problems.

Many of the problems faced by the Northwest are found elsewhere. Even in Texas, American Rivers listed the Rio Grande as America's most threatened river in 1993, in part because of a World Bank proposal to finance timber cutting in the Rio Conchos headwaters, a Mexican river that contributes 70 percent of the Rio Grande's flow.

While loggers on Forest Service land must comply with at least a modicum of controls, private landholders often don't. The Plum Creek Timber Company, once a part of Burlington Northern Railroad, controls 1.5 million acres of forests resulting from an 1864 railroad grant of free public land. The company now clearcuts large tracts, devastating streams as its chainsaws, bulldozers, skidders, and helicopters advance across Montana, Idaho, and Washington. Large timber-cutting consortiums in the state of Washington respond to citizen lawsuits with countersuits designed to intimidate environmental opposition, and they do; citizens fighting clearcuts were turned back by the raw financial power aligned against them.

Some states, such as California and Oregon, enacted laws governing timber practices on private land—especially industrial forest land. Many states, however, have no laws on forest management, and even those that do often fail to protect streams. The 1971 Oregon State Forest Practices Act, for example, does not apply to streams if the fish are less than six inches long. Under this biological absurdity, loggers can remove most or all waterfront vegetation if the fish are simply short enough.

The question of jobs rises to the forefront of any efforts for better regulation of logging or even the tiniest reservation of old growth. While the media cover unemployment in the timber industry with all the attendant social ills that occur when people are out of work, a coalition of northwestern commercial fishermen and conservation groups reported that 90 percent of Washington and Oregon's most critical fish habitat lies in old-growth forests. Reflecting on the politics of ecosystem versus irrigation issues on the West Coast, House Interior Committee Chair George Miller said, "It changed the argument right around when the commercial fishermen got off their boats and came to the capitol and asked, 'What about *our* jobs?'"

Workers by the thousands have in fact been laid off from the lumber mills, creating regrettable economic hardship in spite of increased logging in the 1980s. Importantly, the unemployment statistics correspond not to old growth locked up in reserves but to the increase in exports of logs to Japan for milling and the retooling of sawmills for labor-saving automation. In Mendocino County mills of northern California, for example, seven jobs were needed to produce a million board feet of lumber in 1975; only three jobs were required for the same production in 1985.

Resolution of ecosystem issues, so critical to Northwest rivers, hinges on many factors surrounding modern-day logging. It involves the question of timber availability—little old growth is left, leading Dr. John Osborn of Spokane to say, "We're not up against the spotted owl. We're up against the Pacific Ocean." Resolution involves the reform of regulations and subsidies—hundreds of millions of dollars per year could be saved by simply letting national forests be. Support is growing to subsidize job retraining and conversion to a sustained-yield economy rather than to subsidize clearcutting of public forests.

Alternative methods of harvesting are available, including select cutting of individual trees with less disturbance to watersheds, use of helicopters to minimize erosion, elimination of cutting altogether on steep slopes and riverfront zones, and harvesting at rates that can be continued in perpetuity. Seeking better safeguards for streams, conservationists press for water quality standards, with operators being held responsible not just for following prescribed "best management practices" but for the real-world results on waterways. The new standards would not allow siltation beyond an acceptable and specified level. But even those reforms will fail to provide the extent of old growth needed for regionwide ecological diversity. Regarding old growth, Andy Kerr of the Oregon Natural Resources Council said, "We think that since we're down to 10 percent of ancient forests, it's inappropriate to log any of it."

Since that last share of the old growth will be gone in a decade at the cutting rates of the 1980s, the choice is one of adjusting to the inevitable changes in local economies in ten years, or making the identical adjustment now and having a remnant of virgin forests and streams intact as rare and valued habitat.

Now that we have dismantled the ecosystems of the continent for 300 years, support is growing to save the small pieces that remain. And beyond saving the best of what is left, the job of reassembling the fragments into connected corridors needs to start—a task that appropriately begins along the waterways that can someday link habitats together in a reconnected whole.

✌ Whole Ecosystems

While the importance of watersheds is undeniable to the health of rivers, and while rivers are vital to the rest of the ecosystem, the challenges inherent in proper care for the larger system cause one to pause, if not give up and retire from any contemplated service to rivers. After all, the far more limited goals of stopping unnecessary hydroelectric dams, reducing polluted runoff from farms, restoring flows to depleted rivers, and preserving thin strips of riparian habitat are all hard enough and still unachieved by any standard. While the movement to protect rivers can claim some success in all of these realms, new requirements for protecting watershed areas tower far above the achievements of the past. Yet river protection efforts offer a model for approaching the difficult goals in the incipient era of widespread species extinction. As American Rivers president Kevin Coyle said in 1993, "River conservation is probably the closest we've come in terms of national policy to actually protect ecosystems."

The popular emphasis on ecosystem protection arose about the same time environmental restoration objectives came into vogue in the late 1980s, and these two themes of the environmental movement have much in common. Striking the imagination of many, the new goals meet an intellectual need in the environmental community to move on, to advance beyond the stage of preservation of the last remnants of natural America and beyond the grim fights against the vilest pollution and wanton abuse, even though unlimited work remains to be done in those areas. In practice, both ecosystems management and restoration demand new commitments where people are already overcommitted just trying to do comparatively simple things. Without doing it all, however, remedial needs arise again and again.

The idea of ecosystem protection is unalterably sound, but what people end up *doing* about it may not be a lot different from the piecemeal approaches to conservation in the past. We realize, for example, that an entire biological corridor must be protected. We might begin to accomplish that goal through the familiar program of zoning the flood plain against new land development. And simply zoning the flood plain may be an ambitious task. Perhaps now, however, we have a clearer view of how the parts must fit together. Perhaps now that people are more aware of ecosystem needs, the traditional tasks of river conservation will take on a new and justified urgency.

Going one step beyond the protection of individual areas and toward a complete-systems approach, the National Wild and Scenic Rivers System is intended to safeguard whole riparian and canyon corridors by banning damaging federal projects and licenses and by encouraging better land use. The program incorporates both public and private land in a mosaic where the mingling of acquisition, easements, land use regulation, and voluntary protection enter into a management formula. Other models can be seen in "greenline" approaches, such as at New York's Adirondack Mountains, the New Jersey Pine Barrens, and the Santa Monica Mountains of southern California. At these sites, people recognized that all the land will never be in parks, but protection is nonetheless desired.

To safeguard any but the smallest ecosystem, management will necessarily involve complex strategies such as those of the wild and scenic rivers and the greenline parks. Integration of private and public property into a protected whole must be pursued. Efforts of the Greater Yellowstone Coalition, striving to guarantee biological integrity to a large area, contribute to a growing bank of experience in addressing ecosystems. Though the results in all these cases fall short, each offers hope that broader effectiveness in protection is possible.

When we look at the network of rivers across America, it is apparent that designated wild and scenic rivers, greenline parks, and regions of the Greater Yellowstone's stature will always be rare. Instead, we see the everyday streams, the home watersheds, the common riverscapes—some well loved, some totally neglected. Yet the lessons remain the same: identify the most valuable places and qualities, consider the relationship between what we do and the fitness of the land and water, pursue reform with whatever political tools lie at hand, and strive always to communicate and convince others that the rivers and their landscapes must be respected.

In making the difficult crossing from safeguarding isolated tracts of land to protecting entire ecosystems, rivers can be the medium of influence, much as they were the means of travel to early explorers, who likewise strived to bridge vast areas of land, though their purpose was much different. By traveling on the rivers, our ancestors explored the continent and established a nation. By protecting the rivers, today's generation can begin to save the ecosystems that have made America what it is.

The rivers link landscapes together. As linear corridors, waterways house the complexity of large natural communities, and they run as lifelines of critical habitat. In learning to care for our rivers, perhaps we will expand our perspectives and capabilities until it is whole ecosystems we have carefully sustained for the future.

Chapter Nine
A Time for Rivers

❧ In Search of a Vision

With a greater knowledge of the importance of rivers and the threats they face, the questions remain: What will bring about change? What can people do? Each chapter of *Lifelines* explores problems facing waterways and also reports on progress to prevent further damage and to correct past mistakes. But beyond that collection of cases, our society needs a vision of a protected and respected riverscape if reform is to graduate from isolated successes to a whole new future for American rivers. Clear vision, unfortunately, remains one of the harder things to find in a complex society in complicated times. Perhaps each person's view begins in his or her youth, from some eye-opening experience along a stream or from the day-to-day exposure to a river's vitality.

The land where I grew up, in the Appalachian foothills of Pennsylvania, included a stream. It wasn't large, but it never dried up. It began on our property, at a spring.

My grandfather, George Gremer, and his brother, John, lived just up the hill from us, and in the summer they shoveled out mud from the bottom of the spring, sometimes resetting stones as a lining so that we could dip a bucket there and fill it. With only the strength to carry half-pails of water, I followed them on the blackberry-bordered path between the spring and the garden during the droughts of August, when our well would have gone dry if it were tapped too heavily. It was possible, this way, to water ten tomato plants, beans, corn, squash, and other crops that gave us our summertime vegetables with a lot left over for canning.

My grandfather and great uncle didn't talk much about the spring, but I sensed an importance attached to it by the way they cared for it, by the way they used it. They would not have called it reverence at that time, for that was a term reserved for church. But today, *reverent* is how I remember our regard for the spring.

In time I noticed that the spring had a life of its own going beyond its useful purpose to us. Even after we had carried away our bucketfuls, water miraculously reappeared and overflowed into a rivulet. Though small and at first covered by grass and sedges, it held status in my mind as the *source*. Water soon accumulated as a trickling brook, gurgling through our own private swamp before leaving our property and riffling into the unknown. Where did it go? Gaining courage as time passed, I felt compelled to follow the stream.

Through important years of that childhood, my age could have been measured in the length of the stream I had come to know. I wandered down through the hollows, all of them undeveloped. The water led me past girthy oaks, soggy bottoms ripe with skunk cabbage, abandoned apple orchards, overgrown fields that once had been farmed but then lay thick with a crop of scarlet hawthorn, and deep into woods of red maple, black cherry, and the occasional hemlock. Farther and farther I explored, year by year. Then one day I emerged at a road near my stream's culverted, industrialized, dumped-upon confluence with the Ohio River, at that time the world's largest barge-floating cesspool. Seeing my stream and then seeing where it ended up, I gained a sense of what a river should be and what it shouldn't.

The vision grew on days when my grandfather—I called him "Pa"— said, "Timmy, get your fishing pole." I'd drop everything, go scrambling for my hand-me-down rod, jump in Pa's dusty blue car, and we'd head for Little Beaver Creek, across the state line in Ohio. There we walked on paths through humid undergrowth of jewelweed in the woods and milkweed in the fields, emerging at grassy banks beneath umbrellas of sycamores. Pa set up a lawn chair but I roamed up and down as we fished for bluegills. In moments of pure rapture I pictured myself floating down Little Beaver Creek in a canoe—something I was so desirous of that I quickly put the fantasy aside, as though it were some forbidden fruit. It was torture to imagine it too clearly.

Capstone to those youthful visits to rivers, my family returned every few years to my father's ancestral homeland along the Youghiogheny River in the heart of Pennsylvania's Appalachians, where relatives lived in the village of Ohiopyle. The river there was too wide for me to swim across, and white with rapids. Somehow just the sound of them thrilled me and instilled dreams of epic adventure. I wandered as a wild boy along the rushing, rapid edge, scrambling on rocks far taller than myself and leaping bravely from one to another, uncontainably excited by something I couldn't quite define. Now, I can: here was a wild river.

Later, as a thirteen-year-old, I sat on a slab of Youghiogheny sandstone one balmy evening when the Appalachian air was fragrant with blooming rhododendron, the river streaming by. At dusk, colors faded to shades of blue-gray in humid air, and the scene became one of simplified beauty and motion—nothing but the river and its world existed around me. It was there that I realized with utter clarity: this place is perfect. Why was it perfect? I knew. The river was perfect because it existed the way God made it—it was natural.

Each person who grows up under the influence of rivers and streams may have his or her own vision of that perfection. And youth is surely not essential to this kind of insight. No matter what age they are, people needing solace find it along waterways. Casting lines while peering through the reflective sheen of water and into the mystery below, anglers for generations have recognized that it is the person doing the fishing who gets hooked, not the fish. Other people return from rafting trips, whether on the upper Hudson or in the Grand Canyon, and say, "That experience changed my life." Visions of the natural riverscape have their roots in all sorts of personal experience.

Living in Cincinnati, Ohio, Mike Fremont did not exactly take the Little Miami River for granted. He saw the river nearly every day as it wound down through the midwestern countryside to its confluence with the Ohio River. He paddled his canoe there several days a week, training for long-distance races, but he never saw an important part of the scene—the part about the future. "Then one day in 1969 my neighbor flagged me down," Fremont recalled. "He was president of a conservation group called Little Miami Incorporated, and asked, 'Do you know what they're going to do to your river?' I had no idea, but then learned that a major freeway was planned for the banks of the Little Miami—*my* river. I got out of the canoe and started working for that river."

The highway has not been built, and after twenty-five years of activism for his local stream, after starting the organization called Rivers Unlimited, and after working to safeguard a wide collection of Ohio waterways, Mike Fremont, at age seventy-two, was honored with the Lifetime Achievement Award from American Rivers in 1993. His vision, like that of many people, was based on a personal relationship with one place, with one river, and needed only a gentle nudge to become a vision encompassing responsible action as a steward of that place.

The vision of a personal river can be expanded to community rivers that serve a local society, to rivers sustaining whole ecosystems, and to the rivers of the continent. Collectively, these describe the homes of all North Americans, just as the stream emanating from the spring described the home where I grew up. Imagine, for a moment, the network of all rivers—blue, green, and brown—articulated veins issuing forth from every corner of the landscape. These are the pathways of life. They mark the original America, a base map on which all of the roads, farms, villages, and cities might be seen simply as overlays.

We built our society around rivers, but so much of what we did was wrong—not maliciously wrong, but fatally shortsighted. The rivers were seen as pipes and conduits, an infrastructure likened to hardware whose purpose was to supply the perpetual boom and to transform the landscape into something new and different, into something that it *wasn't*. The vision of rivers, in both a practical and aesthetic sense, related more to ditches, sewers, water tanks, railroads, and highways than to the heartbeat of an ecosystem. What would this country have looked like if we had chosen a different vision? As Christopher Manes wrote, "We need to consider the path not taken, the path of environmental sanity and accommodation." Imagine, for a moment, all rivers as blue-and-emerald corridors of river life, around which a vibrant planet thrives. Does that vision have any chance of becoming reality? Is there hope?

If someone in 1970 had said that the age of building big dams would soon be over, many people would not have believed it. River conservationists at that time fought dozens of big dams, from Tocks Island on the Delaware in New Jersey to High Ross on the Skagit in Washington. We were so accustomed to damming rivers. Congress had authorized hundreds of projects; boosters envisioned thousands more. Yet very few large dams are now being built. Likewise, to draw our drinking water from the Merrimack River was unthinkable in 1960. Now we do it. Can the other goals of river conservationists be met as well? Except for a tiny percentage of protected mileage, rivers are under fire as a result of hydroelectric proposals, pollution, diversions, riparian habitat loss, and watershed damage. This fragmented destiny of our rivers represents one phase of American history. It does not have to represent the indefinite future. Ample precedent exists for hope, spelled out in many cases cited in this book.

The fundamental and ultimate hope lies with people who embrace the blue-and-emerald vision of river life and who become involved in safeguarding their own streams. River Network director Phil Wallin reflected, "There are now more groups working on river protection than there ever were—an explosion of interest. It's conceivable that in every valley we'll see organized river guardians." When that happens, what we do to our rivers will be very different.

❧ Formulas for Success

The river protection movement has diverse and urgent needs of many kinds: organizational, financial, legislative, and activist. But several reforms stand out as having the potential to effect greater change while either saving money or costing little, and at the same time using existing programs.

As relics of a bygone era, the remaining federal incentives backing large dams can be dropped, including 70 percent taxpayer shares for local flood control dams and subsidies to irrigators that top 90 percent. If the government must subsidize those practices, more effective aid could be provided by helping people who are chronically flooded to relocate from flood plains and by paying for irrigation efficiency improvements instead of new dams.

For hydroelectric projects, the moderate notion of equal consideration for fish and wildlife, as required by the Electric Consumers Protection Act of 1986, would eliminate most bad proposals that still wend their way through the licensing process. When power from new dams in Canada is planned for export southward, individual states or the U.S. government could reasonably require environmental impact statements to be prepared to U.S. standards, only then letting consumers, public utility commissions, and utilities decide if the power should be imported. The Federal Energy Regulatory Commission and state public utility commissions could require that benign alternatives for electric generation be exhausted before allowing new dams or diversions. An energy tax would result in conservation of existing supplies and less need for troublesome new generation facilities. In renewing licenses of dams that have been in operation for the past fifty years, FERC can require modification of projects for better stream flows and can eliminate projects causing river destruction disproportionate to the gains in generated power. The law now allows for this.

Great advances can be made in water quality. Nitrate pollution, the scourge of the latter twentieth century, can be cut by reducing the use of chemical fertilizers. Incentive and regulatory programs could seek to roll back the use of pesticides and petroleum-based fertilizers to levels predating 1970, when a good job of farming was done with far less chemical dependence and far less pollution. A tax on pesticides and fertilizers harmful to public waters could generate revenues to help cope with the epidemic of polluted runoff from those sources, otherwise requiring taxpayer funds for correction. Agricultural pollution could be fairly regulated without the customary exemptions that are granted to farmers in most water quality laws. Billions of dollars of federal crop subsidies could be redirected from payments intended to curtail production to improvements in water efficiency and control of runoff.

The flows in dried-up rivers could be improved dramatically with a conscientious application of the "beneficial" and "reasonable" use requirements already contained in western water law. Where diverted waters are not being used for needed crops and not being applied efficiently, the "saved" water could be set aside for long-neglected instream uses. If voluntary initiative is not taken by the irrigation community to solve the instream flow problems that irrigation has created, a wider application of the public trust doctrine is inevitable, one in which courts have already recognized that rivers are good for more than irrigation and hydropower production.

Acreage on which irrigation causes land and water damage, such as fields laced with selenium and salt, should be retired from use through water quality regulation and by water purchase. Incentives are needed to permanently return those tracts to native vegetation and wildlife habitat rather than continuing to subsidize surplus crops on unsuitable soils that never should have been irrigated in the first place.

Because the public is paying for the big federal water projects, the dams should be reauthorized or reprogrammed for broader public values, including equal consideration for fish, wildlife, and other instream uses. A reasonable target may be to restore at least half the lost habitat of the affected rivers.

The quality of riparian habitat would be vastly improved with sensible reform of grazing on public land in the West. Grazing fees should be raised to cover administration of the program so that the ranchers pay their own way. Requirements that land and water not be degraded should be enforced—a practice that would benefit hundreds of thousands of miles of waterways. This reform is simple when compared to most other river conservation needs and would yield the greatest improvement to American waterways for the least cost.

Riparian protection would be an extraordinary side effect of good flood plain zoning. This can be accomplished through a federal flood insurance program that halts harmful development on an entire 100-year flood plain, rather than the current ban only on land where damages are the most frequent and severe.

Entire watersheds and ecosystems would benefit if the U.S. Forest Service discontinued below-cost timber sales that lose the government money. Another quantum leap would be made if the agencies with responsibilities for timber sales enforced requirements on polluted runoff.

Official listing of the disheartening backlog of candidate endangered species should be expedited as intended in the Endangered Species Act.

This sizable sampling of the legacy of our country may otherwise be eradicated.

Far from constituting a radical approach, most of these proposals can be carried out either by cutting wasteful and destructive subsidies and thus saving the taxpayers money, or by implementing laws already on the books—laws intended to do a job but failing. The effect of simply cutting damaging subsidies would solve a multitude of problems on the rivers and would mark a new and brightening future for these universally loved but universally abused highlights of the landscape.

Stepping back to take stock of the future, American Rivers president Kevin Coyle predicted that river conservation will become more biological, more political, and more focused on restoration. Regarding the challenges of the coming decades, he said, "We need to preserve the headwaters of our streams in order to have rivers worth protecting and restoring, we need to get water back into rivers that have been diverted and dried up, and we need to sustain and restore the riparian zones along rivers."

Similarly reflecting on the prospects, River Network director Phil Wallin identified urgent needs to better deal with a rising chorus of opposition from private landowners and organizations representing people who develop, extract, and commodify the land and waters. "We're losing the contest of public opinion in rural communities," Wallin warned, "and those communities control the destiny of most of America's rivers." He itemized the need for new arguments that address the benefits of jobs and property values through river conservation, as well as the need for grassroots support, alliances with traditional rural interests, and leadership to establish statewide river organizations coast to coast.

Considering the gains of the past and the needs of the future, it is apparent that a lot of river contests have been won, but how many of those streams are really protected? Expansion of the National Wild and Scenic Rivers System can guarantee long-term health for many more rivers. State scenic river programs can do the same, and a new national "registry" of rivers could confer protection from new dams without addressing the more nettlesome issue of land use along the waterways.

A nationwide assessment of rivers could do much to document the condition of America's river estate and substantiate the case for protection. This type of study was advocated by the National Research Council in 1991 and by other groups. Free-flowing qualities and biological health would be comprehensively assessed for the first time nationwide. The cause of wetlands protection benefited greatly from an assessment process begun in the 1950s and may serve as a model for rivers.

Regarding dams, channelization, and pollution from point sources, the changing times and the effectiveness of river conservationists have lessened the curve of destruction in recent years. Now, restoration of riparian corridors should be pursued before the seeds of vigor are lost. Restoration can involve flood plain zoning with insurance incentives to eventually reclaim open space by attrition of the most damage-prone development; habitat conservation in lieu of expensive channelization and riprap; razing of useless and unsafe dams; better management of grazing and logging; and acquisition of riverfronts by land trusts or the government, but only when owners desire to sell. Looking at further needs, the Pacific Rivers Council reported on the urgency for an ecologically based national policy on rivers and recommended a National Riverine and Riparian Conservation Act that would mandate the protection and restoration of ecosystems for every river nationwide.

To provide the federal funds needed for restoration, Congress can shift money from outdated military expenditures. This may be possible with the new global politics and the emerging priorities of humankind. In the early 1990s, 50 percent of our tax dollars went to defense-related expenditures and only 3 percent went to environmental and natural resource problems, though the latter represent the most serious threats to our security, civilization, and lives. A few days' worth of the military's budget per year could solve many of the river restoration goals of the nation and give people something of true value.

All of these approaches could help rivers, but in an era of economic limits, it is not new laws, new bureaucracies, or new programs that are most feasible. Needed first are the obvious, cost-effective reforms: eliminate damaging subsidies, enforce existing laws, pursue superior alternatives when public money is being used, and protect public trust values from blatant greed and vested interests that too often have been fed by government policies of the past.

To make any progress in river conservation, the most important principle is to build broad community support. Reaching out beyond the usual supporters has become essential in an era when newly organized opponents fight protection measures. The opponents purport to defend basic American values, such as personal freedoms, while in fact furthering the interests of people who profit at the expense of the rivers, the taxpayers, and the larger community, including future generations.

The community support so necessary to conservation sometimes comes from economic incentives inherent in healthy rivers, but short-term economic arguments cannot and should not always be the underpinning of successful campaigns. University of California economist Dr. Richard Norgaard explained, "A community first needs to decide what kind of future it wants. Then, economics can be used as a means of realizing their goals." Yet an economic case for river conservation carries political freight. In gaining protection for the Gauley River in West Virginia, advocates repeated in every press release the message that the natural river was worth $16 million annually to the local economy.

Stressing the importance of local economies to the Northwest, where resource debates have taken on the sting of a cultural clash, the Pacific Rivers Council pointed out that arguments concerning forest and river ecosystems are not environment versus jobs but jobs versus jobs. The Council pushed for consideration of the "long-term, sustainable, riverine-related or dependent jobs . . . as opposed to short-term jobs that degrade the resource." Bob Doppelt, executive director of the group, wrote, "The constituency for environmental protection will remain limited in scope and effectiveness until the core jobs and economic growth issues are addressed. It is no longer enough to organize concerned environmentalists to lobby for a bill. Those who have suffered most directly from the nonsustainable use of natural resources must be brought into the environmental constituency, along with those concerned about human and economic productivity."

With 10,000 conservation groups in the United States and 300 new ones forming each year, the support for river conservation is growing. However, as conservationists learn to be more effective, the opposition learns to be more effective too. In the end, rivers are a political resource, and to achieve great strides it is necessary to broaden the national base of support.

Seeking to do this, former American Rivers president Ken Olson said, "The thing that drives people to protect rivers is a love of the rivers, but idealistic people are not the limiting factor. The limiting factor is money. In America, $115 billion is given in private charity each year. More than $100 billion of this goes to religious and educational institutions. Culture and the arts receive large amounts from the remainder. All other categories total 3 percent, of which conservation is some portion. That's the limiting factor in river conservation."

Even with limited funds, local river conservation groups accomplish much. As simple as the following solution may seem, experience shows that rivers always benefit when an organization hires a full-time staff— even one person. While many ingredients must be present in any campaign, a common denominator of success seems to be a full-time steward whose job is to tend to the river.

In *People Protecting Rivers*, the River Network concludes with a list of actions that can guarantee success:

Form a coalition.
Focus on a key issue.
Find a possible solution.
Establish an organization.
Raise some money and hire a director.
Survey the resources of the river and create a conservation plan.
Work cooperatively with public agencies.
Recruit people with technical experience.
Propose an alternative to the project that threatens your river.
Advertise the economic value of a free-flowing river.
Build local support through public events.
Put out a regular, informative newsletter.

Set up a network of citizen monitors.

Put yourself in a position of strength to negotiate with the powers-that-be.

Choose the right forum for action.

Look to state and local government for land use control.

Consider protection of truly critical areas through land acquisition.

Keep a "watch dog" organization on the scene.

These jobs constitute the nuts and bolts of success, but only if people first become motivated by a personal vision and a world view that recognizes rivers as lifelines of value that must be treated well.

?? The Story of the River

Before and beyond all the practical needs for conservation, there is a greater need: fundamental changes are necessary in the outlooks of individuals and society if the future of rivers is to be much different from the past era of loss. American Indian activist Winona Laduke pointed out, "We must change from a society based on conquest to one based on survival." Though it has characterized our past, an existence built on the eradication of entire systems of life, the wholesale liquidation of natural assets, and the consumption of resources for frivolous use need not be our destiny. Reaffirming life, rather than causing death, must be the major point of our existence.

Recognizing the same need for a fundamental change going beyond patchwork approaches, Walt Anderson pessimistically noted in 1976 in *A Place of Power* that conservationists "may succeed in halting the construction of a dam or getting a ban on DDT, but they do not penetrate or change the network of cultural values and managerial practices that culminate in dams and pesticides." In *Small Is Beautiful*, economist E. F. Schumacher responded to this theme and wrote, "The task of our generation, I have no doubt, is one of metaphysical reconstruction. . . . We are suffering from a metaphysical disease, and the cure must therefore be metaphysical." So it is: we need not only to fix the chemistry of the river but to fix the river as it exists in our minds.

Part of the reconstruction of the world view and hence the world's well-being may lie in the story of our river—of every river. Each has a biography, an epic of birth, wonder, use, abandonment, new importance, revitalization, biological dependency, and all-powerful permanence. Do we know that saga? Philosopher Thomas Berry stressed the importance of this theme. "Tell me a story," he wrote in *Dream of the Earth*, "that will be my story as well as the story of everyone and everything about me, a story that brings us together in a valley community . . . that brings together the human community with every living being in the valley. . . ."

Running through our civilization, the river's history lies central to local culture, and the tale of each of our rivers must be learned and told to every member of that river's society. People can then recognize the role they play on this larger stage of life. Knowing the chronicle of the flowing water, we can establish a mature relationship to it, and when we do, we can find life enriched because we will be caring better for our part of the earth. After we know of the abundance that once thrived in the river and of the network of life radiating from the water, the changes of the past century and even the past decade will sharpen in focus. Knowing what once was, it is easier to imagine a new dawn when the river, once again, will truly provide sustenance and inspiration. The river then becomes a feature to be revered, or at least deeply respected.

Perhaps the river's story can be a starting point in a new regard for all waterways and for the planet. The new attitude must embrace a deeper commitment to the well-being of a place based on its history, on its role in life, and on the security, joy, and wonder that we know while living in that corner of the universe. In short, it is *love* of place that is needed, based on revealing knowledge that can be unearthed in the story of the river.

From the James River, where European settlers established their beachhead upon America, to the western streams whose waters so essentially underpin that irrigated and urban civilization, the rivers must emerge from decades of personal and philosophical neglect to be a focal point of local culture. Environmental protection, then, will not be an adjunct to society's workings and not an amenity to be polished as a promotional showpiece if the funds allow, but the centerpiece and fundament to all that we so tenuously possess while we briefly make use of the earth through each human lifetime.

Rivers, flowing large or small almost everywhere, can idealize a new kind of conservation of the American environment. Here, the riffling current and the riparian greenway are the water and land where we *live*—the home landscape. At once incorporating the arteries of the ecosystem, our own water supply, the heart of recreational space, and the centerpiece of communities, rivers hold magnetic appeal running deep in our society and psyche. The time to recognize their importance has come. Who will do this?

Major national environmental groups led the fight to save rivers in many of the early conservation battles, but these organizations have not recognized river protection as a primary goal in recent years. Their programs more typically gravitate to air pollution, toxins, parks, forestry, wilderness, and endangered species—all of them important issues but ones that include rivers only from time to time. Filling the void, American Rivers lobbies for action in the nation's capital, the River Network aids local and state activists wherever they are, a score of statewide groups organize for protection of streams within their boundaries, and more than 2,000 smaller organizations work at the local level. These local groups represent the dynamics of the environmental movement at the end of the twentieth century—a decentralization of power for political action. As former Assistant Interior Secretary Nathaniel P. Reed wrote, "Today, the real battle lines are no longer in Washington."

Seeing success at the local and state level, Huey Johnson, former Secretary of Resources for California and a perceptive observer of the American scene, expressed confidence that our nation has turned the corner with outlooks that are now beneficial to the earth. Explaining his confidence, he said, "The public is now with us, and economics have reversed and joined our side of the argument." Yet the lag between those sweeping changes and a reversal of destructive forces will last a long time. Recognizing that the job isn't easy, Johnson foresaw the restoration of environmental quality as a national purpose "that will be accomplished by investing in a nationwide hundred-year plan of resource recovery."

Many different paths can be taken during the next century of sustaining and restoring living rivers, but the central point is that we must make wise decisions now and act on them without delay. The health of rivers and therefore the well-being of life on earth demands a new commitment of heart and soul that leads to positive reform at the individual, community, and national levels.

Because the hydrologic cycle is indomitable, waterways will remain in one form or another no matter what we do. But time is short to secure a future of abundance—one that recognizes and provides for the rich reward of rivers not as pipelines but as lifelines.

Only with the involvement of people at their home waters and their adopted streams will the vision survive of a river running glassy and silver in reflected light, of children splashing at its sunlit edge, of a woman and man walking along the green and flowered shore and remembering many years of dreams that flow as the water does, constantly reborn and renewed. Only by changing the blight of past shortsightedness can we sustain a vision of myriad creatures that swim in elegant grace, that soar overhead and then descend to the water, and that croak, splash, leap, hide, crawl, dive, and simply drift with no destination except that of the current.

With a reformed and responsible regard for what we do and where we live, perhaps we will embrace this new vision of permanent value rather than one of passing wealth. Drawing on the wisdom of the ages, perhaps we will recognize that the grand cycle of life must be sustained along rivers everywhere.

Sources

For the information in *Lifelines*, I drew from government reports by the various resource agencies; accounts in reliable magazines, journals, and newspapers; books on the various aspects of rivers and water; newsletters of organizations such as American Rivers, Friends of the River, and the River Network; and on many interviews. *High Country News* was a valuable source for the West, as this excellent biweekly draws on journalists throughout a fifteen-state region. The National Wildlife Federation's *Leader* was likewise valuable for information on water policy and habitat issues nationwide. Some of the more important sources for each chapter are listed below, with an emphasis on books or articles that are easy to find. Other sources may be available only in government libraries, offices, or from the files of conservation organizations.

Lifelines represents an accumulation of experience and writing on rivers that spans twenty-four years and involves hundreds of interviews with scores of government representatives, conservation organization staff, and others. These are not listed in the following sources, but some are apparent in the text. Many written sources are likewise mentioned in the text as they occur, especially in places where the information may be controversial or where conflicting data exist. Where the subjects of particular sources in the following lists are not obvious, my citations are followed by a note about the type of information gleaned.

Chapter One ☙ Sustaining the Lifelines of a Continent

Much of the material in this introduction is covered in more detail in later chapters, where more sources are listed. Citations for information not covered elsewhere and those of a more general nature follow.

Amos, William H. *The Infinite River*. New York: Ballantine, 1970. The ecology of natural rivers.

Cahn, Robert, ed. *An Environmental Agenda for the Future*. Washington, D.C.: Island Press, 1985. Information on a wide range of environmental issues.

Conservation Foundation, The. *Protecting America's Wetlands: An Action Agenda*. Washington, D.C.: The Conservation Foundation, 1988.

McKibben, Bill. *The End of Nature*. New York: Doubleday, 1989. Atmospheric warming and global environmental issues.

Olson, W. Kent. *Natural Rivers and the Public Trust*. Washington, D.C.: American Rivers, 1988. Essay on the need for conservation.

Palmer, Tim. *Endangered Rivers and the Conservation Movement*. Berkeley: University of California Press, 1986. The history of river conservation.

Rienow, Robert, and Leona Train Rienow. *Moment in the Sun*. New York: Ballantine, 1967. Environmental issues as our society became aware of them in the 1960s. This remains a classic and relevant volume.

U.S. Department of Interior, Bureau of Outdoor Recreation. *Outdoor Recreation: A Legacy for America*. Washington, D.C.: Bureau of Outdoor Recreation, 1974. Recreational use of rivers.

U.S. Department of Interior, Fish and Wildlife Service. *The 1985 National Survey of Fishing, Hunting, and Wildlife-Associated Recreation*. Washington, D.C.: Fish and Wildlife Service, 1988. Data on recreational use of rivers.

U.S. Department of Interior, National Park Service, Rivers and Trails Conservation Assistance. *Economic Impacts of Protecting Rivers, Trails, and Greenway Corridors*. Washington, D.C.: National Park Service, 1990. Economic values of natural rivers.

van der Leeden, Frits; Fred L. Troise; and David Keith Todd. *The Water Encyclopedia*. Chelsea, Mich.: Lewis Publishers, 1990.

Wilson, E. O., ed. "The Current State of Biological Diversity." In *Biodiversity*. Washington, D.C.: National Academy Press, 1988. Endangered species.

Chapter Two ❧ The Embodiment of Rivers

Brown, Bruce. *Mountain in the Clouds*. New York: Simon and Schuster, 1982. Salmon of Washington State.

California Advisory Committee on Salmon and Steelhead Trout. *1988 Annual*

Report: Restoring the Balance. Sausalito, Calif.: California Committee on Salmon and Steelhead Trout, 1989. California salmon.

Collins, Brian. "Salmon Were an Afterthought to 136 Columbia River Dams." *High Country News,* July 13, 1992.

Daniel, John. "Dance of Denial." *Sierra,* March/April 1993. Columbia River salmon.

Ford, Pat. "Endangered Fish: Status Report." *Idaho Rivers Update.* Boise: Idaho Rivers United, October 1990. Salmon in Idaho.

Ford, Pat, ed. "Northwest Salmon at the Crossroads." *High Country News,* April 22, 1991, entire issue.

Harrison, John. "Unanimous Vote for Salmon." *Northwest Energy News,* January/February 1992. Available from the Northwest Power Planning Council, Portland, Oreg.

House, Freeman. "To Learn the Things We Need to Know." *Whole Earth Review,* Spring 1990. Mattole River, California, restoration efforts.

Idaho Department of Fish and Game. *Saving Idaho's Salmon.* Boise: Idaho Department of Fish and Game, 1991.

Idaho Office of the Governor. *Snake River Salmon.* Boise: Idaho Office of the Governor, 1993.

Kauffmann, John M. *Flow East.* New York: McGraw-Hill, 1973. Atlantic salmon.

Nehlsen, Willa; Jack E. Williams; and James A. Lichatowich. "Pacific Salmon at the Crossroads: Stocks at Risk from California, Oregon, Idaho, and Washington." *Fisheries,* March/April 1991.

Netboy, Anthony. "The Columbia Salmon's Upstream Fight." *Sierra Club Bulletin,* August/September 1975.

Northwest Power Planning Council. *Northwest Energy News,* 1989–1992 issues. Available from the Northwest Power Planning Council, Portland, Oreg.

Palmer, Tim. *The Snake River: Window to the West.* Washington, D.C.: Island Press, 1991. Columbia and Snake River salmon.

Stuebner, Steve. "Can a New Plan Save the Fish?" *High Country News,* March 9, 1992. Columbia River salmon.

Wilkinson, Charles F., and Daniel Keith Conner. "The Law of the Pacific Salmon Fishery: Conservation and Allocation of a Transboundary Common Property Resource." *Kansas Law Review,* vol. 32, 1983.

Chapter Three ❧ Breaking the Concrete Fix

Christensen, Jon. "Thirsty Sunbelt Cities Target Water in the Virgin River." *High Country News*, December 14, 1992. Dam proposals near national parks.

Clifton, Charles S. "Saving the South Platte." *Trout*, Summer 1990. Two Forks Dam proposal.

Committee to Save the Kings River. *The Kings River: A Report on Its Future.* Fresno, Calif.: Committee to Save the Kings River, 1987. The Rogers Crossing Dam proposal.

Dawdy, Doris Ostrander. *Congress in Its Wisdom: The Bureau of Reclamation and the Public Interest.* Boulder, Colo.: Westview Press, 1989.

"The Endless Summer?" *Newsweek*, July 11, 1988. Drought and global climate change.

Gottlieb, Robert. *A Life of Its Own.* San Diego: Harcourt Brace Jovanovich, 1988. Water supply issues.

Hundley, Norris. *The Great Thirst: California and Water, 1770s–1990s.* Berkeley: University of California Press, 1992. History of water development in California.

Jones, Andrew, and Jim Dyer. "The Water Efficiency Revolution." *River Voices*, Spring 1993, entire issue. Publication of the River Network.

Marshall, Andy. "Oldman Dam: Battle Rages on at Feds' Inaction." *Calgary Herald*, May 22, 1992.

Obmascik, Mark. "Water: From Growing Crops to Growing Cities." *Denver Post*, July 19, 1992. Water transfers.

Obmascik, Mark. "Water Policy: Some Farmers Paid Twice." *Denver Post*, July 21, 1992. Irrigation and subsidies.

Palmer, Tim. *Endangered Rivers and the Conservation Movement.* Berkeley: University of California Press, 1986. History of water development and river conservation.

Palmer, Tim. *Stanislaus: The Struggle for a River.* Berkeley: University of California Press, 1982.

Roper, Cyndi, and Jonathan Scott. "America's Water Industry: Time for Reform." *Clean Water Action News*, Spring 1990. Water supply proposals.

Rosapepe, John Vincent. "Should This Dam Rise, or Fall?" *High Country News*, April 20, 1992. Elk Creek Dam in Oregon.

White, Gilbert, ed. *Environmental Effects of Complex River Development*. Boulder, Colo.: Westview Press, 1977.

Chapter Four ❧ The Myth of Hydropower

American Rivers. *Small Hydroelectric Projects at New Dams and Diversions.* Washington, D.C.: American Rivers, March 1989, unpublished paper.

Busby, Chris. "Bourassa's Dream for Quebec." *Borealis*, Summer 1991. James Bay Project.

Clark, Wilson. *Energy for Survival*. Garden City, N.Y.: Doubleday/Anchor Books, 1975. The use and conservation of energy sources.

Echeverria, John D.; Pope Barrow; and Richard Roos-Collins. *Rivers at Risk*. Prepared for American Rivers. Washington, D.C.: Island Press, 1989. Overview of hydropower and how citizens may intervene.

Egan, John. "Hydropower Group Battles 'Typical Yuppy' Recreationalists." *Energy Daily*, October 10, 1990.

Hall, C. J. Cleveland, and R. Kaufmann. *Energy and Resource Quality: The Ecology of the Industrial Process*. New York: John Wiley and Sons, 1986.

Hinchman, Steve. "Can Innovation and Efficiency Replace Dams, Power Plants and Coal Mines?" *High Country News*, June 29, 1992. Energy alternatives.

Huth, Hans. *Nature and the American*. Lincoln: University of Nebraska Press, 1957. Niagara Falls protection.

Johnson, Huey D. "Environmental Quality as a National Purpose." In *Crossroads*, edited by Peter Borrelli. Washington, D.C.: Island Press, 1988.

McCutcheon, Sean. *Electric Rivers*. Montreal: Black Rose Books, 1991. James Bay Project.

Mouvement Lumière Sur L'Energie. *Energy Development in the Quebec Context*. 1993. Publication of the Mouvement Lumière Sur L'Energie, C. P. 282, succ. E, Laurier, Montreal, Quebec H2T3A7. James Bay Project.

Reisner, Marc. "Waste in the West, Part II." *Natural Resources Defense Council Newsletter*, January 1978.

Richardson, Boyce. *Strangers Devour the Land*. Post Mills, Vt.: Chelsea Green, 1991. James Bay Project.

Rifkin, Jeremy. *Entropy: Into the Greenhouse World*. New York: Bantam, 1989. Problems of energy use.

Skinner, Pete N. "Hydro Relicensing." *Trilogy*, Fall/Winter 1989.

U.S. Army Corps of Engineers. *National Hydroelectric Power Resource Study, Vol. I*. Washington, D.C.: U.S. Army Corps of Engineers, May 1983. Inventory of hydroelectric potential.

U.S. Department of Energy. *The Potential of Renewable Energy*. Washington, D.C.: U.S. Department of Energy, March 1990.

U.S. Federal Energy Regulatory Commission. *Hydroelectric Power Resources of the U.S.* Washington, D.C.: FERC, January 1988. Hydroelectric inventory.

Wallin, Phillip, and Rita Haberman. *People Protecting Rivers*. Portland, Oreg.: River Network, 1992. Gauley River and conservationists' response to hydropower threats.

Chapter Five ❧ The Elusive Goal of Quality

Adler, Robert W.; Jessica C. Landman; and Diane M. Cameron. *The Clean Water Act 20 Years Later*. Washington, D.C.: Island Press, 1993. Excellent coverage of all water quality issues.

Ashworth, William. *Nor Any Drop To Drink*. New York: Summit Books, 1982. Excellent overview of water quality.

Batie, Sandra F. *Soil Erosion: Crisis in America's Croplands?* Washington, D.C.: The Conservation Foundation, 1983.

Becker, C. Dale, and Duane A. Neitzel, eds. *Water Quality in North American River Systems*. Columbus, Ohio: Battelle Press, 1992. Case studies of twelve river systems.

Brown, Lester; Christopher Flavin; and Sandra Postel. *Saving the Planet*. New York: W. W. Norton, 1991. Global water quality and quantity issues.

Coffel, Steve. *The Lifesaving Guide to Good Water*. New York: Ivy Books, 1989. Excellent reference, including toxics.

Commoner, Barry. "The Environment." In *Crossroads*, edited by Peter Borrelli. Washington, D.C.: Island Press, 1988. Status of water quality and effectiveness of abatement efforts.

Conniff, Richard. "The Transformation of a River—From 'Sewer' to Suburbs in 20 Years." *Smithsonian*, April 1990. The Connecticut River.

"Conservationists' Clean Water Agenda." *Leader*, April 1991. Publication of the National Wildlife Federation.

Gilbert, Bil. "Earth Day Plus 20, and Counting." *Smithsonian*, April 1990. Status of water quality improvement.

Haberman, Rita. "Solar Aquatics, Alternative Wastewater Treatment Technology." *River Voices*, September 1992. Publication of the River Network.

Harris, Tom. *Death in the Marsh*. Washington, D.C.: Island Press, 1991. Selenium problems.

Hinchman, Steve. "River Users in a Pickle." *High Country News*, November 20, 1989. Salinity.

Izaak Walton League of America. *A Citizen's Guide to Clean Water*. Arlington, Va.: Izaak Walton League, 1990.

Marston, Ed, ed. "The West's Fouled Waters." *High Country News*, November 20, 1989, and December 4, 1989, entire issues. Water pollution in the West.

Merrimack River Watershed Council. *The Merrimack River: Water for All?* West Newbury, Mass.: Merrimack River Watershed Council, October 1988.

Mosher, Lawrence. "Soiling Our Water." *Outdoor America*, Summer 1985. Polluted runoff.

National Research Council. *Restoring Aquatic Ecosystems*. Washington, D.C.: National Academy Press, 1992. Overview of water quality problems.

National Wildlife Federation. "Waters at Risk: Keeping Clean Waters Clean." Washington, D.C.: National Wildlife Federation, 1992, unpublished paper. The need to designate waters of exceptional quality.

Nudel, Martha. "Water Everywhere, But Is It Clean?" *Leader*, June 1990. Publication of the National Wildlife Federation.

Odgers, Ed. "Wisconsin's 'Bad Actors' Program: Controlling Agricultural Runoff." *River Voices*, September 1992. Publication of the River Network.

Pennsylvania Department of Environmental Resources. *Local Protection of High-Quality Streams*. Harrisburg: Department of Environmental Resources, 1981. Booklet on local government action for clean streams.

Powledge, Fred. *Water*. New York: Farrar, Straus, and Giroux, 1982. Overview of water quality.

Reilly, William K., Jr. "A View Toward the Nineties." In *Crossroads*, edited by Peter Borrelli. Washington, D.C.: Island Press, 1988.

Rennicke, Jeff. "The Clean Water Act Turns 20." *Backpacker*, June 1992.

Rienow, Robert, and Leona Train Rienow. *Moment in the Sun*. New York: Ballantine, 1967. Water quality in the 1960s.

Rifkin, Jeremy. *Entropy: Into the Greenhouse World*. New York: Bantam, 1989. Estimated costs of environmental cleanup.

Smith, Richard A.; Richard B. Alexander; and M. Gordon Wolman. "Water-quality Trends in the Nation's Rivers." *Science*, Vol. 235, March 27, 1987.

Sosin, Mark, and John Clark. *Through the Fish's Eye*. New York: Harper and Row, 1973. Effects of water pollution on fish.

Speth, Gus. "Environmental Pollution: High and Rising." In *Crossroads*, edited by Peter Borrelli. Washington, D.C.: Island Press, 1988. Water quality status.

U.S. Department of Agriculture, Soil Conservation Service. *Soil Erosion by Water*. Washington, D.C.: Soil Conservation Service, 1987.

U.S. Environmental Protection Agency. *National Water Quality Inventory: 1990 Report to Congress*. Washington, D.C.: U.S. Environmental Protection Agency, 1992. Water quality status.

U.S. Environmental Protection Agency. *Nonpoint Sources*. Washington, D.C.: U.S. Environmental Protection Agency, 1989.

Chapter Six ❧ The Remains of Rivers

Barlow, Thomas. *Federal Flood Control Programs Are Failing to Prevent Flood Losses*. New York: Natural Resources Defense Council. Undated (about 1976) brochure.

Bates, Sarah F.; David H. Getches; Lawrence J. MacDonnell; and Charles F. Wilkinson. *Searching Out the Headwaters: Change and Rediscovery in Western Water Policy*. Washington, D.C.: Island Press, 1993.

Belt, C. B., Jr. "The 1973 Flood and Man's Constriction of the Mississippi River." *Science*, August 29, 1975. Effect of levees aggravating flooding.

Bishop, Jim. "A Water-based Electric Empire Is Hit by a Flood of Criticism." *High Country News*, July 13, 1992. Glen Canyon hydropower.

Bradley, Cheryl E. "Modifications by Dams of River Regimes in North America." Paper presented to conference on water management, University of Lethbridge, Alberta, Canada, November 1988.

Collins, Katharine. "Fear of Supreme Court Leads Tribes to Accept an Adverse

Decision." *High Country News*, October 19, 1992. Indian water rights on the Wind River.

Committee to Review the Glen Canyon Environmental Studies. *River and Dam Management*. Washington, D.C.: National Academy Press, 1987.

Echeverria, John D.; Pope Barrow; and Richard Roos-Collins. *Rivers at Risk*. Prepared for American Rivers. Washington, D.C.: Island Press, 1989. Diversion problems at hydroelectric dams.

Dunning, Harrison C. "Confronting the Environmental Legacy of Irrigated Agriculture in the West: The Case of the Central Valley Project." *Environmental Law*, vol. 23, p. 943, 1993.

Fradkin, Philip L. *A River No More*. New York: Knopf, 1981. The Colorado River.

Diringer, Elliot. "President Signs Water Bill." *San Francisco Chronicle*, October 31, 1992. Central Valley Project reform act.

Harrison, David L., and Robert Wigington. "Water Rights: A Protection Tool for the West." *Nature Conservancy Magazine*, August 1987.

Hinchman, Steve. "Animas–La Plata." *High Country News*, March 22, 1993, entire issue.

Judy, R. D., et al. *1982 National Fisheries Survey, Vol. 1*. Washington, D.C.: U.S. Fish and Wildlife Service, 1984.

Kazmann, Raphael G. *Modern Hydrology*. New York: Harper and Row, 1972. A hydrology textbook.

Malick, Amy. "Scaled-down A-LP Nears Go-ahead." *Durango Herald*, September 8, 1991. Animas–La Plata project.

Marston, Ed, ed. *Western Water Made Simple*. Washington, D.C.: Island Press, 1987. Articles on diversion problems and water rights.

Morisawa, Marie. *Streams: Their Dynamics and Morphology*. New York: McGraw-Hill, 1968. General background on stream hydrology and morphology.

Nebraska Game and Parks Commission. "Platte River Instream Flow—Who Needs It?" *Nebraskaland*, December 1992.

Obmascik, Mark. "Water Policy: Some Farmers Paid Twice." *Denver Post*, July 21, 1992. Water subsidies.

Palmer, Tim. *The Snake River: Window to the West*. Washington, D.C.: Island Press, 1991. Instream flow problems and diversions on the Snake River.

Reed, Scott. "The Other Uses for Water." *Idaho Yesterdays*, Spring 1986.

Reisner, Marc, and Sarah Bates. *Overtapped Oasis*. Washington, D.C.: Island Press, 1990. The case for water marketing.

Sheer, Daniel P. "Managing Water Supplies to Insure Water Availability." In *National Water Summary*. Washington, D.C.: U.S. Geological Survey, 1985.

Shoemaker, Thomas G. *Wildlife and Water Projects on the Platte River*. New York: National Audubon Society, 1989.

U.S. Department of Interior, Geological Survey. *National Water Summary*. Washington, D.C.: U.S. Geological Survey, 1985. Water use data.

Wahl, Richard W., and Frank H. Osterhoudt. "Voluntary Transfers of Water in the West." In *National Water Summary*. Washington, D.C.: U.S. Geological Survey, 1985.

Williams, Garnett P., and M. Gordon Wolman. "Effects of Dams and Reservoirs on Surface-Water Hydrology—Changes in Rivers Downstream from Dams." In *National Water Summary*. Washington, D.C.: U.S. Geological Survey, 1985.

"The Winters Doctrine." *Wilderness*, Fall 1987. Indian water rights.

Worster, Donald. *Rivers of Empire*. New York: Pantheon Books, 1985. Historical basis and social effects of water diversions.

Chapter Seven ᴥ The Riparian Edge

Bellow, Dan. "Massachusetts Property Owners Defeat Wild and Scenic Designation for Farmington River." *Appalachia Bulletin*, May 1992.

Boly, William. "The Sagebrush Rebels." *New West*, November 1980. Grazing in the West.

Brumback, Barbara C. "Restoring Florida's Everglades." In *Restoring the Earth*, edited by John J. Berger. Washington, D.C.: Island Press, 1990.

Chaney, Ed; Wayne Elmore; and William S. Platts. *Livestock Grazing on Western Riparian Areas*. Washington, D.C.: U.S. Environmental Protection Agency, 1990. Excellent source on riparian grazing problems and solutions.

Diamant, Rolf; J. Glenn Eugster; and Christopher J. Duerksen. *A Citizen's Guide to River Conservation*. Washington, D.C.: The Conservation Foundation, 1984. Handbook for citizen action.

Elmore, Wayne, and Robert L. Beschta. "Restoring Riparian Areas in Eastern Oregon." *Free Flow*, Fall 1990. Publication of the Pacific Rivers Council.

Ferguson, Denzel, and Nancy Ferguson. *Sacred Cows at the Public Trough*. Bend, Oreg.: Maverick Publications, 1983. Excellent coverage of grazing problems in riparian areas.

Flather, C. H., and T. W. Hoekstra. *An Analysis of the Wildlife and Fish Situation in the U.S.: 1989–2040, General Technical Report RM-178*. Fort Collins, Colo.: U.S. Department of Agriculture, Rocky Mountain Forest and Range Experiment Station, 1989.

Haberman, Rita. "The Resource Abuse Movement and River Conservation Efforts." *River Voices*, June 1992. Publication of the River Network.

Hoffman, Chuck. "Addressing Landowner Concerns in the River Conservation Planning Process." *River Voices*, June 1992. Publication of the River Network.

Hunt, Constance Elizabeth. *Down by the River*. Washington, D.C.: Island Press, 1988. Excellent coverage of riparian issues related to federal water projects.

Johnson, Steve. " 'Disaster, Disaster on the Range,' Reports Say." *High Country News*, April 20, 1992. Grazing in western riparian areas.

Kusler, Jon, and Larry Larson. "Beyond the Ark." *Environment*, June 1993. Excellent article on flood insurance.

Lavigne, Peter. "Reforming National Flood Insurance." *River Voices*, September 1992. Publication of the River Network.

Mitchell, John G. "The Hiding-Place Tree." *Audubon*, May 1986. Essay on sycamore trees.

National Research Council. *Restoration of Aquatic Ecosystems*. Washington, D.C.: National Academy Press, 1992. Excellent source on riparian issues.

North, Douglass. "Countering the Resource Abuse Movement." *River Voices*, June 1992. Publication of the River Network.

Pashley, David. "Restoring Bottomland Hardwoods." *Leader*, September 1990. Publication of the National Wildlife Federation. Protection of riparian forests of the lower Mississippi.

Pollock, Sarah. "The Charge of the Brook Brigades." *Sierra*, November/December 1989. Citizen action to protect creeks.

Swift, B. L. "Status of Riparian Ecosystems in the United States." *Water Resources Bulletin*, vol. 20, no. 2, April 1984.

U.S. Department of Interior, Bureau of Outdoor Recreation. "Flood Plains for Recreation." *Outdoor Recreation Action*, Spring 1976.

Van Tighem, Kevin. "The Curse of the Cow." *Borealis*, Summer 1991. Effects of cows on riparian areas.

Wallin, Phillip, and Rita Haberman. *People Protecting Rivers*. Portland, Oreg.: River Network, 1992. Citizen action to protect riparian areas.

Wilkin, D. C., and S. J. Hebel. "Erosion, Redeposition, and Delivery of Sediment to Midwestern Streams." *Water Resources Research*, vol. 18, no. 4, 1982.

Williams, Florence. "National Forest Grazing Cuts Are Stalled by Politics." *High Country News*, June 1, 1992. Grazing in the Sawtooth National Forest.

Chapter Eight ⠠⠄ The Heart of the Ecosystem

Allan, J. David, and Alexander S. Flecker. "Biodiversity Conservation in Running Waters." *Bioscience*, January 1993.

Barker, Rocky. *Saving All the Parts: Reconciling Economics and the Endangered Species Act*. Washington, D.C.: Island Press, 1993. Endangered species in the Northwest.

Benke, Arthur C. "A Perspective on America's Vanishing Streams." *Journal of the American Benthological Society*, March 1990.

Ehrlich, Paul, and Anne Ehrlich. *Extinction*. New York: Ballantine, 1981. Endangered species.

"Forests in Distress." *Oregonian*, October 15, 1990. Logging and watershed damage in the Northwest.

Hume, Mark. "The Color of Copper." *Alaska Magazine*, August 1992. Tatshenshini and Alsek rivers.

Inlands Empire Public Lands Council, P.O. Box 2174, Spokane, Wash. 99210. Newsletters, 1988–1992. Logging in the northern Rockies and Northwest.

Jones and Stokes Associates. *Sliding Toward Extinction: The State of California's Natural Heritage*. Sacramento, Calif.: The Nature Conservancy, 1987.

Karr, James R. "Protecting Ecological Integrity: An Urgent Societal Goal." *Yale Journal of International Law*, Winter 1993.

Kohm, Kathryn A., ed. *Balancing on the Brink of Extinction*. Washington, D.C.: Island Press, 1991.

Master, Larry. "The Imperiled Status of North American Aquatic Animals." *Biodiversity Network News*, vol. 3, no. 3, 1990.

Matthiessen, Peter. *Indian Country*. New York: Penguin Books, 1979. Includes an excellent chapter about Tellico Dam.

National Research Council. *Restoration of Aquatic Ecosystems*. Washington, D.C.: National Academy Press, 1991. Excellent coverage of aquatic ecosystem issues.

Nehlsen, Willa; Jack E. Williams; and James A. Lichatowich. "Pacific Salmon at the Crossroads: Stocks at Risk from California, Oregon, Idaho, and Washington." *Fisheries*, March/April 1991.

Pacific Rivers Council. *Entering the Watershed*. Washington, D.C.: Island Press, 1993. Overview of ecosystem problems, with proposals for new national policy.

Rauber, Paul. "No River Wilder." *Sierra*, January/February 1993. Tatshenshini and Alsek rivers.

U.S. Fish and Wildlife Service. *Swimming Upstream: The Endangered Fish of the Colorado River*. Denver: U.S. Fish and Wildlife Service. Undated (about 1992) brochure.

Chapter Nine ❧ A Time for Rivers

Barrow, Pope. "Sorting Through River Conservation Tools." *River Voices*, June 1991. Publication of the River Network.

Bolling, David. *How to Save a River*. Prepared for River Network. Washington, D.C.: Island Press, 1994. Excellent handbook for river activists.

Cahn, Robert, ed. *An Environmental Agenda for the Future*. Washington, D.C.: Island Press, 1985.

Giffen, R. Alec, and Drew O. Parkin. *American Rivers Conservation Agenda: 1990 and Beyond*. Prepared for American Rivers et al. Washington, D.C.: American Rivers, 1989.

Manes, Christopher. *Green Rage*. Boston: Little, Brown & Co., 1990. The environmental movement in the 1990s.

Palmer, Tim. *The Wild and Scenic Rivers of America*. Washington, D.C.: Island Press, 1993. The National Wild and Scenic Rivers System and other means of protection.

River Network. *People Protecting Rivers*. Portland, Oreg.: River Network, 1992. Case studies of river activism.

Organizations Involved in River Protection

American Canoe Association
7432 Alban Station Boulevard
  Suite B-226
Springfield, VA 22150

American Fisheries Society
5410 Grosvenor Lane
  Suite 110
Bethesda, MD 20814

American Rivers
801 Pennsylvania Avenue, S.E.
  Suite 303
Washington, DC 20003

American Whitewater Affiliation
136 13th Street, S.E.
Washington, DC 20003

Clean Water Action Coalition
1320 18th Street, N.W.
Washington, DC 20036

Friends of the River
128 J Street, 2nd Floor
Sacramento, CA 95814

Izaak Walton League of America
1401 Wilson Boulevard
Arlington, VA 22209

National Wildlife Federation
1400 16th Street, N.W.
Washington, DC 20036

Pacific Rivers Council
P.O. Box 309
Eugene, OR 97440

River Network
P.O. Box 8787
Portland, OR 97207

Sierra Club
730 Polk Street
San Francisco, CA 94109

Trout Unlimited
800 Follin Lane
Vienna, VA 22108

The Wilderness Society
900 17th Street, N.W.
Washington, DC 20006

Lifelines: The Case for River Conservation

For additional organizations, including twenty that operate at statewide levels, see the *River Conservation Directory*, available from the National Park Service, Rivers and Trails Conservation Assistance Program, P.O. Box 37127, Washington, D.C. 20013. Also see the *River Activists Directory*, available from the River Network, P.O. Box 8787, Portland, OR 97207, or write to the River Network or American Rivers.

Acknowledgments

Hundreds of people contributed to this book by talking with me during the past several years. A few of the important interviews were with Pope Barrow, Brent Blackwelder, Cheryl Bradley, Christopher Brown, Howard Brown, Tom Cassidy, Ed Chaney, Bern Collins, Dave Conrad, Bea Cooley, Kevin Coyle, Frank Craighead, David Dickson, Bob Doppelt, Mark Dubois, John Echeverria, Glenn Eugster, Scott Faber, Pat Ford, Mike Fremont, Donn Furman, Karen Garrison, Jack Griffith, Hugh Harper, Jack Hession, Phil Huffman, Peter Lavigne, Luna Leopold, Leslie McCarty, Kent Olson, Peter Pacquet, Ed Pembleton, William Platts, Scott Reed, Dale Robertson, Richard Roos-Collins, Signe Sather-Blair, Don Shields, Scott Sparlin, John Turner, Stewart Udall, Kevin Van Tighem, Cliff Wallace, Phil Wallin, Del Wehrspann, and Wendy Wilson.

Reviewers of the manuscript included Tom Cassidy, Jerry Meral, Ann Vileisis, and Jamie Williams, all of whom dedicated valuable time and expertise to this effort. Chapters or portions of chapters were reviewed by Michael Black, Charles Casey, Peter Enticknap, Steve Evans, Jeff Fereday, Matthew Huntington, James Karr, Peter Lavigne, Lori Potter, Charlie Ray, Ron Stork, and others who contributed expert knowledge. Mark Anderman printed the photos. Keri Brown was a great help with word processing of the early drafts.

For hospitality during my work and travels, I'd like to thank the Teton Science School in Kelly, Wyoming; the Colorado Outward Bound School in Jensen, Utah; Jane and Chuck May of Beaver, Pennsylvania; David and Janet Murray of Issaquah, Washington; Becky and Steve Schmitz of Charlottesville, Virginia; Mark and Janet Taylor of Southbury, Connecticut; and Jamie and Florence Williams of Steamboat Springs, Colorado. My mother, Jane May, was vitally important in forwarding mail to me during my lengthy and continuous travels, in her encouragement, and for many other reasons.

Support for writing this book was provided by the Richard Mellon Foundation with a grant to American Rivers, and by Patagonia, Inc., with a grant to Friends of the River. These grants made it possible for me to work full time on this project in 1992 and 1993.

Barbara Dean, my editor at Island Press, never failed in her attention both to the big picture and to detail, and always provided a source of enthusiasm, experience, and good judgment. Her work on scores of books by many authors over the past ten years has immeasurably benefited the entire field of environmental literature. Linda Gunnarson did an excellent job copyediting the manuscript.

I especially want to thank Ann Vileisis, an environmental historian, writer, and educator, for her thoughtfulness on many questions that arose, for her passion for rivers, and for her companionship throughout this project.

Index

About the Author

Tim Palmer has been involved in river protection since 1970 as a writer, photographer, planner, conservationist, speaker, and consultant to citizen organizations. He has written nine books about rivers and conservation, including *The Wild and Scenic Rivers of America, Endangered Rivers and the Conservation Movement, The Snake River: Window to the West,* and *Youghiogheny: Appalachian River.*

In 1988 Palmer received the Lifetime Achievement Award from American Rivers in recognition of his writings on river protection. He has canoed or rafted on 300 different streams nationwide, and his collection of color and black-and-white river photographs is extensive. He is currently completing a book on the river geography of America.